AMZN 2.95 -5

D1015666

This is an entirely new book

PROFIT WITH OPTIONS

Book

PROFIT WITH OPTIONS

Essential Methods for Investing Success

LAWRENCE G. McMILLAN

JOHN WILEY & SONS, INC.

Published by John Wiley & Sons, Inc., New York.
Published simultaneously in Canada.

This publication is designed to provide accurate and authoritative information in
regard to the subject matter covered. It is sold with the understanding that the
publisher is not engaged in rendering professional services. If professional advice
or other expert assistance is required, the services of a competent professional
person should be sought.

Wiley also publishes its books in a variety of electronic formats. Some content that
appears in print may not be available in electronic books. For more information
about Wiley products visit our Web site at www.Wiley.com.

ISBN 0-471-22531-2

Printed in the United States of America.

10 9 8 7 6 5 4 3 2

PREFACE

Over the years, I've written two thick books on options trading that have a combined page count over 1,500. I write a weekly advisory newsletter, as well as a daily fax service. So what, you may wonder, do I have left to write about on the topic of options trading?

With this book, my goal is not necessarily to cover a lot of innovative new ground, but to present material in a new way that will enhance the ability of traders to master a variety of option trading techniques and become more successful at incorporating them into their overall trading program. My first book, *Options as a Strategic Investment* is, at 998 pages, a complete reference text that covers nearly every aspect of options trading in depth. *McMillan on Options* is more focused on how to apply various options strategies, including the ones I personally prefer and use frequently. What has been missing—based on feedback received from my readers, seminar attendees, and subscribers—is a book that covers each phase of the options trading process step-by-step, reinforces individual concepts, and thus allows you to hone and refine skills—in essence, a workbook or study guide.

In *Profit with Options* I have attempted to provide an overview of the options trading process in a more concise, hands-on way. Each chapter covers a specific concept and ends with a set of review questions and answers that will assist you in absorbing and implementing the material covered.

While the introduction does address basic terms and the building blocks of option trading concepts, the book as a whole is written for someone with some degree of investment and trading experience. The first chapter also moves right into the components of option price, using historical and implied volatility to formulate your option trading strategy, and understanding the advantages an option model can provide. Plus, LEAPS, futures, and trading technology are each treated in detail.

Chapters 2 and 3 explain how to use options as both direct and contrary indicators, with examples showing how each can predict market direction and help you decide which options to buy under both scenarios.

Chapter 4 teaches you how to incorporate system trading into an overall options game plan and illustrates the value of taking the system approach. A variety of systems types are outlined that are applicable for both short-term and long-term investors.

Chapter 5 presents powerful methods for using options as "insurance" and portfolio protection, which is one of their key strengths.

Chapters 6 and 7 conclude with various strategies for profiting from trading volatility. I start by viewing volatility as a strategic indicator, and then move into both forward and reverse "skew" and spreading strategies. I then provide a more in-depth look at volatility analysis, the reasons behind volatility changes, and highlight my own favorite strategy plus personal criteria for buying straddles, "follow-up" action, and selling naked options.

Each chapter of the workbook can stand on its own, but taken together, they form the basis of a well-rounded options trading program. With the end-of-chapter questions provided, you can test your knowledge of the concepts, techniques, and systems featured in *Profit with Options* before you need to put them into action in the real trading world. And this learn-by-example workbook should prepare you for making the right moves at the right time, while reacting swiftly to opportunities that arise in the fast-paced options arena.

It is my hope that this hands-on guide will complement my previous two works. You can now access a comprehensive resource on options, a product devoted primarily to strategies in action, and a manual that helps to reinforce tactics and refine option trading skills.

I have devoted much of my career to educating investors on the fundamentals and the benefits of trading options. I think they provide enormous wealth-building potential for anyone who has mastered a proficiency in trading options. And I hope, after completing this handbook, that you will have a better working knowledge of how to use options to diversify and enhance a portfolio. nonsense)

LAWRENCE G. MCMILLAN

April 2002

CONTENTS

———

1

INTRODUCTION

LEARNING OBJECTIVES

The material in this chapter will help you to:

- Become familiar with the terms and concepts of option trading.
- Analyze the components of option price.
- Use historical and implied volatility to formulate your option trading strategy.
- Understand the benefits an option model can provide.
- Understand the advantages and disadvantages of trading futures.

A call option gives you the right to purchase something at a specified price, and that option is normally "good" for only a predetermined length of time. There are options in many facets of life—real estate, executive stock options, and the focus of this book: listed options. The "something" that you may purchase is called the **underlying instrument** (the **underlying**). It could be a stock, it could be an index, or it could be a futures contract.

The specified price at which that underlying instrument can be bought is called the **strike price.** Finally, the date by which the option must be used is called the **expiration date.** These three terms completely define the option. For example, an IBM July 120 call is an option to buy IBM (the underlying instrument) at a price of 120 (the strike price) at any time through July (the expiration date).

For stock and index options, the last trading day is the third Friday of the month, so the expiration date is that day. (Actually, for legal reasons, it's technically the next day—but that's a Saturday, so for all intents and purposes, Friday is considered to be the expiration date.) For futures options, expiration dates vary within the expiration month. We'll talk more about them later. The material in this chapter lays the groundwork for your development as an option strategist.

IMPORTANT TERMS AND CONCEPTS

An important concept is that of a **put option.** A put option allows the holder to *sell* the underlying security at the strike price up until the expiration date. Thus, call options increase in price when the price of the underlying security *rises,* and put options increase in price when the price of the underlying security *falls.*

> *Options were traded over-the-counter for years, but in 1973 the Chicago Board Options Exchange (CBOE) was formed and the innovations that they brought to the marketplace have resulted in the huge market we now have for listed options.*

The biggest innovation was the introduction of a liquid market in options. Options can be bought and sold at any time, just as shares of stock can be bought and sold. It is not necessary to

Table 1.1 Derivative Types

Equity options	(e.g., LEAPS)
Index and sector options	(e.g., S&P 500, OEX; oil and gas, gold)
Listed warrants	(similar to option but behaves more like stock)
Futures options/serial options	
Over-the-counter options	(e.g., Swaps—interest-rate trades)

hold the option until its expiration date. Therefore, if you were to buy that IBM July 120 call, and then IBM stock price rose shortly thereafter—perhaps rising well above the strike price 120—most likely the call would gain some value. You could just phone your broker and sell the call to take your profit. You would not have to worry about whether or not IBM was above the strike price of 120 at expiration.

Options are a **derivative security.** That is, their price movements are taken from the movements in another security (the underlying stock, for example). Over the years, since listed options began trading on the Chicago Board Options Exchange (CBOE), there have been many different types of listed securities. **Index and sector options** are merely options on an index or a sector index (for example, the S&P 500 Index or the Semiconductor Index). **Warrants** have been listed on the New York Stock Exchange (NYSE) for years, but the current type of warrants being traded—particularly on the American Stock Exchange (AMEX)—generally play either currencies or the market as an option security. With warrants, you can own the market without much risk. **Over-the-counter options** are options that are traded directly, generally by big firms such as Morgan Stanley or institutions such as mutual funds. See Table 1.1 for a summary of derivative types.

Here are a few other terms that may be of interest:

- **In-the-money/out-of-the-money.** When the underlying is trading *higher than* the strike price of a call option, the call option is said to be in-the-money. If the underlying is *below* the strike price, the call is said to be out-of-the-money. Conversely, a put option is in-the-money when the underlying instrument is trading at a price *lower than* the strike price and out-of-the-money when the underlying is trading *above* the strike price.

- **Exercise the option.** Converting the option *into* the underlying instrument is exercising the option. A person who exercises one IBM July 120 call would get 100 shares of IBM in his or her account, and those shares would cost $120 apiece—a total transaction cost of $12,000, plus commissions. Exercising a futures option yields one contract of the underlying instrument.

- **In-the-money-amount.** The amount by which the underlying exceeds the strike price of a call option is called the in-the-money amount; for put options, the in-the-money amount is the distance by which the underlying instrument is *below* the strike price.

- **Intrinsic value/time value.** An option's complete price is composed of two things: intrinsic value (which is the in-the-money amount or zero for an out-of-the money option) and time value. The **time value** of an option decreases as time passes until, at expiration, the option's price is either equal to the in-the-money amount or zero (if it's out-of-the-money at expiration). Out-of-the-money options are composed *entirely* of time value premium, while a deeply in-the-money option is composed almost entirely of intrinsic value with very little time value premium. An option buyer must be careful not to continually buy too much time value premium and too little intrinsic value. Such a strategy may lead to ruin because the probability of an out-of-the-money expiring worthless is greater than 50%.

OPTION PRICE

Six components of the price of an option are:

1. Underlying price.
2. Time remaining until expiration.
3. Dividends (not applicable to futures options).
4. Strike price.
5. Short-term interest rate.
6. Volatility.

Of these, volatility is the only one that is not a predetermined, fixed quantity. That is, you know what all the others are at any one point in time, but volatility is *not* known. Hence, fluctuations in the market's perception of volatility will affect the price of the option.

Volatility

There are two kinds of volatility: (1) **historical volatility,** a measure of how fast the underlying instrument *has been* moving around in the past and (2) **implied volatility,** the volatility component built into an option's price. Implied volatility is really an attempt to determine how volatile the underlying *will be* during the life of the option. As implied volatility increases, so does time value premium, so that an option with a very high implied volatility will be a very costly option, and it will have a great deal of time value premium—perhaps even if it is an in-the-money option.

The word *volatility* is used with great frequency in this book. It is the most important thing that an option trader needs to think about. Rather than say an option is "overpriced" (which is a somewhat subjective term), it is better to say it is trading with a high "implied volatility."

Historical volatility can be calculated by a specific statistical formula—it is nothing more than the standard deviation of the movements of the underlying instrument. Implied volatility, however, can only be determined by the use of an **option model**—a mathematical formula used to give some accurate estimates of an option's price, based on its components.

Option Pricing Models

Option models are important for option traders, and everyone should have some sort of model available. There is a free one at the CBOE's Web site, www.cboe.com. There are some models that are a little fancier and have a modest cost, and then there are some that are part of full-blown portfolio management software systems and are quite expensive. More will be said about these later in this book.

Black-Scholes Model

The most famous option model is the Black-Scholes model, invented by professors Fisher Black and Myron Scholes. At the time, they were working in fairly close concert with another professor, Robert Merton. After a difference of opinion over the basics of the model, Merton went on to do his own research, while Black and Scholes attached their names to the now famous model.

The Nobel Prize for Economics was awarded in 1998 for this model. Fisher Black had passed away, and Nobel Prizes are not awarded posthumously, but Scholes and Merton shared the award.

Do *not* think, however, that option models can remove all the guesswork from option pricing. They can give you a good estimate of the option's price, *if you can accurately describe what is going to happen to the underlying price.* Of course, the latter is an impossible task. Still, the models are useful in providing an estimate of an option's cost and in helping to determine if you are buying an "overpriced" option.

Some users found small problems with the Black-Scholes model and so other models, such as the binomial model, have found some supporters. Generally, these models will not give substantially different estimates of an option's value, thus it doesn't matter much which one you use—*as long as you use some model.* Trading options without the benefit of an option model is foolhardy and will put you at an extreme disadvantage to the best and smartest option traders—a disadvantage that will eventually cost you some serious money.

What model are u using?

Delta

One of the benefits of a model is that it can give an estimate of what-if situations. One of the simplest is the **delta** of an option. That is the amount by which the option will move if the underlying instrument moves one point. A call's delta ranges between values of 0.00 and 1.00. So if the underlying moves up a point, and the call increases in price by half a point, then the call's delta is 0.50. Put deltas range from 0.00 down to –1.00, to reflect the fact that puts move in the opposite direction from the underlying.

In-the-money options have large absolute deltas—reflecting the fact that their movements fairly closely mirror those of the underlying instrument. Out-of-the-money options, on the other hand, have small deltas—indicating that it will take a *big* move by the underlying to cause the out-of-the-money option to gain much value. In some sense, the delta can be viewed as the *probability* that the option will be in-the-money at expiration. Table 1.2 gives some examples with comments.

Are these European or American options?

Table 1.2 Stock Price: 120 on April 1, 1999

Option	Price	Delta	Comment
April 110 call	10.125	0.99	Behaves just like stock.
April 130 call	0.0625	0.01	Not much chance of making a move.
July 120 call	8	0.55	Moves about half as fast as the common.
July 140 call	3	0.25	Smaller moves than the July 120 call.
January ('00) 120 call	14	0.60	Longer-term options have lower deltas at the extremes because they have more time value premium.

Note that a change in one variable will cause a change in some of the others. For example, a sharp increase in implied volatility will change the delta of an option. We discuss this in more detail later in this book.

Profit Graph; Pricing Curve

The graphs shown in Figure 1.1 are **profit graphs** depicting the potential profits and losses from a position. Such graphs can be drawn by many of the option software programs for sale today and by Internet application sites as well. When positions become complex—perhaps involving numerous options as well as a position in the underlying stock—a profit graph may be the only way to discern what your position will do when the underlying begins to change in price, or when time passes. Most of the software applications will also let you observe how a change in implied volatility will affect your position as time passes.

A **pricing curve,** on the other hand, is the picture of a single option's value—depicted over a range of stock prices. One

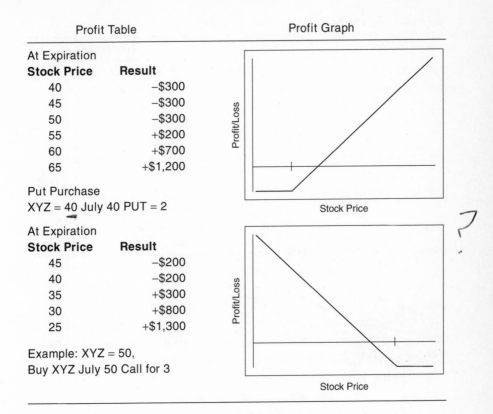

Profit Table		Profit Graph

At Expiration

Stock Price	Result
40	−$300
45	−$300
50	−$300
55	+$200
60	+$700
65	+$1,200

Put Purchase
XYZ = 40 July 40 PUT = 2

At Expiration

Stock Price	Result
45	−$200
40	−$200
35	+$300
30	+$800
25	+$1,300

Example: XYZ = 50,
Buy XYZ July 50 Call for 3

Figure 1.1   Derivative types.

particular graph might contain several pricing curves, usually graphing several options with similar terms (same underlying and same striking price, but perhaps different expiration dates). The graph in Figure 1.2 is such a pricing curve. Four options are shown: a three-month option, a six-month, a one-year, and a two-year. Each one has a strike price of 100. You can see that the curves are similar, but the more time remaining in the option, the higher the curve resides on the graph. Thus, it is easy to see the time value—and the *effect* of time value—with this pricing curve.

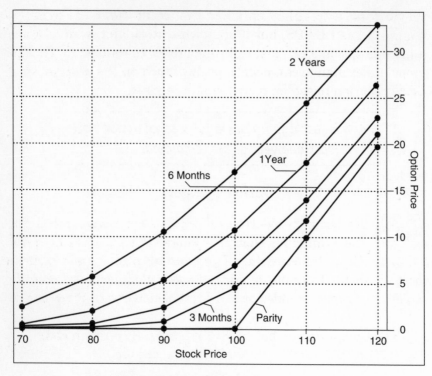

Figure 1.2   LEAPS call pricing curve.

OPTION DESCRIPTORS

LEAPS

When equity options were first listed by the CBOE (and subsequently, the other option exchanges), the longest time in the life of an option was nine months. As the years went by, institutions demanded a longer term option. Thus, LEAPS were created. **LEAPS** is an acronym for some lengthy name, but in reality it is nothing more than a name for an option that has more than nine months of life remaining. When LEAPS are first issued, they have expiration dates of between two and three years. Eventually that time dwindles down to nine months or so, and they become a "regular" option at that point. Not *every* underlying stock has LEAPS, but if you own a stock and want to trade a LEAPS option on it, just tell your broker to request it. The appropriate exchange can decide, pretty much on the spot, to list a LEAPS option based on a customer's request.

LEAPS is just a fancy name for a stock option that has at least one year of life remaining.

Option Symbols

To quote any security electronically, it is assigned a *symbol*. For example, the symbol for General Motors common stock is, quite logically, GM. Unfortunately, *logic* doesn't play a great part in most symbols. To quote options, a more complex symbology is required. A stock or index option symbol consists of three parts:

Equity option symbol = Base symbol + Expiration code
+ Strike price code

Expiration codes are standardized. The expiration codes for *call options* are:

A = January	E = May	I = September
B = February	F = June	J = October
C = March	G = July	K = November
D = April	H = August	L = December

The expiration codes for *put options* are:

M = January	Q = May	U = September
N = February	R = June	V = October
O = March	S = July	W = November
P = April	T = August	X = December

Strike price codes are *somewhat* standardized, but there are some very strange exceptions to the rules. All of the letters, A through Z, are used for standardized codes. But in the case of some "odd" strikes, caused perhaps by noninteger splits (3-for-2 or 5-for-4, for example), minor stock dividends and the like, the letters can sometimes mean something else. The only way to know for sure is to use a quote system that has the table built in, so it can translate the strike price codes into striking prices. Your broker should have such a system, but Internet quoting services have it too. The "standard" strike price codes are:

A = 5	F = 30	K = 55	P = 80
B = 10	G = 35	L = 60	Q = 85
C = 15	H = 40	M = 65	R = 90
D = 20	I = 45	N = 70	S = 95
E = 25	J = 50	O = 75	T = 100

If the underlying is trading at levels greater than 100, the strike prices codes refer to the last two digits of the strike price. For example, IBM might be trading near 150. Then J would stand for 150, L for 160, and so forth. Or the $OEX Index might be trading near 650, so in that case J would stand for 650, L for 660, and so on.

Originally, all stocks and indices had strike prices 5 points apart. Now, many stocks have strike prices that are 2½ points apart, so another sort of semistandardized convention has been used, involving the remaining letters of the alphabet:

U = 7.5	or	37.5	or	67.5
V = 12.5	or	42.5	or	72.5
W = 17.5	or	47.5	or	77.5
X = 22.5	or	52.5	or	82.5
Y = 27.5	or	57.5	or	87.5
Z = 32.5	or	62.5	or	92.5

These semistandardized codes quickly become confusing. That's why it is best if you need to find the option's symbol to go to your broker, or perhaps to use the "delayed quotes" page at the CBOE's Web site, www.cboe.com.

LEAPS Symbols

To make matters even more complicated, note that the expiration codes used earlier *do not specify a year.* That is, "January" is assumed to be the *next* January on the calendar. It cannot also represent the following January. Since LEAPS options expire a couple years in the future, *complete new base symbols are used for LEAPS options.* Thus, for IBM, the symbol *VIB* is used to designate IBM options expiring in the year 2003 with *LIB* for IBM options expiring in the year 2004. So, the IBM Jan 2003 LEAPS with a strike price of 160 would have the symbol VIBAL.

Every stock that has LEAPS options has additional symbols associated with it that designate the later year options. This is particularly cumbersome. Once again, your broker or the CBOE site should be able to supply any symbol you want. On a sophisticated option quoting system, if you type in "IBM," the quote system should give you back *all* of the IBM options, including the LEAPS, so that all of the symbols can be found in one place.

FUTURES

Futures Contracts

First, futures *contracts* will be described. Then, futures *options* will be discussed. For those not familiar with futures contracts, it is easiest to think of them just like shares of stock. They can drop to zero (in theory, but not really in practice), and they can rise to great heights. The main differences between futures and stocks are that (1) futures require far less margin, and therefore have far greater leverage; and (2) futures have an expiration date.

Most of the "older" commodity contracts have a real commodity underlying them—corn, wheat, soybeans, orange juice, and so on. By the expiration date, the *actual physical* product changes hands in accordance with the terms of the contract as specified by the exchange where the futures are traded. For example, one contract of corn involves 5,000 *bushels* of corn.

The newer "financial" contracts may have a *cash* settlement, in some cases. That is, the futures contract is marked to market each day (i.e., your profit or loss is totaled by your brokerage firm), and on the last day the contract just disappears from your account, leaving you with only the cash profit or loss from having owned it.

Futures Option Symbols

A futures option symbol consists of two parts:

$$\text{Futures option symbol} = \text{Futures base symbol} + \text{Expiration code}$$

Futures base symbols are quite logical (usually). For example, LC = Live Cattle, SP = S&P 500 Index, SM = Soybean Meal, and so on. Both futures contracts and futures *option* contracts need to have expiration codes.

Expiration codes are somewhat different for futures and their options:

F = January	K = May	U = September
G = February	M = June	V = October
H = March	N = July	X = November
J = April	Q = August	Z = December

Also, since futures contracts can span several years, a single digit is used to describe the expiration date. Therefore, the symbols "H3" would indicate March of the year 2003. So the futures option symbol for S&P futures expiring in March 2003 would be SPH3.

Futures Options Terms

This section provides a brief review of some terms related to futures options. All futures contracts have an expiration date. *Physical commodities* (such as corn, gold, sugar, etc.) have a **first notice day** as well, that is, the first day that the holder of a long futures contract can be made to take delivery of the physical commodity. Thus, speculators usually exit the market by that date. Options expire *before* the first notice day so that all exercising and assignment of options is out of the way before physical delivery begins in the commodity. The expiration dates of the options are thus different for each commodity each

Table 1.3   Futures Options Terms

Exercise	For futures or cash.
First notice day	Earliest date holder can be made to accept delivery of the commodity.
Option expiration	Before FND.
Delivery	At seller's option.
Option expiration date sources	Futures magazine. Chart books. Broker's notice.
Commissions	Round turn. Per side. Flat rate.
Settlement price	Middle of the closing range at the end of the day.

month, and it would be very useful for the trader to get a calendar of expiration dates.

Both futures and futures options have a **settlement price**—a price that the market makers post as the "middle" of the closing range at the end of the day. Nothing actually trades at that price, but it gives an idea of where the market makers think the options would be trading.

Table 1.3 presents a brief summary of futures options terms.

Futures Options Symbols

Symbols for futures options are a lot easier to master than stock options. In fact, there is hope that some day *all* symbols—futures, stock, and index—will be handled in this manner:

$$\frac{\text{Futures}}{\text{option symbol}} = \frac{\text{Futures}}{\text{symbol}} + \frac{\text{Strike price}}{\textit{as a number}} + \text{Designator}$$

$$= \frac{\text{Base}}{\text{symbol}} + \frac{\text{Expiration}}{\text{code}} + \frac{\text{Strike price}}{\textit{as a number}} + \text{Designator}$$

A call with strike price 1350 on the March 2003 S&P futures contract would have the symbol: SPH3 1350c. Note that the strike price is a number and the letter designation "c" is used for call; "p" would be used for a put.

These symbols are much more logical and straightforward than the convoluted method used for stock and index options.

Serial Options

Another concept that sometimes arises in futures options is that of the **serial option,** an option on a futures contract that has an expiration month different from that of any of the futures contracts. This is an attempt by the exchanges to have options trading at nearly every month of the year, even though there is not an underlying futures contract that expires in the same month.

For example, S&P 500 futures expire in March and June (there is no contract for April or May). However, during the months of April and May, the exchange lists options with those expiration dates, because short-term option traders are accustomed to trading them then. The underlying futures contract is the *June* contract (i.e., the next contract available) for these serial options. So in April:

Option	April S&Ps	May S&Ps	June S&Ps
Expiration date:	4/17/98	5/15/98	6/19/98
Underlying future:	June future	June future	June future
If exercised:	June future	June future	Cash

Quote Machines

If you are paying for quotes, there *may* be some differences on various quote systems regarding futures options. For example, the "c" for call or "p" for put may be required to be placed *before* the strike price on some quote systems, but that is a minor thing. If you should encounter a quote system that requires symbology *significantly* different from that described here—for either stocks, indices, or futures—I would seriously consider switching your account to another quote vendor.

It is very useful to know what option position is equivalent to a position in the underlying stock. *If an investor buys a call and sells a put with the same terms—same expiration date and strike price—then that investor has a position equivalent to a long position in the underlying stock.* Conversely, if the investor *sells* a call and *buys* a put with the same terms, the position is equivalent to a short position in the underlying stock. Table 1.4 summarizes options as substitutes for the underlying stock.

Table 1.4 Options as Substitutes for the Underlying Stock

Buy call + Sell put = Buy stock
XYZ stock = 50; XYZ July 50 call = 3; XYZ July 50 Put = 3A

Stock	Profit if Long Stock	Buy Call Profit	Sell Put Profit	Total Option Profit
40	−$1,000	−$300	−$700	−$1,000
45	−$500	−$300	−$200	−$500
50	0	−$300	+$300	0
55	+$500	+$200	+$300	+$500
60	+$1,000	+$700	+$300	+$1,000

Investment	Options: 20% + Put premium = $1,000 + $300 = $1,300, initially.
	Stock: $5,000 cash, or $2,500 on margin.
Debit balance	Options: None; stock on margin: $2,500.
Disadvantages	No dividends on options position (but earn interest?).
	Two commissions.
	Two bid/asked spreads.
Shorting stock without an uptick	Sell call + Buy put = Sell stock
	Smaller margin requirement.

Equivalent Positions

Two or more option trading strategies are equivalent if they have the same profit potential. Alternately stated, they are equivalent if they have profit graphs with exactly the same *shape*. While there are many equivalent positions—literally hundreds of pairs of strategies—a few are quite important and should be understood by the well-versed option trader. The following pairs are equivalent:

Position 1 . . . is equivalent to . . . Position 2

A long call	Long stock + Long put
Long stock	Long call + Short put
Short stock	Long put + Short call

Among other very important equivalents is this one: *A covered call write . . . is equivalent to . . . the sale of a naked put.* Many (unsophisticated) investors think that a covered call write is a conservative strategy because they have heard their brokers say so, and they know it is allowed in the most conservative retirement account. However, nearly every option trader—even the novice—knows that naked options have big risks and are not conservative strategies. How can this be? Are the two strategies *really* equivalent? Yes, they are: Both have limited upside profit potential and both have large potential downside risk if the underlying stock should suffer a serious decline. It's just that brokers and government regulators feel that owning a stock is conservative—so what if it can drop to zero!

TRADING FUTURES

Many more investors and traders trade stocks rather than futures. This fact, however, should not dissuade you from investigating futures trading as a potential source of trading income. As you will see, there are a certain number of factors regarding options—volume, price, volatility, and so on—that apply equally well to futures and stock (as well as index) option trading. Thus, if you were to ignore futures (or either of the other two as well—stocks and indices), you would be ignoring a section of the marketplace that offers the potential for profitable option trades.

One of the major differences between futures and stock trading is that there are *daily price limits* on nearly every futures contract. Once the futures reach that price, they cannot advance or decline any further in that direction. For example, suppose that May Soybeans closed at 660 on a particular day. The daily limit move in Soybeans is 30 cents. That limit is established by the exchange where the futures trade—the Chicago Board of Trade, in this case. So, on the following day,

May Soybeans would not be allowed to trade above 690 or to trade below 630. Once they reach one of those prices, the marketplace remains open, but no trades will be occurring.

For example, suppose May Soybeans trade down to 630, down the 30-cent limit from the previous night's closing price of 660. There will be offers to sell at 630, but no bids to buy. Thus, trades won't occur. The market is still open, however, and if some news or other market-moving information should come to light, soybeans could begin to rally off the limit down condition.

However, if May Soybeans *don't* trade up off the limit down condition, that could be a psychologically depressing factor for the next day's trading. In fact, the market might just open straight down the limit again—another 30 cents—to what would then be a price of 600. It is possible that the contract could *open down the limit again, with virtually no trading taking place* at all on that day. In fact, a series of these limit moves might occur. When they do, the "average" futures trader is stuck. If you happened to be long while this was going on, you *could not* sell your futures contract to get out of the position, which is worsening every day.

Fortunately, there is a way around this situation—it is the use of the equivalent position. Since the dangers of getting caught in a series of limit moves are so devastating, **understanding this option strategy is mandatory—not optional.**

Specifically, a futures position that is locked limit down— meaning that it cannot be sold because there are no bids—can be sold "equivalently" by using the equivalents that we saw earlier. The investor could buy a put and sell a call with the same terms. The reason that this can be done is that the *options* continue to trade until they, too, reach their limits—which means that, in most cases, the at-the-money options will still be trading even though the futures are locked limit. See the summary provided in Figure 1.3.

Assume May beans: 630, down 30 (limit down)

Options are still trading: May 625 call: 8
                                May 625 put: 16

Implied futures price: = Strike + Call − Put
                                = 625 + 8 − 16
                                = 617

Use this price in your model or for any analysis.

Mandatory Knowledge   Taking the loss on a locked limit position

If you're long futures, you can "sell" them by:
    Buy the 625 put @ 16
    Sell the 625 call @ 8
    Total Debit: 8 points

Eventually, you sell the futures at 617:
    Exercise put or assigned on call @ 625
    Less the 8-point debit
    Net sale price: 625 − 8 = 617

Figure 1.3   Price discovery of futures locked limit.

Futures Margin

One other point about futures trading is the margin required and the daily mark to market. When you buy a stock, even if you buy it on margin, there is no further money that goes into or comes out of your account until you sell the stock (or until you get a margin call, if that should occur). In the futures market, however, the initial margin requirement is a very small fraction of the total value of the contract. For example, earlier we saw that May Soybeans were trading at 600 cents ($6.00). One contract of Soybeans represents 5,000 bushels of Soybeans, so a one-point move in Soybeans is worth $50 per point. Hence, the full value of the Soybean contract is $30,000 (50 times 600). However, the initial *margin* required to buy or sell one contract of Soybeans is merely $1,200—or just 4%! Obviously, there is a lot of leverage in this contract.

A one-day limit move of 30 cents is worth $1,500 (30 times $50 per point of movement), so a one-day limit move could wipe out your margin completely! At that point, your brokerage would ask for more margin. In fact, in a futures account, each position is marked to the market every day and the cash profits or losses added to or subtracted from the account. In this manner, it is easy for the brokerage firm to identify margin problems. I find this method of record keeping useful for the short-term trader as well because it forces viewing of profits and losses daily in actual dollar terms. Sometimes, when you own stocks, for example, and they begin to go down and lose money, it doesn't seem like "real" money because no debits are being subtracted from your account. In this manner, you might be lulled into holding a position that you should really be jettisoning. A futures trader wouldn't have that problem because he or she sees (and *feels*) the losses daily.

TRADING TECHNOLOGY

Data Services

Probably nothing better demonstrates the advances that have been made in communication technology than the myriad of possible ways that stock and futures market data can be brought into the individual's home. It used to be fairly difficult and costly to get data—so costly in fact that it was relegated to trading and brokerage firms almost exclusively. Now, however, access to data is becoming less and less expensive—much of it free—and can be delivered to a home office in several different ways.

In addition, the Internet has added another beneficial dimension to these services. Now, with sites such as the CBOE (www.cboe.com), delayed stock and option prices can be obtained free. Competitors are springing up in many places. In fact, the sites mentioned on this page might be outdated within just a matter of months. However, having said that, both www.quote .com and www.gfds.com (Genesis Data) provide good, free quoting capabilities as well. Meanwhile, www.ino.com offers analytical capability as well.

At the risk of sounding commercial, I encourage you to visit McMillan Analysis Corp's Web site at www.optionstrategist.com. The site provides some very valuable *free* services—such as:

1. A complete summary of implied and historical volatility on *every* underlying instrument upon which listed options are traded; updated weekly.
2. Option and stock quote chains.
3. Earnings estimates.
4. A probability calculator for simple what-if probability.
5. A calculator for computing returns on covered call writes.
6. A service that pages, faxes, or e-mails you (your choice) if a stock hits a predefined price.
7. Plus many other informational services, such as an option chat room, a *large* question and answer area, the ability to order free trials of our newsletters, and more.

In real-time prices, there are two costs involved: (1) the fee that is paid to the data provider service itself (e.g., eSignal) and (2) the fee that is paid to the exchange that disseminates the prices. Real-time exchange fees are modest for stocks and stock options, but escalate rapidly for futures and futures options. See Table 1.5 for a summary of data services and means of access.

Software

Getting data into your computer is only half the battle if you're trading from home or from your office. You need something to analyze that data—software. Such software can range from

Table 1.5 Summary of Data Services and Means
of Access

Fees	Exchange, service
Option quote pages	
Data connection	Satellite
	FM radio
	Direct phone link
	Cable TV
	Internet
Delayed prices	Signal closing
	DTN
	Telescan
	www.cboe.com
Real-time prices	eSignal
	Realtick
	ILX
	Bloomberg
	PC Quote
Software	PowerAnalyzer
	Option Vue
	AIQ
	Track Data
	Option Station

simple programs that cost $100 or less to complex, full-blown
systems that attach to a real-time data feed and perform a myriad of calculations and portfolio management functions, and
which cost quite a bit more. There is nothing wrong with the
simple programs, especially if that is really all that you need. In
these software programs, the user must generally type in the
stock price, strike price, expiration month, and so on, because
the software does not attach to the data gathering service. I use
a simple calculator like this quite often when I just want a quick
view of the analytics on a specific option. McMillan Analysis

Corp. sells such a calculator, as does Ken Trester. Mantic Software also has an excellent version.

The most well-known "big" option analysis programs are shown in Table 1.6. Soon, similar programs will be available on the Internet. The advantage to using the Internet version will be that you won't have to maintain any data on your own computer. All of the data maintenance, dividends data, strike price values, stock splits, and so on, will be handled by the Internet vendor. You, as a fee-paying subscriber to the Internet service, merely log on, calculate whatever you want, view the results, and log off. No software installation, no data files clogging up your hard drive—just pure options analysis. This is the future of the software business for option traders, and it's not far off. PowerAnalyzer is the current leader in this technology.

Even the simplest software program should be able to calculate an option's implied volatility and its delta. If you want something like portfolio management—that is, the ability to see the profits and losses on your option positions, and possibly to analyze the risk of the aggregate option positions in your portfolio—then you will need more expensive software. Portfolio analysis is not normally included in any low-end option software.

Table 1.6 Option Analysis Programs

Theoretical value calculations	Implied volatility Delta
Portfolio management system	Profit and loss Exposure of portfolio to market
Types of option models	Black-Scholes—faster calculation Binomial model: Cox, Ross, Rubenstein—slower calculation (Use 0% for futures options)
Internet (free) analysis	Implied volatilities on www.optionstrategist.com Futures subscription site: www.optionsanalysis.com

The most important thing about buying software for option analysis—and remember, as we said earlier, you *must* have some sort of model available, for trading without a model will cost you money—is to *buy what you need.* If you buy something more complex than required, you probably won't use it.

SUMMARY

This chapter introduced the concepts and terms basic to option trading strategies. Familiarity with such concepts as volatility, symbols, option pricing models, and equivalent positions is essential for success in option trading. Also essential are tracking and understanding information about the instruments you plan to trade. Gathering pertinent information has become easier recently thanks to new communication technology.

REVIEW QUESTIONS: INTRODUCTION

1. Which of the following would *not* be a dealer in over-the-counter-options?

   a. Merrill Lynch.

   b. Salomon Brothers.

   c. Options Clearing Corp.

   d. Trust Bankers.

2. Which are advantages of exchange-traded options? Choose all that apply.

   a. Lower commissions.

   b. Secondary market.

   c. Larger open interest.

   d. More reputable brokers.

3. Which are differences between CBOE-listed stock options and NYSE-listed warrants? Choose all that are true.

   a. Warrants must be borrowed before they can be sold, while options don't require borrowing.

   b. Stock options are for 100 shares of stock, while warrants are typically for one share.

   c. For one particular stock, there is generally only one warrant strike price, while there are many strikes for stock options.

   d. Stock options have an expiration date, but warrants do not.

4. Which strategies have the *possibility* of much larger profits than losses? Choose any that apply.

   a. Call buying.

   b. Straddle buying.

   c. Covered call writing.

   d. Naked writing.

5. Which three-month stock option would normally have the *least* time value premium?

   a. A call that is 10% in-the-money.

   b. A put that is 10% in-the-money.

   c. An at-the-money put.

   d. An at-the-money call.

6. About which of the following would there likely be some disagreement among traders?

   a. The correct way to measure 20-day historical volatility.

   b. The correct way to measure implied volatility.

   c. The correct way to measure statistical volatility.

   d. The correct way to estimate implied volatility.

7. Choose all that apply. If a stock has been trading with a 20-day historical volatility of 30%, then:

  a. It is likely to rise or fall 30% in the next 20 days.

  b. It is likely to rise or fall 30% sometime during the next year.

  c. Its options should be trading with an implied volatility of 30%.

  d. It is more volatile than a stock with a 20-day historical volatility of 20%.

8. Given the criteria that follows, choose the option with the highest implied volatility:

Given: Stock price = 100

    Current date = April 1

    Dividends = $0.00

  a. April 100 call trading at 5.

  b. July 100 call trading at 5¼.

  c. April 90 call trading at 10.

  d. July 110 put trading at 10¼.

9. Which options *don't* have their last trading day as the third Friday of the expiration month? Choose all that apply.

  a. Corn options.

  b. S&P 500 futures options.

  c. CBOE-listed index options.

  d. Stock options.

10. Currency futures options expire in March, June, September, and December. Which of the following would be *serial* options? Choose all that apply.

  a. D-mark options expiring in June.

  b. Yen options expiring in April.

   c. British pound options expiring in December.

   d. Swiss Franc options expiring in November.

11. Choose the *one* position that is *not* equivalent to the others.

   a. Long one July 50 call, and short one July 60 call.

   b. Long one July 50 put, and short one July 60 put.

   c. Long 100 shares of stock, long a July 50 put, and short a July 60 call.

   d. Long one July 60 put, and short one July 50 put.

12. If your trading supervisor wanted to see a "picture" that would describe the risk and rewards of a complex option position that you had in place, would you show a profit graph or a pricing curve? Why? What other simple option measure might you show to explain the potential risk of the position?

13. State the position that is equivalent to shorting 100 shares of stock and buying one call.

14. State the position that is equivalent to buying a put and selling a call with the same terms—same underlying, strike price, and expiration date.

15. Using the two equivalent positions from Question 14, what are the two main advantages of the option position?

16. May cotton futures are trading up the limit at a price of 76.50. Given the following option prices and the fact that these options are trading freely,

     May 76 call: 8.00   May 76 put: 2.20

     May 77 call: 7.50   May 77 put: 2.70

     May 78 call: 7.10   May 78 put: 3.30

   a. Where would you say that the futures *would be* trading if they could trade freely?

   b. If you were short *five* contracts of May cotton futures, and a one point move in cotton is worth $500, what option position (and in what quantity) would you establish to completely hedge yourself—effectively removing the position at current prices?

17. Which of the following data connections can deliver the most data, fastest, to your computer?

    a. FM radio.

    b. Cable box.

    c. Satellite.

    d. Internet via standard phone line.

18. Arrange the following four items in order of their *monthly* cost, from lowest to highest:

    a. Obtaining delayed NYSE quotes.

    b. Obtaining real-time quotes on all of the major stock, option, and futures exchanges.

    c. Having a Bloomberg Terminal in your office.

    d. Having an Internet account with AOL.

19. Which of the following would you *not* be able to obtain from using the Black-Scholes model? Choose all that apply, from the five choices listed.

    a. Implied volatility of the option.

    b. Delta of the option.

    c. Historical volatility of the underlying stock.

    d. Implied dividend of underlying stock.

    e. Theoretical price of the option.

20. You are trading option positions for a member firm. To keep software costs down, your boss wants you to use the free model that exists on the CBOE Web site and the delayed quotes that are also on that site for your modeling and analysis. List at least five points you would make to him or her to justify purchasing a sophisticated option analysis software program.

2

OPTIONS AS DIRECT INDICATORS

LEARNING OBJECTIVES

The material in this chapter will help you to:

- Use options as predictors of market behavior.
- Distinguish between direct indicators and contrary indicators.
- Use price and volume as technical indicators.
- Read the signs of insider trading.
- Filter out noise from insider trading activity.
- Determine whether to buy options or the underlying stock.
- Understand event-driven straddle buying.

Most people associate options with a few basic concepts—leverage, some sort of protection, or perhaps a way to reduce absolute risk. But the use of options as a technical indicator in their own right is not something that is widespread. Some of the concepts discussed in this chapter *have* become a little more common in recent years—particularly the use of the put-call ratio for making broad market predictions—but most investors do not know how to employ these concepts. In addition, some of the people attempting to use options as predictors are actually making incorrect use of the material. So, in this chapter, you learn specifically, and *correctly,* how to use options to help you in predicting the movement of the underlying stock, futures, or index. Just think of this as learning about a new technical indicator.

TECHNICAL INDICATORS

Any technical indicator is either a direct indicator or a contrary indicator. A **direct indicator** means that whatever the indicator says about the market is the way that the market is going to move. With options, there is really only one direct indicator— the one we are going to discuss first—and that is the tracking of illegal insider trading. A **contrary indicator** is one that says the practitioner should take a market position *opposite* to what the indicator is predicting. Most contrary indicators measure market sentiment, and that is true for the options as well. Unfortunately, most of our fellow option traders are wrong most of the time—especially at major turning points in stocks, futures, and indices—so if we can measure what they are doing, and then do the opposite, we should make money. Table 2.1 summarizes the ways in which options can be used as predictors.

Price: Implied Volatility

All of these option technical indicators rely on one of two things—price or volume—as the foundation for the analysis. Remember that *implied volatility* reflects itself in the price of the options, so that expensive options have high implied volatility, and cheap options have low implied volatility. Therefore, when

Table 2.1 Using Options as a Predictor

Direct indicator	Stock option volume.
	Insider trading.
Contrary indicator	Option prices.
	Option volume.
Theory of contrary indicator	The masses are wrong at major turning points.
	Option activity is a good way to measure what (uninformed) speculators are doing.

we talk about using option price as a technical indicator, we might also say that we are using implied volatility as a technical indicator. They represent the same thing in this case.

Carrying this thinking one step further, also recall that implied volatility is the volatility that the marketplace is using as the *prediction* of the volatility of the underlying instrument during the life of the option. So, implied volatility is a matter of opinion among traders; no one knows for sure what it's going to be. It is the culmination of all the guesses of all the traders. If, for some reason, implied volatility moves to one extreme or the other, there is a great likelihood that it can be used to make decisions about upcoming movements of the underlying instrument. Again, if there is insider knowledge, we should heed what the implied volatility is saying, but in most cases it is the reflection of the opinion of the (uninformed) public, and we should be prepared to treat it as a contrary indicator. This chapter and the next will contain many examples of how and where to use these important technical indicators.

Volume

The other indicator is volume. If we spot the activity of illegal insider traders as they barge into the option market—perhaps inflating normal trading patterns five- or tenfold—then that is a direct indicator. On the other hand, if we measure the public's trading volume in call options versus put options on a particular stock or relative sector of stocks, then we might have a useful contrary indicator.

Insider Trading

If someone on Wall Street gets advance knowledge of a takeover or some other important information that will greatly affect the price of a stock (earnings surprise, new product announcement, etc.) greed often takes over, and the person will rush to buy the stock or the options to make a "sure" profit. **Insider trading**— trading with advance knowledge of a corporate event—is illegal, but that doesn't keep it from happening. It is as if these investors have tomorrow's newspaper and they want to act on it. (But, if you ever *do* come across tomorrow's newspaper—play the lottery! Forget options!)

They often buy options instead of the underlying because of the great leverage available when a quick move occurs. We have seen this type of activity for ages, and we look for signs of it so that we might know what these insider traders are doing. It is perfectly legal for us to use their activity as a direct technical indicator and to attempt to "piggy-back" on their trades. Most commonly, their activity shows up as dramatically increased trading volume, but it may also show up as an increase in price levels— implied volatility—as well. On *some* occasions, which we'll discuss shortly, the increase in implied volatility is our only clue as to their activities; volume does not increase in those cases. There are several examples coming up that will clarify these situations.

Simplistically, we want to look for one day's option activity on a particular stock's options to at least *double* its average activity for a day. The average activity is the 20-day moving average of option volume on that stock. In addition, we want there to be some sort of *absolute* volume measure. So, we arbitrarily set 500 contracts as a minimum number. This would eliminate wasting our time looking at situations where the average volume is 20 contracts a day, and one day that stock's options total 50 contracts. Insider trading activity will normally generate volume well in excess of 500 contracts, as long as there is a reasonable amount of liquidity in the stock options. Once this situation is identified, we want to buy calls (or buy the underlying stock) if there is a heavy preponderance of call volume by whomever is trading these options, and we want to buy puts (or *short* the underlying stock) if there is heavy put trading by these insiders.

One other thing to look for is some confirmation by the price of the underlying stock itself. If insiders are buying many calls, the stock should begin to move up. This happens for at least two reasons: (1) institutions pick up these rumors, too, and they often play them by trading stocks; and (2) the market makers who sell the options to these insiders are not stupid; they want to hedge themselves after selling the options, and often the best hedge is to take an offsetting position in the underlying stock. That is, if the market makers have been selling calls to the insiders, then the market makers might go into the stock market and buy stock to hedge themselves.

From an outsider's perspective, like ours, what we want to see is some technical confirmation by the underlying stock. For example, if there's a small resistance area above where the stock is trading, we want to see the stock break through there, thus giving a technical confirmation to the call buying that we have been observing and are attributing to insider call buying. *If the stock can't at least go up while all these calls are being bought, then perhaps this is not a true insider trading situation.* Table 2.2 shows how insider trading provides signs of changes in the option market.

These insider-trading situations tend to manifest themselves as rumors in the marketplace. They may appear in chat rooms, on bulletin boards, or in newsletters devoted to this type of activity (such as our *Daily Volume Alerts*). If you take the time to carefully study the option and stock activity in these situations, you can often weed out the "bad rumors"—those

Table 2.2   Options as Direct Indicators

Volume Alerts

Fact	Insiders buy options for leverage.
Signs	1. Daily option volume is more than 2 times average option volume.
	2. Total option volume is more than 500 contracts.
Action	1. Filter out noise: covered writes, spreads, arbitrage.
	2. Look to buy if call volume is heavy.
	3. Look to sell if put volume is more than or equal to 40% of total volume.
	4. Use technical confirmation as well: don't take a position until previous day's range is exceeded.

Note: This process doesn't really work for futures.

created by someone who wants to move the stock to liquidate his or her own position. This type of trader often feels that the best way to move the stock is to start a false rumor. Here is an example: A stock suddenly falls dramatically, perhaps on bad earnings. It is now trading at 10 when it was just trading at 20 a few days ago. Suddenly, a rumor appears that such-and-such a company is interested in acquiring this stock because its low stock price is extremely attractive. The stock then rallies from 10 to 13 on heavy volume. Who do you suppose is selling at 13? Right! The trader who started the rumor at 10, who holds a lot of stock bought near 20 and wants to unload it! That is a false rumor, and it can often be identified because it does not fit into the typical pattern of activity of an insider.

Noise

There may also be **noise**—trading volume that has nothing to do with insider trading activity. In that case, we must filter out that noise lest we be misled into buying stocks on which there really isn't any insider trading. This becomes something of an art. It's hard to say what a typical day is, because the market is so dynamic, normally there are between 60 and 100 stocks that trade more than double their average option activity on any given day. Of those 60 to 100 stocks, only about 5 to 8 have any sort of insider trading. The rest are just noise. That is, the volume in the rest is a result of other types of market activity that inflate trading volume but are not related to any sort of inside information on the company.

There are three main types of activity that we classify as noise, including:

1. *Covered call write.* Often an institution (mutual fund, hedge fund, etc.) decides to write calls against a large block of stock. They may already own the stock, or if the institution is in the business of hedged option strategies, they may buy the stock and sell the calls at the same time. In any case, the option trade is often large and occurs all at one time. Insiders would not be able to buy 5,000 option contracts at one time from a market maker because they would not have the proper representation by an institutional broker. What normally happens is that, say, Morgan Stanley comes to the trading floor and says to the market makers, "We are going to cross 5,000 IBM Jan 120 calls to a customer. Do you guys want any?" The market makers will often take a good portion of the trade if they think it is priced favorably for them, and Morgan Stanley will take the rest in their firm's account. They will also cross the stock if necessary, and the covered write is in place. Moreover, it is unlikely that an insider would be coming in through Morgan Stanley's institutional desk and even more unlikely that Morgan and/or the market makers would sell an insider that many calls at *any* price. This often results in almost all of the day's option volume being in one particular option series—and it is normally one that is a few months out in time. This is not the type of option that an insider would buy. If you

have access to time and sales, you can easily see this; but even if you don't, you can still see that there was little activity in any other options on this stock.

2. *Arbitrage.* Recall that we earlier saw which option positions were equivalent to what stock positions. **Long stock** is equivalent to a long call and a short put with the same terms, and **short stock** is equivalent to a short call and a long put with the same terms. If we observe that most of the heavy option activity in a particular day's trading is an approximately equal number of puts and calls with the same terms, then we can probably surmise that an arbitrage took place—particularly if there is little or no option activity in other options on this stock.

These trades, too, often occur in large blocks. Say someone buys 50,000 shares of common, sells 500 calls and buys 500 puts (with the same terms). Do not bother yourself with *why* someone is doing this—it is arbitrage, and it is not available to commission-paying customers like yourself. This activity can be easily identified with a time and sales screen, but if you don't have a time and sales screen, you can still observe that these large blocks dominate that day's option trading and are therefore most likely noise. An insider wouldn't buy calls and sell puts—selling puts takes too much capital and the reward is limited. This is not what the insider's interested in.

3. *Spread.* Many traders of all kinds do spreads. Spreads generally limit risk in one manner or another, but also tend to limit profit potential (you can't get something for nothing—especially on Wall Street). However, not wanting to limit profit potential, an insider wouldn't bother with a spread. So, if you observe that there has been a heavy increase in option activity, but then you notice that most of it is involved in two options that look like a **vertical spread** (same expiration month, different strikes) or perhaps a

calendar spread (different expiration months, same strike), then it is most likely that a spread was transacted and that this is *not* a candidate for insider trading analysis. If you have time and sales, it is often easier to identify spreads because you can see that both sides of the spread were transacted in equal quantities and at the same time. Otherwise, you can make an educated guess.

Table 2.3 provides a summary of option trading patterns that signify noise rather than insider trading.

Before getting into the actual examples, let me point out a couple of other things. The information that these insiders have normally leaks out of corporate offices inadvertently—perhaps through an outside contractor, such as a printer, law firm, or accounting firm. Not *every* takeover is leaked in advance. One of the largest in history—Disney's takeover of Cap Cities Broadcasting—was conceived by the two CEOs at a conference.

Table 2.3 Option Trading Patterns: Noise, Not Insider Option Activity

Assume the average option volume in each of these stocks is 200 contracts on a given day.

Covered writes	XYZ:	50	April 50 call	Volume:	50
			May 55 call	Volume:	20
			July 55 call	Volume:	1,500
Arbitrage	ABC:	60	May 50 call	Volume:	1,000
			May 50 put	Volume:	1,000
			April 55 call	Volume:	30
Spreads	XXX:	25	April 20 call	Volume:	800
			April 25 call	Volume:	800

			April	May	June	July
The ideal pattern	XYZ:	50	April	May	June	July
		45	300	100	50	20
		50	800	300	100	75
		55	600	350		50
		60	200	100		

They brought in only a handful of top advisors on both sides, so very few people knew about the pending deal, and all of them were extremely trustworthy. When the deal was announced, there had not been even the slightest bit of increased option activity in advance of the announcement. "Quiet" deals like this happen all of the time, but so do the "loud" ones—ones where we have a chance to play.

This type of analysis only works on stock options. It does not work on futures options, or on index options. We have tested it on both, but there is apparently no meaningful information that can move futures or index markets that is known to only a few and leaked in advance. We had at one time thought that important analysts at major firms, who might be ready to upgrade an entire sector, might tell their best clients in advance, and we would see activity in the sector index options. But this has not proven to be true.

Over all, even with all of the work necessary to weed out noise, bad rumors, and so on, this strategy produces about 45% to 50% winners, but if you use stops to limit your losses, the profits can often be large. Adhere to your stops and sell out when the news that was anticipated actually hits the tape.

Some Examples

The charts in Figures 2.1 through 2.9 depict the situation in the stock and option markets just before takeovers or earnings surprises were announced. The "option volume" data on the chart doesn't show the breakdown as it occurred by strike and expiration month. Therefore, that data is included in the text portion that follows.

American Cyanamid

The first example, shown in Figure 2.1, is that of American Cyanamid (**ACY**). By late July, the stock was trading near 60,

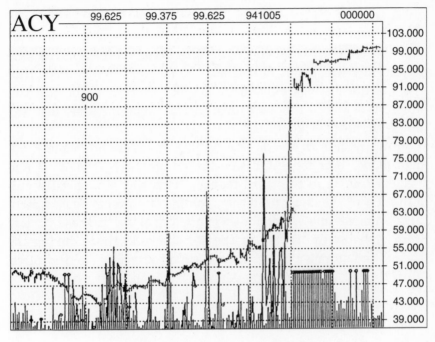

Figure 2.1 American Cyanamid.

and option volume then proceeded to reach the highest levels ever. On July 29 (a Friday) and August 1 (the following Monday), the option volume accelerated to extreme levels. The following table shows the option trading data for July 29, but a very similar pattern occurred on August 1:

ACY: 63

		Expiration Month			
		August	September	October	January
Strike price	55 calls	100	33		
	60 calls	542	315		
	65 calls	1,189	369	45	29

A total of 2,622 calls had traded. A total of 297 puts also traded, scattered among five different series. Average volume at the time was 697 total contracts. So option volume on this particular day was about four times the average. You can see that the speculative look existed in the distribution of the call volume. Most was in the near term, August, options and most was in the highest strike (65).

Finally, late in the day on August 1, American Home Products made their bid. ACY was halted on the NYSE at 63 and reopened at 91 in the third market. This was a successful culmination to the story for option volume observers. Since watching option volume is a short-term trading activity, these traders were probably in and out of the stock several times during the spring and summer of 1994, each time garnering small profits, until the big strike in early August.

Southern Pacific Railroad

On July 26, 1995, Southern Pacific Railroad **(RSP)** suddenly spurted a point higher, from 19 to 20, in one day. See the graph in Figure 2.2 for an illustration of this data. Option volume was heavy. Nearly 2,600 contracts traded that day—almost all of which were calls—as opposed to an average volume of less than 900 contracts daily. August expiration was more than three weeks away, so there was plenty of trading in the August options. The call option volume looked like this:

		Expiration Month		
		August	September	November
Strike price	12½ calls			30
	15 calls	25	50	
	17½ calls	220	88	
	20 calls	1,100	580	120

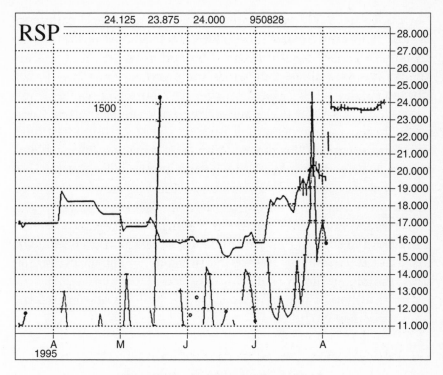

Figure 2.2 Southern Pacific Railroad.

Only a few puts had traded: 140 of the Aug 17½ puts and 230 of the Nov 230 puts. The strike price of 20 was the highest strike price available. Note the preponderance of call volume at that strike. That is good. Also, note how the August calls are the most active at the two highest strikes; that is also good. In addition, the put volume doesn't seem to indicate much, if any, arbitrage was going on since there is very little matching of call volume and put volume in the same series. Finally, there doesn't really seem to be much, if any, spread activity either, even if all of the in-the-money calls were related to spreads against the calls with a striking price of 20 (and they most assuredly are not *all* in that category), that would still leave a lot of speculative activity in both the August 20 and September 20 calls. In fact, it is more logical to assume that the Nov 20 calls and many of the in-the-money calls were bought by market makers as a hedge against the August 20 and September 20 calls they were selling to the public.

All in all, this is a classic volume pattern, and it was justified. Option volume remained high as the stock oscillated back and forth around 20 for the next five days. Then, on the sixth day, the stock received a takeover bid from Union Pacific Railroad.

Chipcom

Chipcom **(CHPM),** shown in Figure 2.3, closed at 26 on Friday, July 21, 1995, and option volume surged. As shown in the following table, option volume that day had a speculative look to it as well, although it wasn't as classic a pattern as some of the ones described earlier:

CHPM: 26

		Expiration Month		
		September	October	January
Strike price	22½ calls	77	31	28
	25 calls	338	1,482	59
	30 calls	n/a	69	66

A total of 2,014 calls had traded (and 562 puts traded also). This total volume of 2,576 was huge compared to the average volume of 280 total contracts per day—more than nine times the average.

This volume pattern has some slight anomalies in it. First, the heaviest volume is in the September options, even though the August options had four weeks of life remaining at the time.

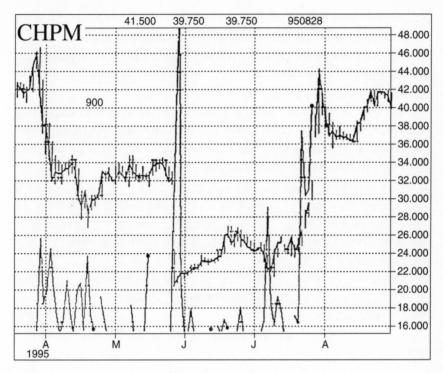

Figure 2.3 Chipcom.

Second, the majority of the volume is in the at-the-money strike (25) instead of out-of-the-money (30). Both of these facts are slightly different from what we would hope to observe in an ideal situation. Note that there were *not* any August 30 calls available for trading at the exchange. Because the pattern was not perfect, technical analysis was relied on: if CHPM could break out over the 26 level, CHPM should be bought. Surprisingly, even after the breakout, the volume never did develop the classic pattern, as more September and October options traded than did August options.

There is one other trait of the Chipcom situation that is interesting—a trait that occurs with some frequency in takeover situations: the stock, while trading down, becomes a takeover target because of its low stock price. It's sort of a Catch-22 situation. The target company is doing poorly and its earnings are bad, so the stock sells off. However, if they have a good basic business, product, and so on, the low stock price itself may raise the eyebrows of cash-rich companies in its field. These cash-rich companies can then step in and buy the relatively low-priced stock for what they feel is a reasonable price. In the case of Chipcom, the stock had traded as high as 51 in late 1994 (not shown on Figure 2.3), before plunging to a low of 20 in May 1995. This vast decrease in stock price obviously attracted the attention of Three Com, who apparently saw an opportunity to buy a (mismanaged?) company at a price well below its highs of the previous year.

Federal Paperboard

Option activity, shown in Figure 2.4, in Federal Paperboard **(FBO)**—since it came from essentially zero volume to heavy activity in just a matter of a day or two—does not need to be shown in detail to verify that it was of the speculative type. You can rest assured that any explosion in activity like that over the course of several days is speculative activity. What is perhaps more interesting here is how the expensiveness of the options dictated a slightly different strategy—one that paid off with optimum returns in this case.

With FBO at about 41 in early November 1995, option volume was very strong, so that a purchase was in order. However, the options were extremely expensive:

FBO: 41	
Call option: Price	November 40 call: 4
	November 45 call: 2
	November 50 call: 1

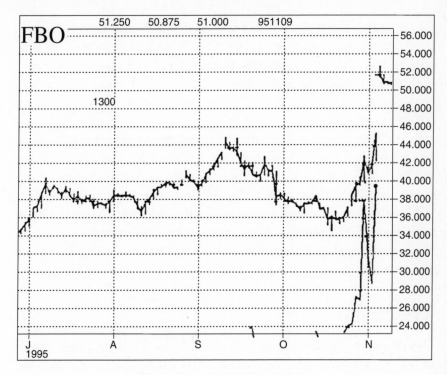

Figure 2.4 Federal Paperboard.

These options had only a couple of weeks of life remaining, so you can see how heavy the speculation was. We recommended that our customers purchase the Nov 45 to Nov 50 call bull spread. This cost a point, or perhaps 1¼, the next day. Within a week, the stock was taken over, and it traded at 53. The spread was removed for 4⅞. This is a classic case of why a bull spread is sometimes useful.

For comparison purposes, let's say the spread was sold for 5, and any of the other options could have been sold at parity with the stock at 53. Then the following table compares the various returns that would have been available from various purchases:

Purchase	Cost	Sale Price	Return
Bull spread	1	5	400%
November 40 call	4	13	225
November 45 call	2	8	300
November 50 call	1	3	200
Common stock	41	53	29

Thus, the spread was the best choice, by far, in terms of returns realized. The reason that it was able to outperform the other calls was that each individual call was so expensive to begin with that it hampered the overall returns. However, at least in the bull spread situation, we were both buying and selling an

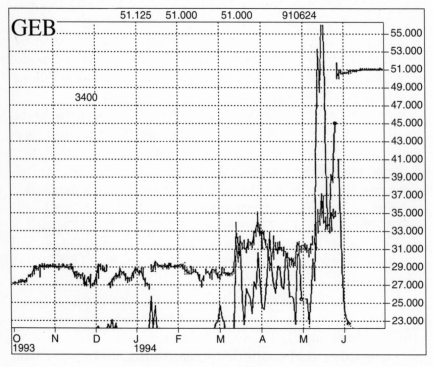

Figure 2.5   Gerber.

expensive option, and that balanced itself out somewhat. Had the takeover been at a much higher price, the spread would not have been the best winner, but it would still have done very well, and its initial cost was small—only one point.

Gerber

Gerber **(GEB)** is an interesting story because it illustrates both ways that a takeover can be signaled in advance by option trading: (1) volume and (2) price. This example, illustrated in Figure 2.5, deals with the volume example. The price example will follow in a few pages.

Until early March 1994, Gerber was trading in a very tight range of 27 to 29 with no option volume on most days. Then, in March the stock broke out to 33, accompanied by heavy call volume. A couple of weeks later, the stock managed to move up to 35 intraday, and option volume remained relatively heavy on most days. Rumors of a takeover were rampant, and when nothing happened, traders began to exit the stock. So Gerber fell all the way back to 29 by mid-April.

Then, on May 6, the stock jumped two points, from 31 to over 33, and option volume hit its highest levels ever. This was a clear signal that the stock was in play once again. On that day, option volume looked like this:

GEB: 33⅝

		Expiration Month			
		May	June	July	October
Strike price	25 calls	78	15	40	2
	30 calls	1,909	414	268	29
	35 calls	4,112	1,079	584	252

This is another classic example of what speculative option volume looks like in advance of corporate news. Nearly 8,800 calls traded that day, and about 400 puts traded as well. At the time, average daily option volume was 2,770 contracts. This tripling of normal volume was an impressive sign that something was happening in Gerber.

The stock continued to climb higher over the next two weeks, and option volume rose to ever loftier levels. The peak price was 37, and by Friday, May 20 (option expiration day for the May options), Gerber had fallen back a little to close at 34⅝. The takeover bid was received that Friday night—after the market had closed and after time to file exercise notices had expired. On Monday, Gerber opened at 51.

Much to their chagrin, some option writers were assigned out-of-the-money May 35 calls! They had gone home Friday night assuming that their written May 35 calls had expired worthless. Such an assignment means that someone "knew" enough to exercise out-of-the-money calls that were expiring, *before the takeover bid was made public!* Not *all* of the May 35 calls were exercised, but those that were smacked of some sort of insider knowledge. Why else would someone exercise an out-of-the-money option? That is the height of chutzpah. There were lawsuits filed and investigations begun, but nothing was ever proven regarding any illegal nature of the exercises.

This example illustrates that trading with inside knowledge will probably never cease. Obviously, these people's greed overcame their fear of being caught—even though an option exercise should leave a fairly clear trail. Somehow, they were able to avoid prosecution. I'm not sure why—lack of arduous pursuit by investigators, use of offshore brokers, and so on—but it demonstrates that it pays to watch what these insiders are doing and to mimic it.

Duracell

The story of Duracell **(DUR)** is reflected in Figure 2.6. The insiders were so bold as to buy every option in sight just two days

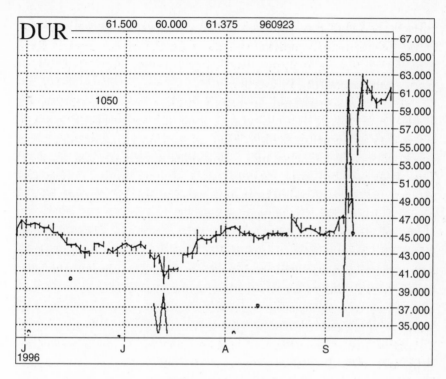

Figure 2.6 Duracell.

before the takeover was announced—inflating option volume nearly tenfold in the process. They bought some options as low as ¹⁄₁₆ of a point ($6.25 apiece) and sold them two days later for $1,100 each. The market makers clamored for justice and the *Wall Street Journal* splashed the news on the front page. Surely, if anyone was ever going to be caught, this was going to be the time. Yet, no one *was* caught. If they ever *had* been, it sure would have once again been splashed all over the *Wall Street Journal's* front page. The crooks hid behind the safety of an off-shore account.

Yet there is no need for us to engage in anything illegal as long as we have the capability of observing activity such as this. In fact, the only people that the SEC has *actually* charged and caught in this regard (besides Ivan Boesky and Michael Milken) are fairly small fry—corporate insiders who tell a relative or a neighbor about some inside information. Then, after the relative makes a completely traceable trade, and after the takeover, or whatever, occurs, and the exchange begins an investigation, the relatives are caught. Usually the penalty is a disgorgement of the profits, plus some sort of fine.

Of course, there's all the bad publicity that goes with it as well. If you should ever be tempted to try to act on some illegal insider information yourself, just ask yourself how you would feel if you opened the local newspaper and read in the headline "Local Man Arrested for Illegal Insider Trading"? I recently had someone call me with information that a family member, who was the CFO of a small NASDAQ-listed company, had told another family member that the earnings were going to be better than expected. Many of the family members were rushing out to buy the stock. *This* particular family member, though, asked me before buying, and I asked him the preceding question. Since he was a fairly well-known public figure locally, he thought about it for a minute, realized he would never make enough money from such a trade to compensate for the public embarrassment of an arrest and probably the loss of his job and therefore refrained from the purchase. If the opportunity ever presents itself, you should also refrain from making an illegal insider purchase.

WHICH OPTION TO BUY

I am often asked whether I buy stock or options when I uncover one of these situations. If there is an in-the-money option with very little time value premium, then I will buy the option. Otherwise, I buy the underlying stock. Since it is often the case that this increased option activity results in the options quickly becoming expensive, I *do not* buy at- or out-of-the-money calls on these stocks. That is just too risky because the premium will disappear if the stock is taken over or if the rumor is denied. You don't want to be holding thin air when that happens. The absolute worst feeling is to be right about a stock being taken over, but to see it advance only a point or two, and to see your options deflate to the point where you lose money.

I also buy the shortest-term option available (unless there's less than a week to go until expiration). This is another way to minimize time-value premium expense. By owning a short-term, in-the-money option, I have one with a very high delta—that is, one that behaves like the underlying stock.

Such an option still provides plenty of leverage should a takeover occur. Moreover, if the stock moves up *at all,* this option will increase in price so there will be some profit in the trade. Sure, if there is a takeover 30 points higher, then this option won't provide the same leverage as one that was well out-of-the-money would have, but how often is a "telegraphed" takeover going to increase that much in price? Not often, I can assure you.

Two examples illustrate these points. First, suppose that there is a takeover rumor in a stock, and the options are *not* too expensive. In that case, the option arrays might look something like this:

Date: September 1
Stock: 44

Options	Price	Delta
September 35 call:	$9\frac{1}{8}$	0.99
September 40 call:	$4\frac{1}{2}$	0.84
September 45 call:	$1\frac{1}{2}$	0.44
September 50 call:	$\frac{1}{2}$	0.13

These options are trading with an implied volatility of 50%. That is fairly high for a regular stock, but not necessarily high for a takeover rumor. In the real world, we would be able to compare the current level of implied volatility with the point at which implied volatility normally trades, but that's not important for this example.

I would probably buy the Sept 35 call because it barely has any time value premium, and its delta indicates that it behaves *just* like stock. The Sept 40 would be a reasonable choice as well, although with less than three weeks remaining until expiration, the loss of the half point of time-value premium is a significant percentage. Neither the Sept 45 nor the Sept 50 call would be an acceptable purchase. In many cases, the stock rises in advance of the actual takeover announcement since the option volume is publicized in newsletters and the media. Hence, a takeover might occur at only a slightly higher price. If this stock were to receive a takeover bid at 46 tomorrow, both the Sept 45 call and the Sept 50 would lose money. The other two would profit.

Now let's look at a similar, but slightly different, example—one where the options are *really* expensive, probably because the rumor has been whipped into a frenzy by the media or perhaps because the insiders are just so obviously aggressive that they have kept buying and buying, thereby forcing prices to extremely high levels:

Date: September 1
Stock: 44

Options	Price	Delta
September 35 call:	$9\frac{3}{8}$	0.92
September 40 call:	$5\frac{1}{2}$	0.74
September 45 call:	$2\frac{3}{4}$	0.49
September 50 call:	$1\frac{1}{4}$	0.27

In this case, things are substantially different. Even the deeply in-the-money Sept 35 call has a little bit of time-value premium. All of the other options have an excessive amount of time-value premium. When I see something like this, my two choices are (1) to buy the Sept 35 call or (2) to buy the underlying stock. Nothing else is a reasonable alternative. You might think that the extremely overpriced options indicate that the stock will be taken out at a very high price, but that's not necessarily so. If the rumors have been circulating heavily in the chat rooms on the Internet, there is a strong possibility that a lot of careless buyers have jumped into these calls, thereby inflating them beyond all reason. Usually the rumored takeover price in these chat rooms is well above what turns out to be the *actual* takeover price. Consequently, the purchase of options with a lot of time-value premium is a risky endeavor and should be avoided.

More Examples

Motorola

This example, illustrated by the graph in Figure 2.7 on page 57, shows how option volume may "predict" earnings surprises. This happens for the same reasons that takeovers are predicted by option volume—someone is privy to inside information in advance, and to take advantage of the leverage, they trade options in fairly large size for their own account prior to the event. This is also illegal, but once again if we are following volume patterns, we can capitalize on the insiders' trading pattern.

The following data is from the first day of increased option volume—July 6—and is representative of the pattern that occurred during each of the four days prior to the actual release of earnings. Since a large volume of puts traded that day, as well as calls, the data that follows details the trading in all options:

MOT: 44½

| | | Expiration Month | | | |
		July	August	October	January
Strike price	40 calls	1,980	52	30	50
	puts	998	167	1,451	42
	42½ calls	122	0	19	
	puts	1,113		46	
	45 calls	1,152	746	103	22
	puts	399	220	125	49
	47½ calls	1,363	504	244	
	puts	322		125	
	50 calls	804	299	122	
	puts	0	290	31	

Just over 7,500 calls traded that day, and almost 5,400 puts traded as well. Average total volume at the time was 5,624 contracts, so the total volume on that day (12,900 contracts) was over twice the average volume.

The volume pattern in this table is not as clear-cut as you might like to see, but since the options were so active, it is worth analyzing. First, you must remember that Motorola options are always active to a certain extent. So, whatever normally causes that activity was probably taking place on July 6 in the normal course of events; then, on *top* of that activity, there was some speculative activity as well in advance of the earnings report. If you only look at the striking prices of 45 and higher, the pattern looks fairly speculative in terms of call volume. There are a number of puts trading at those strikes, but nothing unusual compared to the calls. So, from observing the activity at the three higher strikes, you would figure that the option volume was predicting a positive earnings surprise because of the heavy call volume.

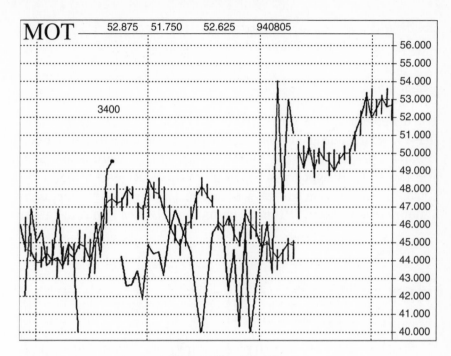

Figure 2.7 Motorola.

This volume pattern continued pretty much the same way for the ensuing three days. Total volume was more than double normal volume, and—while call volume was dominant—there was a lot of put volume trading as well. Finally, on July 12, the earnings were released and were a huge positive surprise. The stock gapped higher on the opening and closed over 5 points higher that day.

This example shows two typical things. First, if you are going to use option volume to predict an earnings surprise, you want to see the option volume reach high levels for several days prior to the actual earnings announcement itself. Second, when option activity increases in a stock where options are normally quite active, then you are going to have extraneous volume clouding the issue; so you must be a little more analytical in interpreting what the option volume is predicting.

Aetna

The other example of an earnings surprise in the video is Aetna **(AET),** which had heavy *put* volume for three days in September 1997 (Figure 2.8). On the fourth day, earnings were below par, and the stock dropped nearly 10 points. Negative earnings surprises, however, don't always occur on the day of the earnings announcement itself. Often, a company will *warn* about negative

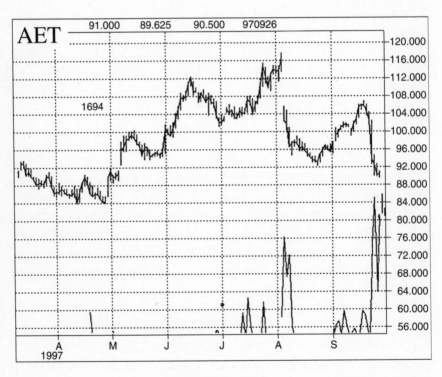

Figure 2.8 Aetna.

earnings a month or so before actual earnings are due. This way, it supposedly avoids some of the lawsuits filed by shareholders when poor earnings come out. These warnings don't have a specific date associated with them like regular earnings announcements do. Thus, traders have no way of knowing, in advance, when such a warning is going to be issued. Or do they? If put option volume is suspiciously heavy, it might indicate that someone knows an earnings warning is due.

That very situation occurred in Sears (**S**) stock options in 1999. This was the trading pattern on the second of two days of heavy put trading:

Date: 9/1/99
Sears: 37¼

		Expiration Month		
		September	October	January
Strike price	35 puts	35	580	54
	40 puts	215	1,146	15
	45 puts	15	2	2

In addition, about 400 calls changed hands that day. Average *total* volume was 1,082 contracts in Sears at the time, so this was a major influx of put trading. On the next day, Sears warned of a negative earnings surprise and the stock not only dropped four points that day, but fell another point the next day despite the fact that the Dow was up nearly 250 points, and Sears was a member of the Dow at the time.

Syntex

Syntex (**SYN**) was a "perennial" takeover rumor, and Figure 2.9 shows three large spikes of option volume. The first two

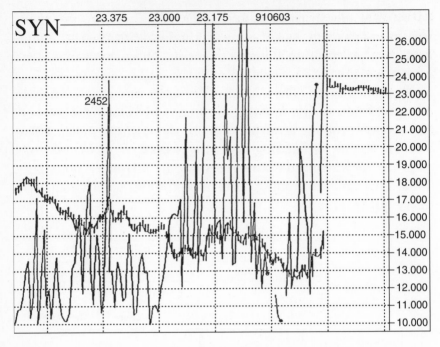

Figure 2.9   Syntex.

proved to be false, as the stock fell to lower lows after each rumor hit and then left the marketplace. The third time was the real thing, however, but probably not many were left to capitalize on it.

For example, during the spate of heavy option volume in February, a "typical" day consisted of something like this: Call volume was a massive 12,851 contracts, and an additional 6,500 puts traded as well. At the time, average daily volume was 3,383, so this was an opportunity for followers of option volume to buy the stock.

Option volume remained very heavy for the rest of February and the first half of March (see Figure 2.9). Unfortunately, the stock did not make much headway. It *did* trade up to nearly 16, but that was in early March. Then, once again, it began another rather nasty descent, eventually falling to 12½ in mid-April. With the decline in the stock price, option volume had almost completely dried up by mid-April. At that time, however, option volume once again returned.

Then, on April 23, both the stock and the options got "heated" together. First, the stock jumped from 12 to 13 in one day, and simultaneously option volume rose to the highest levels since March. Then on April 29, Syntex traded over 15, and option volume once again had an extremely speculative look:

SYN: 15⅛

Strike price		May	June	September	December
	12½ calls	56	85	71	
	15 calls	2,453	3,922	693	34
	17½ calls	436	3,596	370	32
	20 calls	24	741		164

Expiration Month header spans May, June, September, December columns.

Nearly 13,000 calls had traded, and even though over 3,000 puts traded (most of them with a strike of 10), this was a sign that the rumors were back in force.

Those traders who weren't gun-shy from having traded Syntex before were able to buy it and reap the rewards—which were huge in percentage terms—as the stock received a takeover bid and opened at 23½ the next day. In the minds of many traders, Syntex was a "good riddance" type of stock. This was true for short-term traders, who had been burned by many false takeover rumors in the past, as well as for long-term holders who saw the stock taken over at a price that was less than 90% of the highest daily closes over the previous several years. Only the observers of option volume felt somewhat redeemed, and even they had lost money a couple of times before the final takeover occurred.

OPTION *PRICES* AS AN INDICATOR

Most of the time, we can use option volume as our guide to takeovers, earnings surprises, and so on. In many of these instances, the activity of the insiders' option buying forces the options to become expensive. That is, *implied volatility increased.* These option prices are exacerbated not only by the insiders' buying, but by the buying of interested observers such as ourselves who have observed what the insiders are doing.

However, there *are* occasions when option volume is low, yet the prices are high. This occurs when the insiders are unable to buy many calls from the market makers because the issue is thin. In this case, option *volume* will not be high enough to trigger our "alert" signals, but these insiders may have increased the price being paid for options by *bidding* them up to higher prices. Hence, we could observe this as an increase in the implied volatility of the options.

The seasoned observer of option activity who is searching for signs of insider trading should not only watch for increases in option volume in a particular stock's option, but should also look for unwarranted sharp increases in the *prices* of particular equity options. Such a price increase should be a very sharp one, perhaps on the order of seeing implied volatility jump at least 30% above its average in the matter of only a da· or two. In some instances, implied volatility will spike up so quickly that it will *double* the average volatility. By the way, average volatility means the 20-day moving average of daily composite implied volatility. This is a *spike* in implied volatility and is what we are looking for.

Hence we are using expensive options as our main indicator in this case. Recall that high implied volatility means that the options are overpriced. Thus, we call this the *overpriced option method* of determining what stocks might move. As the following examples show, this method might uncover stocks that are going to make an upward move—that is, a directional trade in that we know what direction to expect the stock to move in. Or it might uncover a situation that we know is volatile, but we do not have any idea which way the stock will move. This latter situation would normally result from forces whose influence will be large but unknown, such as a decision by a jury or a government regulatory body like the FDA.

Before continuing, let's insert a definition here so that everyone is on the same page. When I speak of the implied volatility of a particular underlying instrument's options on a given day, it is a **composite implied volatility** of each of the options on that underlying instrument. I weight them by distance from the strike (i.e., how far they're in- or out-of-the-money) with the at-the-money options getting the largest weight. Also, I weight them by trading volume, so that high-volume options get heavier weight. The exact formula for creating this composite volatility is in the book *Options as a Strategic Investment* (L. G. McMillan, New York Institute of Finance, 2002, p. 1001), although most individuals won't need to know that much detail about the process.

So, with this weighting, every stock, index, or futures contract has *one* implied volatility number for each day. We can keep a database of these and compare today's reading with past readings, for example, to see if the options are cheap or expensive. Or we can keep a moving average of these daily readings to see if the current reading is well above or below the moving average. These measures, then, tell us whether implied volatility is high or low.

A *gradual* increase in implied volatility to high levels is not usually as reliable a sign. The reason being that the insiders are anxious to get their hands on the calls and will aggressively bid them up over a short period of time because they know what is going to happen (a takeover, for example). In fact, we often find that strong option volume *and* a spike in implied volatility accompany one another. In that case, we have a double confirmation of the insider activity.

Now we might rightfully question why anyone would want to buy overpriced options at all. After all, aren't we basically taught to use an option model just so we won't do something stupid like overpay for an option? Well, that's not exactly true. We use the option model so that we *know if* an option is overpriced or not. You are quite free to buy an overpriced option, and in this case where the insiders have advanced knowledge and are thus making the option "overpriced," you probably *want* to be buying an overpriced option. In fact, if the insiders are correct, this option is probably not really overpriced at all—it just looks expensive with respect to what has happened in the past. But since the insiders know the future, they know they're not really overpaying for these options.

The problem is that after the rumor spreads you don't know if it's the smart guys who are making the options overpriced, or just a bunch of people reading rumors being spread in chat rooms on the Internet. Therefore, you should be careful about which option you buy when the options get so expensive. It's okay to use the expensiveness of the options as an indicator, but I still prefer to buy an in-the-money option.

Consequently, the same rules that were stated earlier for which option to buy apply with even greater force here. Stick to a short-term, in-the-money option to minimize time-value premium expense. When time passes or implied volatility decreases, the time-value premium of an option shrinks. However, if we already own one that doesn't have much time-value premium to begin with, then the passage of time or an implosion of implied volatility can't affect us much. Of course, those things may make the stock go down, and that will hurt the price of any long call, but at least you can avoid the detriments of decreasing time and implied volatility by owning an in-the-money call. In fact, the higher that implied volatility has jumped prior to buying a position, the deeper in-the-money I would go when buying the call. Try to find one with time value premium of a half point or less. If no such options are available, then perhaps the underlying stock itself would be the better buy.

More Examples

Gerber

In January 1994, implied volatility suddenly increased in Gerber options, even though their trading volume was extremely low—as usual. With Gerber near 29 on one of the early days of Gerber's increased implied volatility, the various measures of volatility stood at these levels:

Daily implied volatility:	51%
10-Day historical volatility:	23%
20-Day historical volatility:	20%
50-Day historical volatility:	28%
100-Day historical volatility:	26%
20-Day implied volatility average:	28%

You can see that the implied volatility has literally exploded as compared to any of the other measures of volatility. Look at the historical volatilities. They are meandering around in the mid-20% range, indicating that the stock has been rather trendless. Not much has been going on. Moreover, the recent moving average of implied volatility is low, reflecting the fact that not much has been happening in the options either.

Obviously, this is a situation that demands some attention—perhaps not right away (because there is always the chance of a one-day fluke), but certainly if the implied volatility keeps registering at such high levels. It *did* persist (see

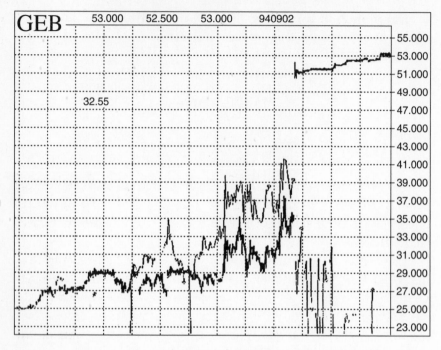

Figure 2.10   Gerber.

Figure 2.10), allowing the purchase of stock at low levels. Note: buying the options at this point in time would probably not have been profitable, for it is unlikely that you would have bought options that expired in June or later. However, a stock buyer would have been buying near the low and could have carried the position profitably all the way until the takeover.

The next example is also of Gerber, but at a much later time—in May, right before the actual takeover occurred. Once again, implied volatility had taken a sudden jump, but from much different levels.

By the middle of May, just a week or so before the takeover, Gerber's stock had rallied to the 35 level and option implied volatility took another jump:

Daily implied volatility: 84%

10-Day historical volatility: 67%
20-Day historical volatility: 55%
50-Day historical volatility: 57%
100-Day historical volatility: 44%

20-Day implied volatility average: 78%

All of these numbers are at vastly increased levels when compared with the prior table. First, note that the daily implied volatility is still much higher than each of the historical volatilities.

The historical volatilities themselves tell an interesting tale, too. Note how much higher the short-term historical volatilities are as compared to the longer term one. This was caused by the fact that the stock moved higher, then fell, and then rallied (see Figure 2.10). The 100-day historical still contained some of the older, stodgy price movements, while the 10- and 20-day contained only the recent, volatile movements. Nevertheless, the daily implied volatility is still higher than any of the historicals.

What is important to recognize from this example is that the takeover occurred within a week, so we should treat the above data as significant. This means that a comparison of *daily* implied volatility and the 20-day *average* of implied volatility need not show a significant difference. It is more important if the various historical volatilities differ substantially from the daily implied volatility. When that happens, we have a situation that is worthy of note.

Salomon Brothers Takeover

The rumor of a takeover in Salomon Brothers **(SB)** first surfaced in late July 1997. Option volume surged and so did implied volatility. However, the rumor was plastered all over the newspapers. It is still one of my "rules" that I am reluctant to believe the rumors when they're printed in the media. The stock market just *isn't* that easy—you can't pick up the morning paper, buy what they say, and sit back and get rich. Even if the media is right about the rumor, invariably many buyers will have pushed the stock higher while the rumor was being widely publicized. Then, even if the rumor proves to be true, the stock barely budges, or maybe even falls, since the public—especially those on the Internet bulletin boards and chat rooms—in its extreme optimism has already pushed the stock to or past the actual takeover price.

    Salomon's first rumor pushed the stock up to about 69 on August 1, with implied volatility jumping as well. See this data illustrated in the graph in Figure 2.11. Both SB and the implied volatility fell back from there. However, about three trading days later, a second surge pushed the stock up to 67 and implied volatility went to its highest level so far. At that time, the papers were carrying stories on the front page of the financial section, speculating on who was going to buy Salomon and what price they were going to pay.

    As the month dragged on, however, no actual takeover news surfaced, and short-term rumor players began to get bored with SB. They sold it down to 60 and the options returned to a more or less normal level of implied volatility. That is typical of these situations as well: if the rumor doesn't come true in a fairly short period of time, and if option activity dries up, too, then sellers usually emerge.

    Then the stock slowly worked its way back up to about 66 by mid-September without any particularly noticeable trading *volume* in the options. However, the implied volatility of SB options suddenly began to rise rather dramatically. Probably what happened was that market makers who had gotten burned the month before weren't about to sell a lot of "fair" valued options once again. They demanded a higher price, and that reflected itself as a sudden increase in implied volatility. Within two days, the

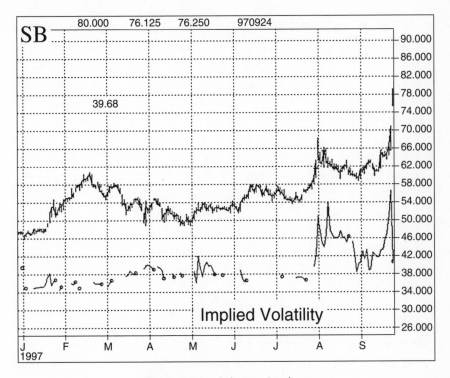

Figure 2.11 Salomon Brothers.

stock broke out over 66 and was taken over at 81. The only real clue to the actual takeover bid had been the increase in implied volatility.

The fact that the first rumor in August had proved false kept many traders on the sidelines the second time around. They figured they weren't going to get burned by the same rumor twice. Yet, it was this *second* rumor that proved to be the real one.

Multicare (MUL)

Figure 2.12 shows the implied volatility (upper line) and option trading volume (lower line) of this stock, leading up to its receiving a takeover bid of $27. This graph doesn't show anything

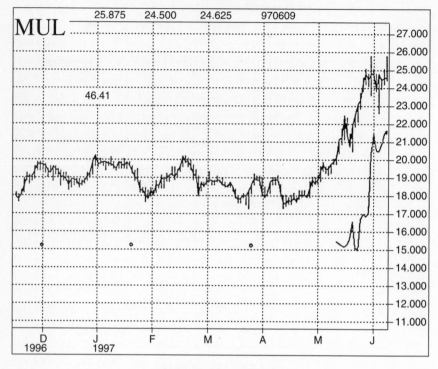

Figure 2.12 Multicare.

particularly different than the others, but it confirms that the two often go hand-in-hand prior to a takeover bid being received.

Event-Driven Volatility

Another way that we can use option prices to predict the underlying's potential movements involves identifying a stock with extremely expensive options as it heads into a major, pre-announced corporate event. These would normally tend to be lawsuits and hearings before federal agencies, such as the FDA. Weeks in advance, the company often announces that a hearing will be held. In the case of a court trial, reporters usually are able to give some idea as to when a judge will rule, or if it's a jury trial, it's easier, because once the jury begins to deliberate, everyone knows it won't be long until a decision is reached. Once the time is made public via one of these forms, the options then begin to increase in expensiveness until right up to that important date. What typically happens then is that the judge or jury returns its verdict or the FDA or FTC hands down its decision, and the stock explodes in one direction or the other as the marketplace rushes to factor in the "new" information that it has suddenly obtained.

There is no way to know in advance whether the stock is going to explode up or down because none of the parties involved in the decision making—judge, jury, FDA, FTC—leak their information in advance. Everyone is on level playing ground here. There is no inside information.

A strategy that often works is to buy a straddle on the stock on the exact day *before* the decision is made public. A **straddle** is the simultaneous purchase of both a put and a call at the same terms. Admittedly, this is an expensive straddle because option-implied volatility will have normally been increasing for several weeks up to that point in time. Nevertheless, the stock usually explodes so violently that it outdistances the price paid for the straddle, and the straddle buyer can make money. This strategy is called **event-driven straddle buying.** The straddle is sold as soon as the news is announced, usually within a day or two.

The chart of Liposome (LIPO) in Figure 2.13 shows the period leading up to an FDA meeting in July 1997. Implied volatility expanded as that meeting drew close, and then the FDA rejected the drug application and the stock collapsed from 25 to 9. The straddle had been selling for about 9 points prior to the news release, so the 16-point drop in the stock price provided nice profits. Note that the stock had mostly been rising before that, so we should be careful to note that the *stock* price is not a good indicator of what will happen at the FDA meeting. *No one knows what the FDA will do,* so we cannot possibly discern price

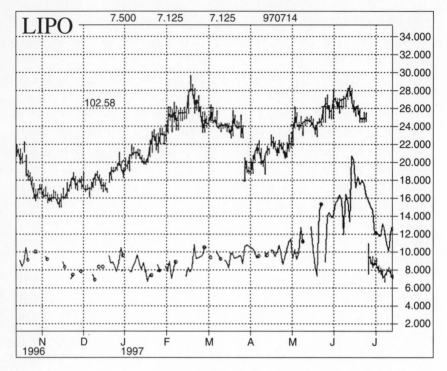

Figure 2.13 Liposome.

clues from the stock itself. All we can do is verify that the options have gotten very expensive, in which case the event-driven straddle buy strategy is called for.

In *The Option Strategist* newsletter, this strategy has been analyzed many times. Results were quite positive. The average move after an "FDA-type" event (FDA hearing, FTC hearing, or lawsuit) was 27% by the underlying stock in one day. That's a *huge* move for one day, but that's the kind of pent-up action that one can expect after the bombshell decisions made by these government agencies or judges and juries. However, if the average straddle costs more than that, this move would not be profitable. Fortunately, the straddle is usually cheaper than that. *In fact, the average profit from buying the straddle is 19%, including commissions.* That is, the event-driven straddle buyer averaged a 19% profit after commissions (in one day) when these events occurred.

In a related study, we measured what the profitability would be if one bought straddles on the day before earnings were announced (and when options were expensive—indicating that traders felt the earnings had some volatility potential in them). In that case, though, the straddle buyer *lost* money. It seems that option traders were overly optimistic about the volatility that the earnings announcement might cause. Hence, *buying straddles in advance of earning is **not** recommended.*

SUMMARY

In this chapter, you saw how options can be used as direct indicators for market predictions. By watching option price and volume behavior, especially as influenced by insider trading, it is possible to determine the movement of the underlying stock, futures, or index. It is important, however, to be able to distinguish between noise and actual insider trading activity.

Sometimes the best investments are the options that appear to be overpriced but are really not, as future "leaked" events will prove. When stock prices are going to be drastically affected by a corporate event such as an earnings announcement or settlement of a lawsuit, an event-driven straddle may be the answer.

REVIEW QUESTIONS: OPTIONS AS DIRECT INDICATORS

1. Your neighbor tells you that his brother-in-law knows the CFO of a small, listed company. He explains that he heard, through this grapevine, that the company is going to report much better than expected earnings. If you buy the stock

based on this information, would you be guilty of illegal insider trading?

  a. No, because you don't even know who generated this information.

  b. Yes, because you acted on material information that had
not been made public.

  c. No, because you have no direct tie-in with the company.

  d. Yes, because you made money on the trade.

2. You observe that two different stocks had heavy put trading, and each stock was down on the day. In the first stock,
almost all of the puts traded were out-of-the-money. However, in the second stock, all of the puts traded were deeply
in-the-money. Would you suspect the option volume in
either or both of these stocks to be the result of insider
trading? Why?

3. Over 2,000 options trade on a particular stock one day,
while the average option volume is only 200 contracts. The
near-term option series is July. The option trading looks
like this:

    XYZ stock: 50 (last sale)

    July 50 calls: 950

    July 50 puts: 900

    July 55 calls: 25

    July 60 calls: 15

    July 65 calls: 10

Is there insider trading going on here? Choose all that
apply.

  a. Probably yes, because all the activity is in July.

  b. Probably yes, and the stock should be shorted because of
the heavy put activity.

  c. Probably not, because of the low volume in the out-of-
the-money calls.

d. Probably not, because it looks like arbitrage caused the volume.

4. Is heavy *sector index* option volume a good predictor of what the underlying index is going to do? Is heavy *futures* option volume a predictor of what the underlying futures contract will do? In essence, the question is "Is there insider activity in these markets?" Why or why not?

5. When insiders are aggressively buying options, why should the stock go up, too?

    a. The insiders buy stock, too.

    b. The stock specialist or market maker hears the rumors and moves his stock quotes higher.

    c. Option market makers, who are selling calls, buy stock to hedge themselves.

    d. All of the above could be true.

6. As a public customer who has been following heavy option volume, you are long calls on a stock that receives a takeover bid at $50 per share. The stock itself reopens for trading at $48. What should your next move be?

    a. Sell your position now that the good news has been released.

    b. Hold your calls until the spread between the takeover bid (50) and the actual share price (48) shrinks to a more reasonable differential.

    c. Short the underlying stock against your long calls to lock in a profit.

    d. Do some research to find more information on the proposed deal.

    e. It depends on whether or not you have a profit in your long calls.

7. With about two weeks to go before expiration, you buy into a heavy option volume situation by paying a point over parity for a slightly in-the-money call, which you value as

expensive. It's now the last trading day before expiration. The stock is about unchanged two weeks later, but option volume has been sporadically high, and the options are still expensive. You still own the calls you bought, and you have a loss of about a point on them. In addition, you see that it will cost about another three-quarters of a point, plus commissions, to roll your options out to the next expiration month. What should you do?

a. Sell the calls you own and limit your loss now.

b. Roll your calls out to the next expiration month.

Explain why you would make that choice.

8. You see heavy put volume in a stock that is due to report earnings in about a month. Assuming that this put volume is being generated by insiders, what do they probably "know"? Choose the most likely answer.

   a. Earnings are going to be worse than expected when released next month.

   b. A financial fraud at the company is about to be made public.

   c. A pre-announcement—warning of bad earnings—is about to be made.

   d. The company is going to have to restate earnings for some past quarters.

9. Bugfree Software is a company that has been the object of several takeover rumors in the past, but none have ever come true. Bugfree recently reported poor earnings, and the stock is trading at $14 a share, down 9 from recent levels before the earnings report, and down over 30 from its yearly high. Suddenly, you see that there is heavy call option volume in Bugfree's options. What do you suspect?

   a. Covered writers are hedging their stock because they figure it is "dead money" for a while.

b. This is probably insider activity, because a takeover is more likely now that the share price is so depressed.

c. A false rumor is being spread by Bugfree holders who want to sell their stock into any rally that the rumor might generate.

d. Any of the above three choices might be true.

10. You spot heavy option trading in a particular stock and notice that the options are very expensive as well. Since the calls are so expensive, you consider selling some puts instead. The relevant prices, with about a month to go until April expiration, are:

    Underlying stock: 40

    April 35 call: 8

    April 35 put: 2

    July 35 put: 4

    Oct 35 put: 6

    What should you do?

    a. Sell the Oct 35 puts to take in the most money possible.

    b. Sell the April 35 puts to take advantage of the greatest time decay rate.

    c. Sell the July 35 puts to get a good balance between high premium and time decay rate.

    d. Not sell any puts at all, but instead buy the April 35 calls or the stock.

11. You own a decent number of shares of a stock, and you begin to notice that its options are getting very expensive. This pattern has lasted for several days. What should you do?

    a. Do some research to find out why the calls are expensive.

    b. Buy more stock because it looks like a takeover rumor is in place.

    c. Sell covered calls against your stock because they're so expensive.

3

OPTIONS AS
CONTRARY INDICATORS

LEARNING OBJECTIVES

The material in this chapter helps you to:

- Recognize and apply a true contrary indicator.
- Interpret OEX and VIX in terms of contrary indicators both for the broad market and for individual stocks and futures.
- Determine when to engage in straddle buying.
- Determine when to buy the underlying or when to sell naked puts.
- Read implied volatility and put-call ratios as signs of market movement.
- Take a dynamic rather than static approach to interpreting put-call ratios.

In the previous chapter, we saw how options can be used as a direct indicator—that is, whatever the option market is "saying" should be the direction in which the underlying then moves. However, that was a fairly narrow application, mostly related to the times when traders with illegal insider information are "operating" in the marketplace. Most of the time, our fellow option traders are unfortunately wrong about their opinions—whether those opinions be on the market in general, or on a specific stock, futures, or index. In these other cases, then, we must treat option statistics as a *contrary* indicator. In this chapter, we'll discuss how to recognize true contrary indicators and use them for successful investing.

CONTRARY INDICATORS

A contrary indicator is one whose signals must be interpreted in an opposite fashion. That is, if the indicator shows that "everyone" is buying, then by contrary interpretation, we must *sell*. Conversely, if everyone else is selling, according to the contrary indicator, then we must *buy*. There are a number of contrary indicators in technical analysis. Most of them have to do with measuring sentiment among the majority of the trading or investing public. The public tends to be wrong at major turning points in the market. So if we can measure public sentiment and determine when it is extreme, then by contrary theory we should be taking positions opposite to those of the majority of the public.

Contrary indicators have an excellent track record. One of the best known is the survey of investment advisor newsletter writers published by *Investors Intelligence*. This is a well-respected gauge of market opinion (in a contrary fashion) and often is quoted on television and in print media. Simply stated, *Investors Intelligence* measures the percentage of newsletter writers who are bullish or bearish. If "too many" are bullish, then watch out for a market correction. On the other hand, if "too many" are bearish, then you should buy the market.

Measuring how many is "too many" is not always easy. In the *Investors Intelligence* community, something like 60% bulls is too many, while something like 70% bears is too many. These levels have been determined by looking at past market movements in relation to the number of bullish or bearish investment advisors.

How Contrary Indicators Work

Why do contrary indicators work? Because once there is a unanimity of opinion about the fortune of a stock or the market, then nearly everyone has already acted on his or her opinion, and there really isn't anyone left to perpetuate it. For example, suppose that we find that there is an extreme bullish sentiment about the market from the general investing public. This means that they have all bought. Who is now going to buy more to push the market higher? Probably no one. In fact, if all the buying is done, the easiest path is for the sellers to drive the market down. Admittedly, this is a simplification of what's really happening, but it illustrates the idea. In fact, we could probably extend this philosophy well beyond the stock market to many other facets of life.

Measuring Market Opinion

The biggest bane of contrary theory is isolating the opinions of the "uninformed" public. We do not want to distort the statistics with noise, such as arbitrage trading or institutional hedging strategies. Those are not market opinion activities, and it is only market opinion that we are interested in measuring for the purpose of contrary investing. Arbitrage or hedging strategies might involve the establishment of short sales or put buying for hedging of long positions. However, those short sales or put purchases shouldn't be interpreted as bearish market opinion for they are merely offsetting bullish arbitrage or institutional positions. In real life, we can't factor out all of this noise, so we must learn to interpret the overall statistics that include such activities.

You will see from our further discussions that it is possible to learn to interpret the statistics with this noise in it and still have a viable tool for market guidance.

PRICE AND VOLUME AS CONTRARY INDICATORS

Options are useful as a sentiment indicator because the public buys options with abandon when it seems like there is easy money to be made. They are usually wrong at these times, and so an astute practitioner of contrary investing can measure the public's sentiment via option trading statistics and use contrary theory to establish profitable trades.

As was the case with using options as a direct indicator, to measure contrary sentiment in options we can use two main factors—option prices or option trading volume. For option prices, we look at the levels of implied volatility of the options on a particular instrument as a good guide for contrary option sentiment. In the case of option trading volume, we will look at something called the **put-call ratio** for our contrary sentiment indicator.

IMPLIED VOLATILITY

Option Prices (Implied Volatility) as Broad Market Contrary Indicators

Any of these option contrary indicators are applicable to the broad market indices as well as to individual stocks or futures contracts. Let's look at the broad market application first. The primary speculative vehicle for option traders who want to trade the broad market is the S&P 100 Index (symbol: $OEX), which is customarily called **OEX.** This index was created in 1983 by the CBOE, using 100 major stocks whose options trade on that exchange. Some years later, Standard and Poor Corporation—

who already had the S&P 500 and the S&P 400, among other indices—indicated to the CBOE that it would like to take over
maintenance of the index. The CBOE agreed and thus the index
then became known as the S&P 100 Index. There are no *futures*
on the $OEX index, so all activity involving that index shows up
in the index options. It should be noted that CBOE market makers of $OEX options use the S&P 500 futures contract to hedge
sometimes—a subject we discuss later in this book.

The S&P 500 Index is actually a more widely followed index
of market performance. It, too, has options that trade on the
CBOE under the symbol $SPX. However, those options never re-
ally caught on with the investing public—they are more of an
institutional hedging vehicle. That may change someday, but for
now the public speculator continues to predominantly trade
OEX options. The S&P 500 Index also has futures and futures
options traded at the Chicago Mercantile Exchange. Those futures are the largest index derivative vehicle in existence today.
Many institutions, arbitrageurs, and traders use those futures
for speculation and hedging. The futures options on that contract trade with some high level of activity as well. However,
these instruments can only be traded via futures accounts and
through brokers who are registered to transact futures. Therefore, the majority of the investing public does *not* trade these—
preferring to stick with something that they can trade through
their regular stock broker. $OEX options can be traded by a reg-
ular stock broker, so they remain the market trading vehicle of
choice for many.

In the early 1990s, the CBOE began to publish a measure of
the *implied volatility* of $OEX options. It is called the CBOE's
Volatility Index and is normally referred to by its symbol, **VIX.**
$VIX can be used as a measure of contrary sentiment. It is most
useful when it gets too high during an extreme market selloff—
normally a swift bearish move or even a crashlike environment.
When the market is falling dramatically and $VIX gets too high
and then peaks, that is a market buy signal.

Think of it this way: the market is falling dramatically, the media is full of bearish news, so the public buys $OEX puts en masse. They are speculating that the market will drop even further. When they rush in to buy these puts, they don't care much about the price—they just want the puts. So they pay very high prices, resulting in an increase in implied volatility, which is shown to us as a dramatic increase in $VIX. When the last bearish investor has paid top dollar for that last put, the market then reverses and rises—crushing the put buyers and making profits for practitioners of contrary investing theory.

Figure 3.1 shows how this happened in 1996 and 1997, but charts of many other market periods show the same thing over and over again. In fact, the $VIX chart in Figure 3.2 of the 1994 to 1995 time period shows similar occurrences, just at different levels of $VIX.

We need to make a *dynamic* interpretation of $VIX. We want to see a spike peak in the index, no matter where it occurs. Thus, in April 1994 there was a spike peak of $VIX at about the 23 level (see Figure 3.2). In 1997, during the "Victor Niederhoffer" crises when the stock market fell over 500 points in one day and had to have trading halted, $VIX peaked at 40 (see Figure 3.1). Note that the $VIX charts in Figures 3.1 and 3.2 use *closing* prices. Intraday, $VIX traded at even higher levels. In both of these cases, the peak in $VIX was an excellent market buy signal—even if you didn't act on it for a day or two, as you were perhaps waiting to confirm that there was actually a spike peak that had formed on the chart.

Thus, we use $VIX dynamically. That is, we *don't* say something like "buy the market when $VIX rises to 23 for that is too high." You can see that that would have worked okay in 1994, but certainly not in 1997. In 1997, $VIX routinely traded at 23 almost daily because the marketplace had a higher opinion of forthcoming market volatility.

In fact, in almost any sentiment indicator, we must use a dynamic interpretation because market conditions change. Those

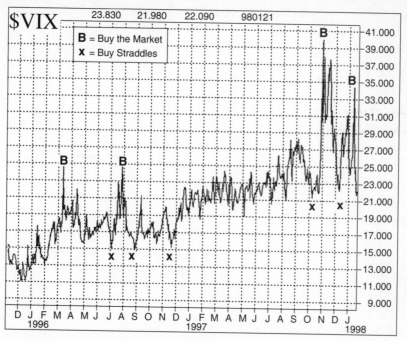

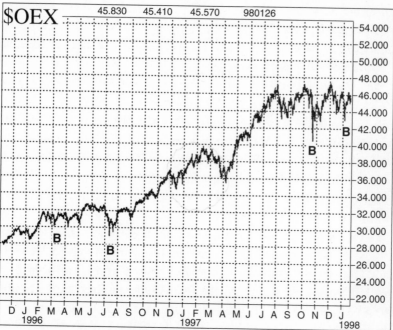

Figure 3.1 $VIX and $OEX.

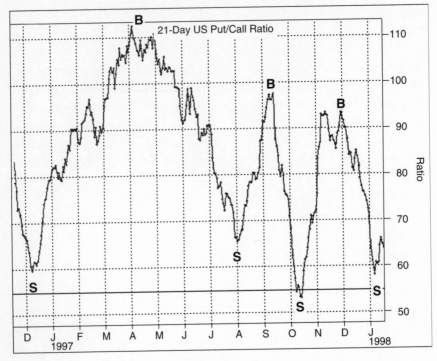

Figure 3.2   VIX.

changing market conditions can alter the "equilibrium" point—the average level of $VIX, for example. But contrary theory will still hold, albeit at differing levels, for when the $VIX shoots higher during a collapsing market and then forms a spike top, you have a good market buy signal, no matter what the absolute level of $VIX is at the time.

$VIX did not exist during the Crash of 1987. However, once the CBOE determined the formula for computing $VIX (more about that in a minute), it then went back and computed $VIX from 1983 onward, using prices from those earlier times to compute $VIX as if it had existed then. With this measure, $VIX would have traded at 110 on the day of the Crash of 1987 and near those levels for a few days afterward. This is the highest level ever recorded for $VIX.

The second highest levels to date occurred in the panicky atmosphere of August to October 1998 when there was a foreign bond crisis and the failure of a major hedge fund. The Dow dropped nearly 20% during that time, and $VIX peaked (on a closing basis) at 48 on two occasions about a month apart. The first peak led to a strong rally of several weeks duration before falling market prices once again produced the second peak at 48. *That* peak led to one of the strongest bull market moves ever seen—from October 1998 to April 1999. By the way, *intraday* $VIX traded up to 60 at that time. Those are very high levels, so a dynamic interpretation was necessary to keep from buying the market too early, before the peak in $VIX had been reached.

$VIX is computed using only eight of the $OEX options, so some traders claim it is a slightly distorted measure of implied volatility. That may be, but as you can see from Figure 3.2, it is a useful indicator nonetheless. $VIX takes into consideration only the two nearest-term options at the two nearest strikes. While it is certainly most likely that those options are the ones that have the heaviest trading volume, and are thus probably most indicative of what speculators are doing, it ignores all other $OEX options in its calculations. Thus, if the current month were April and $OEX were trading at 702, then $VIX would consider the April 700, April 705, May 700, and May 705 options.

You might ask, "Does it use the puts or the calls at those strikes for the purposes of implied volatility?" We would answer: Puts and calls with the same terms—same strike price and expiration date—must have the same implied volatility or else risk-free arbitrage is available. *Different* strike prices on the same underlying instrument can have different implied volatilities; that is called a *volatility skew* and is something we discuss much later in the book. However, at any *one* strike, the put and the call have identical implied volatility.

Novice option traders, and even some with experience, have trouble believing this concept. So, I'll explain it a little further. All arbitragable options (i.e., those in which the underlying actually exists and where the underlying can be borrowed for short sales) with the same terms adhere to the following pricing formula:

$$\text{Put price} = \frac{\text{Strike}}{\text{price}} + \frac{\text{Call}}{\text{price}} - \frac{\text{Underlying}}{\text{price}} - \frac{\text{Fixed}}{\text{cost}}$$

where fixed cost is the cost to carry the position less dividends received.

Fixed costs are constant on any given day, and the strike price is a constant, too, of course. So, if during the trading day, the call rises in price (i.e., its implied volatility increases), then the put price must rise in price as well in order to keep the equation in balance. If the equation falls *out of* balance, then an arbitrageur will step in and make a profitable, risk-free transaction. The arbitrageur's actions will force the equation back into line.

Low $VIX Readings

You will notice that the charts we have been referring to in Figures 3.1 and 3.2 have the small letter x marked at low points along the bottom. This is the opposite of the extremely high $VIX readings. So, does the x denote a sell signal? Actually, it does not, but it is still a contrary indicator of sorts.

When $VIX is too low, that means that the average investor is expecting the stock market (i.e., $OEX) to have low volatility over the life of the options. Buyers of options become timid. Sellers of options become more aggressive. Therefore, the bids and offers simultaneously decline, and a low $VIX reading is the result. Remember, though, that implied volatility is nothing more than the market's guess at what volatility will be over the life of the option. We have already seen that when everybody's guess is too high, the market proves them wrong by not only slowing down its volatility, but usually by rallying at the same time.

Similarly, when everybody's guess is too low, the market normally proves them wrong by exploding in one direction or the other shortly thereafter. Thus, the x marks on the charts indicate periods of potential market explosions. Some of these explosions are to the downside, but others are to the upside. So we cannot tell for sure which way the market is going to move, just that it *is* going to move. The proper strategy in that case is to buy both a put and a call with the same terms (same striking price and expiration date) so that we can make money no matter which way the market explodes.

The charts of $VIX in Figures 3.1 and 3.2 show where straddles should have been bought. Each one of these preceded market explosions in one direction or the other. Later in the book, we discuss this philosophy of straddle buying in much more depth. It is an excellent strategy—when applied properly—for both the novice and experienced option trader, and by its very design it eliminates some of the pitfalls of other option strategies.

High Implied Volatility as a Contrary Indicator for Individual Stocks and Futures

Implied volatility can be useful in predicting which way individual stocks or futures contracts as well as sector indices, will move. The same two concepts that were described with respect to $VIX can be used on these instruments as well.

The first was high implied volatility during a falling market. We can generalize the concept that was seen with $VIX to a more general statement:

> If: A market is collapsing rapidly *and* implied volatility is rising rapidly
>
> Then: When implied volatility peaks, the underlying is ready to rally
>
> So either: Buy the underlying
>
> or
>
> Sell naked puts

This general statement covers all markets. When the options are so expensive, it probably is not a great strategy to buy the over-priced calls. Therefore, the purchase of the underlying is apt to be a wiser strategy. In addition, you might think—especially if you're a stock option trader—"Why not establish a covered call write?" That strategy is modestly bullish and would allow you to capture that expensive call premium. In reality, though, a naked put sale and a covered call write are equivalent strategies (refer to the discussion in Chapter 1 of equivalent strategies). Therefore, it is usually more economical in terms of commissions, and bid-asked spreads, to sell the naked put rather than establish a covered call write. See Figure 3.3 for an illustration of IBM stock movement and implied volatility.

These two strategies—buying the underlying and selling a naked put—have quite different characteristics, though. The former has unlimited profit potential and requires some upward market movement for profitability. The latter has *limited* profit potential, but it would make money if the underlying merely stops going down and begins going sideways. In either case, the underlying has usually moved up a little in price by the time that you verify that implied volatility has peaked. Thus, when you are buying the underlying or selling naked puts, there is a natural stop loss point—if the underlying returns to new lows.

Both of these strategies have large downside risk, but all directional strategies (i.e., strategies in which you are trying to predict the direction of the underlying stock or of the stock

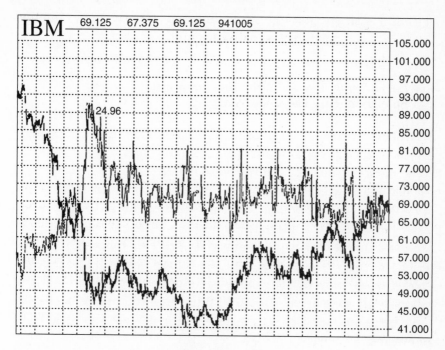

IBM 69.125 67.375 69.125 941005

24.96

105.000
101.000
97.000
93.000
89.000
85.000
81.000
77.000
73.000
69.000
65.000
61.000
57.000
53.000
49.000
45.000
41.000

Figure 3.3 IBM.

market) have substantial risk, so that isn't a negative toward either strategy. In fact, that's why we're using the implied volatility as an indicator—to give us an entry point where supposedly the downside risk is reduced. And if this method of stopping yourself out at new lows is used, then this strategy should be one with good profit potential and limited risk. The only time that risk could be substantial is if there is a large downside gap in prices. But any outright bullish strategy has that same risk.

As for which one of the two strategies to use, there is no ironclad guideline. You would hate to sell naked puts—having only limited profit potential—while the underlying races away to the upside. Yet, you'd like to gain some benefit from the expensiveness of the options. There is an aggressively bullish strategy that can encompass some of the traits of both. The following section describes this strategy.

Buy Out-of-the-Money Calls and Simultaneously Sell Out-of-the-Money Puts

With this strategy, there is unlimited upside profit potential. There is also, if enough puts are sold, the capability of making some money if prices remain relatively unchanged.

For example, suppose you identify a buy point in IBM by observing a peak in implied volatility after the stock has been falling rapidly. It is currently mid-June. IBM bottomed at 118. It is trading at 123 by the time you verify to yourself that implied volatility has peaked and, therefore, the bullish strategy should be employed. You *could* buy stock, or you could sell the (supposedly expensive) July 120 puts, but you are reluctant to buy the (also supposedly expensive) July 125 or 130 calls. The relevant prices are:

IBM: 123

"Average" Implied Volatility: 32%

Option	Price	Implied Volatility
July 120 put	6	43%
July 125 call	7½	45
July 130 call	5½	44

Assume that you want to have unlimited upside profit potential because you feel that IBM might be ready to rebound with a big move to the upside. The calls are quite expensive. A feasible strategy might be to buy some of the July 130 calls and simultaneously sell some of the July 120 puts to "finance" the purchase of the calls. If an equal number of puts are sold and calls purchased, each one will bring a credit of a half point ($50) into the account, less commissions. That's not much profit if IBM remains relatively unchanged, so you might want to sell a few extra puts. The profit graph in Figure 3.4 shows how a couple of probable strategies would look at expiration.

This "doubly" bullish strategy has unlimited upside profit potential, and it can make some money even if IBM is between 120 and 130 at expiration. How much money is made in the unchanged case depends on how much initial credit is taken in. If the quantity of calls bought and puts sold is equal, then there won't be much credit. However, if an extra put or two is sold, then the unchanged results will be more favorable.

The margin required for this type of position is that the calls must be paid for in full, and the puts must be margined as naked options. A naked stock option margin is equal to 20% of the stock price, plus the put premium, less any out-of-the-money amount. The margin required for a naked put sale is generally quite a bit less than that required for buying a stock on margin.

Finally, remember that the risks shown in the IBM chart (Figure 3.3) are unlikely to materialize, because you are going to place a mental stop point at IBM's recent lows. Thus, if IBM were to fall below 118, then you would stop yourself out of the

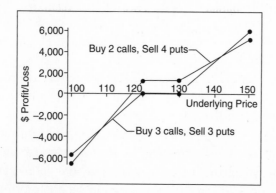

Figure 3.4 Bullish strategy—buy call and sell put at expiration.

position. This would certainly incur a loss, but it would be a limited one.

Meanwhile, the position has unlimited upside profit potential, so that if IBM were to really blast off, the position would have you along for the ride.

This strategy is certainly useful with stocks. What you might find, however, is that the whole market is falling rapidly and many of these similar situations set up in individual stocks at about the same time. If that occurs, you might just want to use the strategy on the $OEX index options or some other broad-based index. However, if a relatively isolated stock decline occurs, accompanied by extremely high implied volatility, then the strategy can be applied to those individual stock options.

The strategy applies equally well to futures contracts. In fact, sometimes futures offer the best opportunities, for many of the futures markets are quite unrelated to each other. Also, futures have a quirk that makes them different from stocks: *When stock prices fall, volatility accelerates and implied volatility increases as a normal function of market movements; however, in futures markets, falling prices are more often accompanied by a decrease in implied volatility.* There are differences of opinion as to why these markets behave this way, but one simple explanation is this: Most futures contracts have a floor (for example, wheat has a government support point, and besides, wheat is always worth something—it can't go to zero like a bankrupt company's stock could), but on the other hand, because of the tremendous leverage available in futures, upside moves are greeted with more euphoria and excitement. That behavior often causes implied volatility to *increase* when futures prices rise and to *decrease* when they fall.

Remember our requirements for using the implied volatility strategy that we are discussing in this section of the course: If a market is declining rapidly *and* implied volatility is rising rapidly, then we take a bullish position when implied volatility peaks. In futures markets, then, we would expect to see this only rarely, so when it occurs, it is usually a *very* good trading opportunity.

The charts in Figures 3.5 and 3.6 show two examples—Live Cattle futures during the Mad Cow Disease scare and Copper futures in the wake of the Sumitomo Bank trading scandal. But others occur—at least a couple a year—and they are equally good trading opportunities for futures traders. If you don't personally trade futures, you may want to open an account just to have the flexibility to trade these situations when they occur, which, as stated above, will not be frequently. The concepts here are those related to *options*—it doesn't really matter what the underlying is.

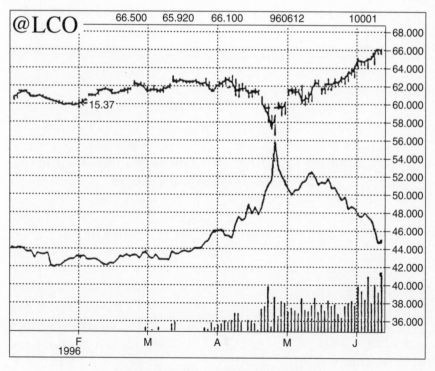

Figure 3.5 August live cattle futures.

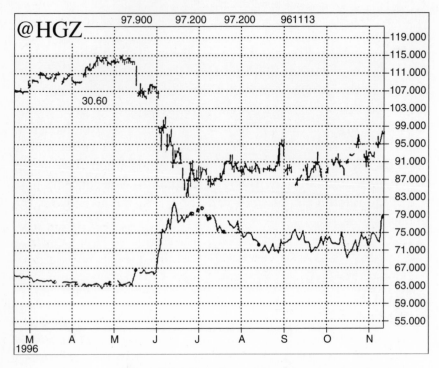

Figure 3.6 December copper futures.

Low Implied Volatility as a Contrary Indicator for Individual Stocks and Futures

We saw earlier with the $VIX charts that when implied volatility is too low, we can expect a market explosion shortly thereafter. It's a contrary theory of sorts: Everyone is too complacent, so the market explodes, confounding the majority once again. This same concept applies with even more veracity to individual stocks and futures. Two examples are shown in Figure 3.7 and more are discussed later in the book. In the case of $VIX, many people are watching it daily, so if it gets too low or too high, a great deal of attention and publicity are drawn to it. However, with individual stocks and futures, far fewer people are watching each issue.

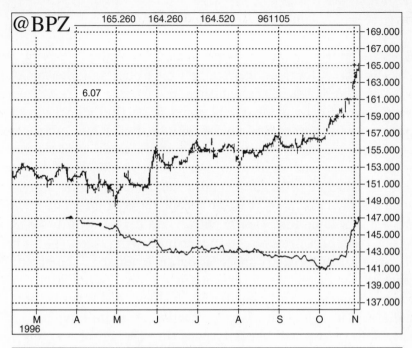

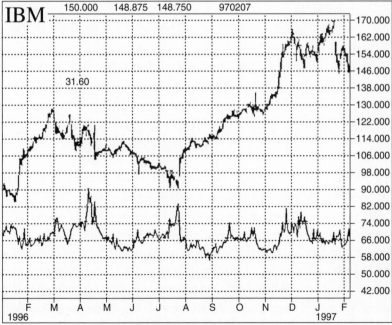

Figure 3.7 BPZ and IBM.

Even the market maker in a stock may not really be paying extremely close attention—especially if his primary market-making stock is a larger, more active issue.

As a result, it is relatively common to find stocks and futures on which straddles can be bought. Recall that a straddle purchase consists of buying both a put and a call with the same striking price and expiration date. Later in this book, we outline the exact steps to go through when attempting to analyze a straddle buy. For now, it is sufficient to say that: (1) we want the options to be historically cheap, and (2) we want to be able to see, from past price action in the underlying stock, that it has the capability to easily move a distance equal to the straddle price in the required lifetime of the option. On any given day, there are perhaps between 10 and 15 stocks and futures that fit the statistical pattern of an attractive straddle buy, but only about one or two will actually pass the scrutiny of a severe inspection. Still, this is quite a good number of opportunities.

In fact, straddle buying in situations where the statistics are favorable is my favorite option strategy. Any surprises will be positive surprises and not negative ones. That is, the only thing that causes the straddle buyer to lose money is time decay, and any gaps in the stock's price—such as might be caused by a negative earnings warning (downside) or by a takeover (upside)—are welcomed by the straddle holder. In fact, a gap is preferred and it doesn't matter in which direction the gap occurs.

I usually favor buying a straddle that has at least three months of life remaining. This gives a sufficient amount of time for the stock to make a move without time decay becoming an immediate problem. While any option constantly loses its time value premium to time decay, the most rapid rate of decay occurs during the last month of life of the options. So, a straddle with three or more months of life remaining at time of purchase can be held for a couple of months before suffering untoward losses—even if the underlying doesn't really move much.

Generally, I recommend buying the straddle, but if the underlying is directly between two strikes, a *strangle* purchase may be better. A **strangle** consists of a put and a call with the same expiration date, where the call has a higher strike price than the put. So, if XYZ is trading at 72½, then one might buy the July 75 call and the July 70 put to form a strangle purchase.

You do not have to constantly monitor the long straddle position because nothing bad can happen in an instant. A simple phone call to your broker once per day is probably sufficient to be able to monitor a straddle buy. More will be said later about which straddles to buy and how to take partial profits, and so on. At this point, it is just important to understand that option prices can become quite cheap, and when they do, that is usually a sign that the underlying instrument is about to make an explosive move in one direction or the other.

PUT-CALL RATIOS

In this section, we discuss the use of option volume as an aid in predicting the direction of the underlying instrument. Option volume is used to total up all the puts that traded on a particular day and divide that by the total of all the calls that traded that day. The result is the **put-call ratio.** It is customary to group options into similar categories when calculating the ratio. For example, a trader might calculate an *IBM* option put-call ratio, or maybe a *gold* option put-call ratio. In order to smooth out the fluctuations of the daily numbers, it is usual to keep track of some moving averages of the put-call ratio.

Technicians have been calculating the put-call ratio for a long time, even before the advent of listed options, because it is known to be a valuable *contrary* indicator. When too many people are bullish (when they are buying too many calls), then contrarians short the market because the majority is usually wrong. Similarly, when too many traders are bearish and buying puts, then a contrarian will look to buy the market. The put-call ratio is a measure of how many puts are trading with respect to calls, so that the contrarian can attempt to quantify his measurements.

When the put-call ratio is at a high level, a lot of puts are being bought, and that indicates a market buy. Then, the put-call ratio declines while the market is rallying. Eventually, bullish sentiment becomes too strong, and the put-call ratio bottoms just as the market is making a top. After that, the put-call ratio rises while the market is falling, until the whole cycle begins again.

For predicting the broad market, the most useful major put-call ratio is the **equity-only put-call ratio.** This is calculated, as the name implies, by using the volume of all *stock* options. There are some other broad measures, but they have become less reliable as institutions have increased their hedging activity. Since we know that traders who like to speculate on the movement of the market as a whole like to trade $OEX options or the S&P 500 futures options, we would hope that those put-call ratios would be useful as contrary indicators. For many years they were, but now the put volume in them is so inflated due to institutional hedging activity that they are not particularly useful market predictors any longer.

In the late 1990s, the public began to transfer its speculative activity into equity options, so that put-call ratios on individual stocks have become a reliable predictor of that stock's movements. The most reliable ratios exist where there is a lot of option volume each day. If we were to calculate the put-call ratio on many individual stocks, there would normally be so little volume that the futures would be quite distorted and would not be useful in predicting the direction of the stock's movement. Very active equities such as Intel or IBM are exceptions, because their volume is large enough to allow calculation of the put-call ratio as a meaningful speculative number.

It should be noted, though, that there is always the chance that a stock could become a takeover rumor, and thus its call volume might be inflated *correctly*. That is, a low put-call ratio would *not* be a contrary sell signal in that case. For this reason,

Table 3.1 Put-Call Ratio as Contrary Indicator

Calculate put-call ratio for:

- Any index or sector.
- All equity options.
- All listed equity and index options ("total" trading).
- All futures options on a single underlying commodity (e.g., all gold futures options).

Use put-call ratios as contrary indicators:

- Too much put buying is bullish for the underlying.
- Too much call buying is bearish for the underlying.

we must be careful about interpreting the put-call ratio on individual stocks. If the stock is very large and well capitalized, it is unlikely to be a takeover candidate—and so those are the best stocks on which to analyze the put-call ratio. Smaller stocks that might be subject to takeover rumors can be expected to have far less reliable put-call ratio signals.

A sort of middle ground exists with futures options. It makes no sense to calculate a *futures* put-call ratio wherein all futures contracts are included, for there is no relationship between grain options and oil product options, for example. However, if futures options are relatively active on a particular commodity, a trader could use the option trading across all months for those specific futures options and, thus, might compute a *gold futures* option put-call ratio or a *soybean futures* option put-call ratio. Table 3.1 summarizes the use of the put-call ratio as a contrary indicator.

The Data

All of the data is available in the newspaper every day, although the equity-only put-call ratio data needs to be obtained elsewhere. The easiest broad ratio to determine is the *index* put-call ratio, because you merely have to divide the total number of OEX puts traded by the total number of OEX calls traded.

These two numbers are reported in the *Wall Street Journal* or *Investors Business Daily* every day. On any given day, there are normally more index puts traded than index calls; this is a result of the fact that many investors and money managers buy OEX puts as protection for their long stocks. Unfortunately, as mentioned earlier, as more and more money managers use this protective feature of index options, the index put-call ratio has become less useful.

The equity-only put-call ratio cannot normally be computed directly unless you happen to have software that analyzes every stock option traded—and such software is normally only available at private companies. However, a very good substitute is readily available. The CBOE publishes the daily equity-only put-call ratio of all stock options traded on its exchange only. While this number may differ slightly from the actual equity-only put-call ratio, the *shape* of the curve will be similar for the two indicators. Thus, the CBOE equity-only put-call ratio can be used as a valid substitute for the true equity-only put-call ratio.

You might think it's not worth the bother to compute the equity-only ratio, since many speculators trade OEX options. It turns out that the equity-only ratio has given some important signals with far better timing than the index ratio in recent years. In fact, some analysts think that the equity-only ratio is the purer one because there is so little arbitrage in equity options anymore and most money managers don't buy equity puts for protection—they buy index puts. Therefore, equity options may represent a better picture for contrarians.

It might be important to point out that in the 1980s, the equity-only ratio was suspect because of the heavy amount of equity option arbitrage that existed then. Moreover, that was before the institutions began to buy index puts heavily to protect their stocks, so the $OEX put-call ratio was actually the best measure of speculative sentiment. But the two reversed positions by the late 1990s. Who knows that they might not reverse positions again someday? So it is probably worth your while to keep both ratios and to be wary of the $OEX ratio as a predictor until it appears that speculators are once again dominating the index.

There are other index options—the Dow-Jones ($DJX), for example, or the NASDAQ-100 ($NDX and QQQ options). They, too, may be useful as broad market predictors. In addition, you can compute the *total* put-call ratio. The major newspapers publish the total option volume of all the exchanges each day. Unfortunately, this number includes all of the equity, sector, and index options as well as the currency options on exchanges where they trade. Hence, the resulting number is something of a hybrid and is useful only as a backup to the other more specific gauges.

The daily put-call numbers can either be expressed as the absolute ratio, or as a percent. For example, if an equal number of puts and calls traded, then the daily number would be 1.00 (absolute) or 100 (percent). I prefer to use percent because, when you're speaking about the ratios, you don't have to keep saying "point" (as in one point fifteen for 1.15, for example). The index put-call ratio tends to have daily numbers in the 100 to 130 range (circa, late 1990s). The equity-only ratio, however, is far different. Since there are normally many more equity calls traded than puts, the equity-only ratio is normally in the 30 to 50 range. That is, only 30 to 50 equity puts trade for every 100 equity calls that trade on a given day.

The total put-call ratio (all options traded) is typically in the 50 to 70 range. These ranges tend to change over time, so one should understand that the above ranges refer to the mid-to-late 1990s time period.

Different technical analysts keep track of different moving averages of the ratios. I prefer to use a 21-day moving average and a 55-day moving average. However, some prefer to keep shorter or longer moving averages. I find that the 21-day average is useful in catching short-term moves that might last from a few days to a few weeks, while the 55-day identifies more intermediate-term trends.

Interpreting the Ratios

The concept of interpreting the put-call ratios is an easy one in theory, but in practice, things become a little more complicated. It is an easy matter to say that when the ratio gets too high, you should buy the market. Conversely, if the ratio gets too low, you should take bearish positions. Quantifying too high and too low is where things get tricky. Past experience has shown that static interpretation of the put-call ratios is an incorrect approach, for investors and traders change their investing patterns. Rather, a dynamic approach is best. A dynamic approach means that one looks for peaks and valleys—at whatever absolute levels they may occur—in the put-call ratio to indicate buy and sell points.

This is a very important concept because if you use static interpretations, you will most certainly be deluded into making an inappropriate trade. For example, we stated earlier that in the 1980s there was heavy arbitrage in equity options. Hence, it was not unusual for the put-call ratio to trade up to high levels, such as 80, 90, or 100, because of the heavy put volume by arbitrageurs. So, in those days, the ratio would have been considered low at 60, say, and that would indicate a sell signal. However, as things changed over the years, the ratio was almost *always* below 60. A blindly static approach would have meant that you would have been short for years—clearly wrong in the market of the 1990s.

No one would be that stubborn, of course, to stay short for years just because one indicator was below some historic level. But, on a shorter term basis, it is important *not* to use static numbers either. For example, most market corrections in the 1990s have been very shallow, so the equity-only put-call ratio's 21-day moving average has only moved up to about 55 or so before peaking out and giving a buy signal (see Figure 3.8).

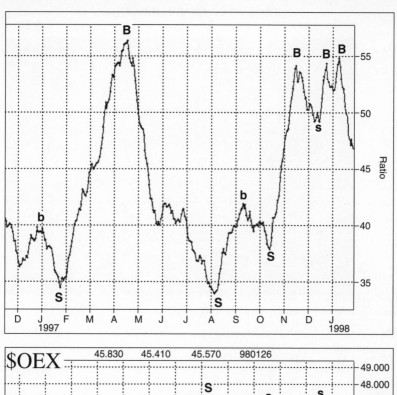

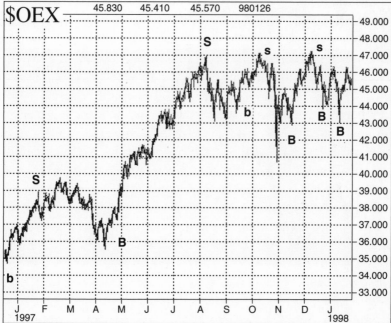

Figure 3.8 21-day equity only put-call ratio.

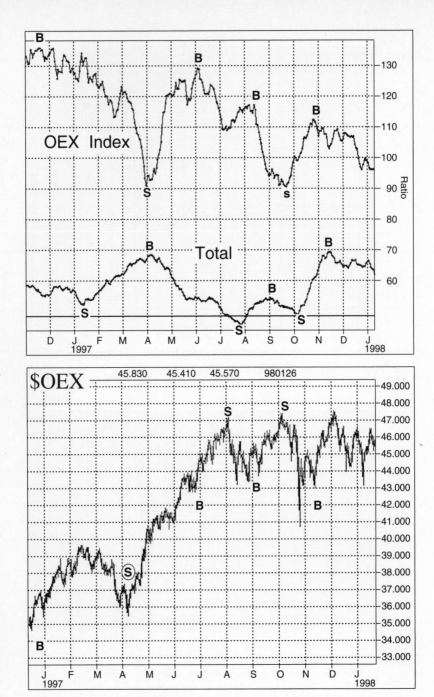

Figure 3.9 21-day put-call ratio.

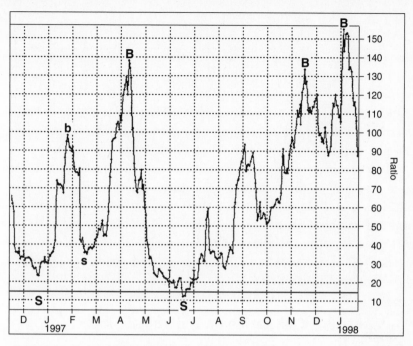

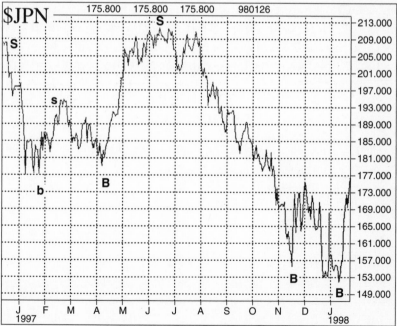

Figure 3.10 21-day $JPN put-call ratio.

However, in 1998, the correction was more severe and the ratio didn't peak until it had gotten all the way up to 65. If you were using a static interpretation, you might have decided to buy the "market" when the ratio reached 55. That would have been disastrous for the most severe pounding came later, accompanying the put-call ratio's rise from 55 to 65 (Figure 3.9).

To correctly interpret the charts that accompany this section, use any local maximum as a buy signal and a local minimum as a sell signal. You can easily observe the buys and sells marked at those places on the charts. Accompanying each put-call ratio chart is the chart of the underlying index, stock, or futures. You can see that the ratio is a good predictor in each of these cases (Figure 3.10).

Put-Call Ratios on Individual Stocks

The ratio works quite well for some of the large-cap stocks. The charts of Dell Computer **(DELL)**, Figure 3.11, and Intel **(INTC)**, Figure 3.12, show their put-call signals have been quite excellent. The following large-cap stocks do quite well with put-call ratio signals:

AOL	America Online	IBM	IBM
AXP	American Express	INTC	Intel
CVX	Chevron	JNJ	Johnson & Johnson
CPQ	Compaq	MCD	McDonald
CSCO	Cisco Systems	MRK	Merck
DELL	Dell Computer	MSFT	Microsoft
DIS	Disney	PFE	Pfizer
EK	Eastman Kodak	WCOM	Worldcom
GE	General Electric	WMT	Wal-Mart
HWP	Hewlett-Packard		

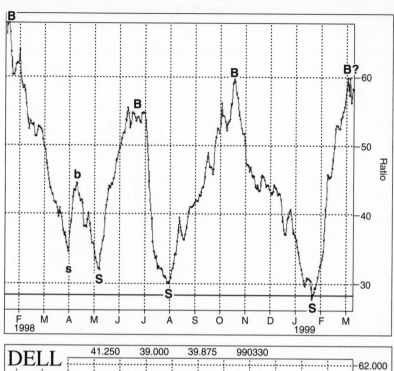

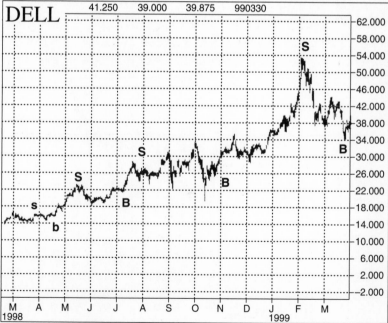

Figure 3.11 Dell computer 21-day put-call ratio.

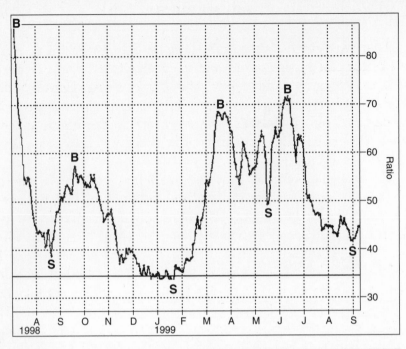

Figure 3.12 Intel 21-day put-call ratio.

There are stocks other than those on this list on which put-call ratios can be computed and used profitably, and you may want to incorporate those into your own trading. However, be aware that heavy speculative activity may indicate some sort of insider trading, or at least a "hot" rumor in the marketplace. When those occur, the put-call ratio will not only be distorted, it may give a wrong signal.

For example, suppose that you are following a stock where the put-call ratio usually ranges from about 50 to 120. For several days, there is heavy call buying and the ratio drops to 30. Should you be *really* bearish (as the put-call ratio might indicate)? Not necessarily. You should probably investigate the call volume to see if it fits with our previous description of insider trading: volume more than double the average, heavy activity in the near-term at-the-money and just out-of-the-money calls. If it does, you may be observing the "tracks" of an inside trader and you would therefore want to go along and buy the stock—not turn bearish on it.

Also, equity options incur a number of noise transactions, as discussed earlier. These include arbitrage, covered writes, and spreads—with the latter two being the most frequent activities. These activities would certainly distort the put-call ratio inaccurately for a relatively thin stock. However, for the big-cap stocks shown in the previous list, these activities might distort the put-call ratio slightly, but it would not be enough to counteract it altogether.

Sector Index Options Put-Call Ratios

Put-call ratios can be used in a similar manner for the more liquid sector options. Since sector options are quite a bit less liquid than OEX and stock options, you would expect the signals to be less accurate—and they are—but they are still quite useful most of the time. At the time this book was written, the following sectors were responding best to put-call ratio signals. The index symbol is given in parentheses (we use a dollar sign to denote that it's an index):

• Banking ($BKX)	• Oil & Gas ($XOI)
• Gold & Silver ($XAU)	• Oil Service ($OSX)
• Hong Kong ($HKO)	• Pharmaceuticals ($DRG)
• Japan ($JPN)	• Russell 2000 ($RUT)
• Morgan-Stanley High-Tech ($MSH)	• Semiconductor ($SOX)
• NASDAQ-100 ($NDX)	• Tech Stocks ($TXX)
• Natural Gas ($XNG)	• Utilities ($UTY)

Specific details of the components of each sector index can be obtained from your broker or from the exchange where the options are listed.

It is interesting to note that three foreign stock markets are among the sectors with active option trading in the United States: Mexico, Japan, and Hong Kong. The put-call ratio has proven to be a good trading vehicle for all three of these sectors.

Futures Options Put-Call Ratios

Put-call ratios can also be calculated for futures options. As stated previously, though, it only makes sense to compute such a ratio for one commodity or set of futures contracts at a time. Thus, to compute the gold futures options put-call ratio, add the put volume for all of the existing gold contracts (February gold futures, April, June, October, and December, for example). Then divide that total by the call option volume totaled over the contracts. The result would be the gold put-call ratio for the day. The number of puts and calls traded is reported, subtotaled by commodity, in the daily newspaper listing of futures option prices.

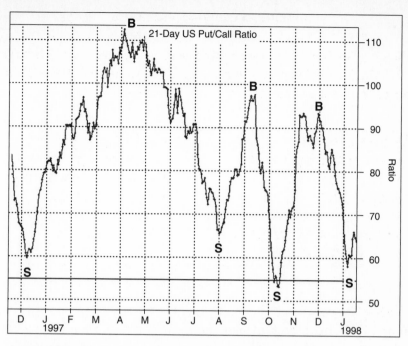

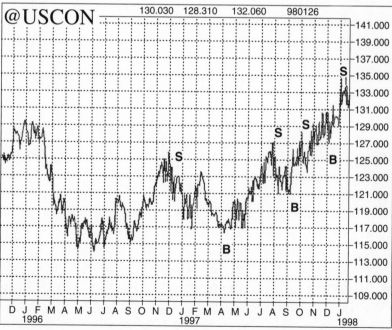

Figure 3.13 USCON T-bond futures.

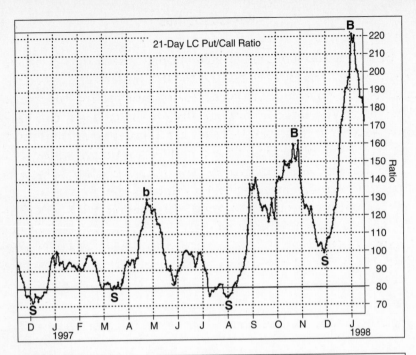

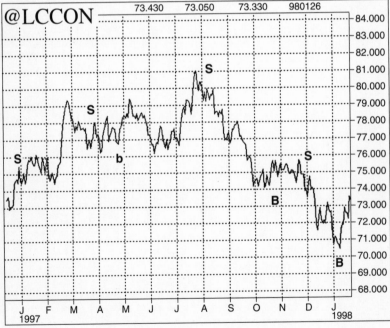

Figure 3.14 LCCON live cattle futures.

Since the total volume of gold options traded in a given day is a very small number compared to OEX options or total equity options, you must be a little careful in interpreting the indicator. One or two large orders can distort the gold put-call ratio daily because volume is relatively thin. Thus, rather than interpreting each local maxima (peak) and local minima (valley) as a sell or buy signal, respectively, you may be better served by looking for *extreme* maxima and minima as signals.

The continuous charts shown in this section [@USCON (Figure 3.13) is the continuous chart of T-bond futures, @LCCON (Figure 3.14) is that of Live Cattle futures, and @JYCON (Figure 3.15) is that of the Japanese Yen futures] are constructed

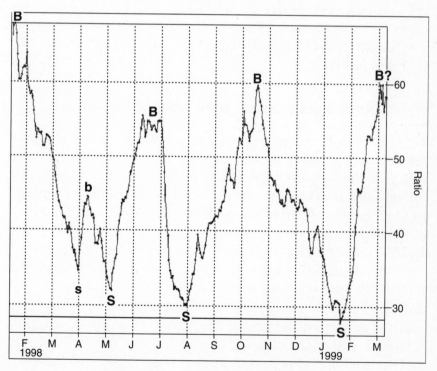

Figure 3.15 JYCON Japanese yen futures.

by sequentially linking futures contracts and eliminating the gap that occurs between them. For T-bonds, for example, during March, April, and May, the price is that of the nearest June futures. Then during June, July, and August, the continuous price uses the nearest September futures, and so forth. However, the price of each sequential contract is adjusted to eliminate the gap that exists (between June and September futures, for example). Essentially, this chart represents the actual results a trader would have experienced had he bought T-bond futures and continually rolled to the nearest contract about a month before expiration. In a situation where the longer term contracts trade at a discount to current contracts (T-bonds, for example), the continuous price chart would have a *higher* price at the end of the chart than the actual December T-bond futures. We use this continuous price chart to evaluate the signals because it reflects how a trader would have done at any time by trading the most liquid contract over the length of the chart, without artificial gaps in prices.

Anticipating a Change in a Moving Average

There is actually a way that we can use the computer to aid in determining whether we are looking at an impending peak or valley on the put-call chart at any moment in time. It works by evaluating a tree of possibilities, based on the expected range of put-call reading in any particular market. However, if you are looking for a more in-depth discussion, please refer to the book, *McMillan on Options* (L. G. McMillan, New York: Wiley, 1996).

Thus, using a computer, we have a good chance of catching a turn in the put-call chart—and hence a buy or sell signal in the market—before it becomes confirmed to the naked eye. We might pick it up on the first or second day after the actual peak is formed, rather than having to wait for, say, a full 10 days to confirm that a 10-day peak or trough was formed. For example, suppose we know that a 10-day moving average of numbers is

140, and we know that the number that is about to come off is 160. Then tomorrow's 10-day moving average will be:

$$\frac{(140 \times 10 - 160 + \text{Tomorrow's number})}{10}$$

Furthermore, suppose that we know that tomorrow's number is likely to be in a range of 120 to 160 (put-call ratios perhaps). If we assume that tomorrow's number can only be 120, 130, 140, 150, or 160 and each occurs with equal probability then:

Tomorrow's Number	New 10-Day Moving Average
120	136
130	137
140	138
150	139
160	140

Thus, there is a 4-out-of-5 chance that 140 is the peak for at least one day. This process can be extended out for any number of days, and a computer can calculate the probability that today's moving average number will subsequently prove to be a peak or valley. Combined with technical analysis, this method can allow you to get in on a trade near the put-call ratio buy or sell signal.

SUMMARY

Because option traders as a group are usually wrong, their trading activity can be read as a contrary indicator—a signal to do the opposite of what the majority of traders are doing. As with direct indicators, price (implied volatility) and volume are the measures to track. Study the $OEX and $VIX for trading statistics regarding volatility. Calculate the put-call ratio to track volume. Effective interpretation of contrary indicators tell you when to engage in straddle buying; when to buy the underlying; and when to sell naked puts. The key is correct interpretation of the indicators.

REVIEW QUESTIONS: OPTIONS AS CONTRARY INDICATORS

1. Which one of the following would *not* be useful as a contrary indicator? Choose all that apply.

   a. Option volume.

   b. Option time value premium.

   c. Option implied volatility.

   d. Stock volume.

2. Which one of the following is *not* an example of an opinion that can be considered contrary?

   a. Nearly all economists expect earnings to increase this year.

   b. Surveys say a certain candidate will win the election.

   c. Small investors are shorting odd lots of stocks with great frequency.

   d. Investment advisors expect another bull market next year.

3. What does the CBOE's Volatility Index ($VIX) measure?

   a. The implied volatility of eight active $OEX options.

   b. The implied volatility of all $OEX options.

   c. The implied volatility of all options traded at the CBOE.

   d. The implied volatility of all $SPX options.

4. Extremes in $VIX indicate what market action should be taken?

   a. Buy after extreme high peaks and sell after extreme low readings.

   b. Sell after extreme high peaks and buy after extreme low readings.

   c. Buy after extreme high peaks and buy straddles after extreme low readings.

   d. Sell after extreme high peaks and buy straddles after extreme low readings.

5. Which of these is a condition for an implied-volatility bullish (buy) signal? Indicate all that apply.

   a. The underlying has been falling rapidly.

   b. Implied volatility has been increasing rapidly.

   c. Implied volatility establishes a peak.

   d. Option volume surges to more than double its average.

6. Which strategies would be appropriate after a buy signal from question 5? Choose all that apply.

   a. Buy an at-the-money put, and sell an out-of-the-money put.

   b. Sell a naked put.

   c. Establish a covered call write.

   d. Buy an out-of-the-money call, and sell an out-of-the-money put.

   e. Buy an out-of-the-money put, and sell an at-the-money put.

7. If implied volatility is too low, what can we most likely surmise?

   a. The underlying should be sold. This is a sell signal.

   b. Insiders are selling options.

   c. The underlying is probably about to explode, but we don't know which way.

   d. Call should be bought because this is a buy signal.

8. What one of the following would *not* be a good group upon which to calculate a put-call ratio?

   a. All gold and silver stock options.

   b. All grain futures options.

   c. All stock options traded on all exchanges.

   d. All S&P 100 Index options.

9. Put-call ratios can be used as a contrary indicator on:

   a. Individual stocks.

   b. A stock sector index.

   c. A single commodity.

   d. All of the above.

10. What volume does the equity-only put-call ratio measure?

   a. Stock options traded on the CBOE.

   b. Stock options for stocks in the Dow-Jones 30 Industrials.

   c. All stocks traded on the NYSE.

   d. Stock options traded on all the exchanges.

11. Explain the difference between a *dynamic* interpretation of an indicator and a *static* interpretation. Specifically, how does it apply to put-call ratios?

12. What has caused the $OEX put-call ratio to diminish in usefulness in the late 1990s? Choose all that apply.

   a. An ongoing, strong bull market.

   b. Arbitrage.

   c. Institutional hedging activity.

   d. Decreasing volume of trading.

13. What might you use to verify a put-call ratio buy signal? Choose the one best answer.

   a. The underlying shows some signs of strength.

   b. Option volume increases dramatically.

   c. The underlying makes a new low.

   d. The underlying makes a new high.

14. Pertaining to a single stock, arrange the following "buy" signals in order of the immediacy of their timing, from

shortest to longest (or from most accurate timing to vaguest timing).

a. Put-call ratio buy signal.

b. Stock price breaks out of a trading range by closing above multiple resistance areas.

c. We believe the stock's corporate earnings will rise.

15. The put-call ratio for XYZ stock has ranged between 30 and 80 over the past six years. Now, a put-call buy signal occurs at the 90 level. Which of the following are true? Mark all.

a. This should be the best put-call ratio buy signal ever for XYZ.

b. This signal should be much better than the previous buy, which occurred at the 60 level.

c. We have no idea whether this will be a better buy signal than any other.

d. We need to research *why* the put-call ratio is so high before we can decide how good this buy signal might be (i.e., *why* were all those puts being bought?).

16. Suppose you are computing the put-call ratio on a relatively illiquid sector index or stock, and on a particular day the total volume consists of zero calls and 100 puts, so the put-call ratio = 100 divided by 0, or infinity. Describe how you would handle this in a put-call moving average.

17. Some mathematicians suggest using the following ratio for the daily put-call ratio calculation:

$$\frac{(\text{Put volume} - \text{Call volume})}{(\text{Put volume} + \text{Call volume})}$$

This, instead of the more normal (Put volume / Call volume). Describe what you see as the major advantages and disadvantages of this approach.

18. Indicate any and all true statements regarding continuous futures charts:

   a. The continuous chart is constructed by aligning a series of futures charts on the same commodity, such as March S&Ps, followed by June S&Ps, followed by Sept S&Ps, and so on.

   b. The continuous chart is the same as answer (*a*), but in addition the gaps between the series of individual futures are removed.

   c. The continuous chart depicts the results that a trader would have if he were long a futures contract and continuously rolled it to the next nearest futures when expiration approached.

   d. The continuous chart and a regular, long-term chart of a commodity have the same shape.

19. Computers can be used to anticipate when a moving average might be ready to roll over because:

   a. There is a simple formula that can be evaluated to find the answer.

   b. Computers can evaluate a large number of outcomes (a "tree") to estimate the answer.

   c. Moving averages can only be calculated with computers.

20. Novice investors often think that if they can find out what a consensus of brokerage firms, investment advisors, and other traders are doing in the market (buying or selling), then they can follow along and profit. What is wrong with this philosophy of trading?

4

SYSTEM TRADING

LEARNING OBJECTIVES

The material in this chapter helps you to:

- Choose the trading system that is right for you.
- Realize the importance of following your system's rules—always.
- Determine the amount of money you need to start short-term trading.
- Understand what makes the market move.
- See and react to index arbitrage at work near or on index option expiration day.
- Compute index fair value.

Much has been written in recent years about day traders. In fact, day trading has been around for ages, but the most common practice has been to day-trade futures because they have large leverage. In addition, some futures contracts are volatile enough that their daily trading range is wide, so that a day trader has a reasonable chance to make (or lose) some money. The kind of day trading that the media fell in love with was day trading of stocks—a realm that used to be reserved strictly for professional traders who paid no commissions. However, with the advent of Internet stocks' volatility, it *appears* to many novice traders that they can make money day-trading these stocks. History will almost certainly prove that to be false for the vast majority of these day traders.

In any case, if you are going to day trade, you need a *system*—you can't just say, "I think I'm going to buy Microsoft today." That is almost certainly the road to ruin. A **trading system** is a methodology that has well-defined rules for entry and exit, plus perhaps some rules for taking partial profits. There are hundreds, perhaps *thousands,* of systems that are profitable. If you are going to trade any of them, you need to pick ones that are compatible with your trading style. The discussion in this chapter will show you how to pick the system that's best for you and use it profitably.

CHOOSING A SYSTEM

In selecting a trading system, you should ask these (and perhaps even more) questions: Does it work in the markets you like to trade? Some systems work much better in certain markets than others (for example, it might work well in bonds, but not in currencies or the S&Ps). Does it require more time than you can give? That is, does it require you to be glued to a screen all day to watch short-term, real-time price movements? Does it have a larger risk than you really want to take? Just because a system has a good track record does not mean that it will make money for you, so you must analyze how much you are placing at risk in case the first few trades all turn out poorly. Are the system's drawdowns too large for the capital you are going to risk? That is, are you risking ruin on a short, unprofitable run of trades by your system? If so, you must either trade with more capital or find a system with a smaller drawdown.

While we are on the subject, let us discuss **drawdown** because it is a term that is not familiar to everyone—although its concept certainly is. I facetiously define drawdown as what happens to your account the minute you begin trading a profitable system. Drawdown is the worst losing period that a system has faced. Even wildly profitable systems have drawdowns—they are inevitable; not every trade can be a winner. You should allow enough trading capital to margin the trades plus allow for the maximum drawdown. In that way, a trader will not be wiped out prematurely, that is, before the system has a chance to become profitable.

Follow the Rules

A system by its very nature has a rigid set of rules. *The hardest thing about system trading is following the rules.* Your emotions will get in your way. You may decide not to take a certain trade because there have been several losing ones in a row, and you figure the system isn't working. That's just when a system will crank out a big profitable trade. Even worse, if the system is working really well, and you have a series of winners, you may be tempted to skip a trade because you figure that it's due to be a loser. Again, you could easily be missing out on a winning trade, or if a *really* long winning streak unfolds, you probably won't get back into the system once you have "gotten out" by skipping that trade.

Even if you enter the trade you're supposed to, you may find it difficult to adhere strictly to the buy and sell points. If you're watching the market in real time, you may be tempted to override a stop loss point, figuring that the market is certainly due to rebound. *Don't do that!* You're almost certain to be wrong—especially in a losing situation—because your emotions are overruling your system's hard statistics. One good approach to system trading is to find a broker who will trade your system for you. Your broker has no emotional ties, especially if you make it clear that the only thing that will make you mad is if he or she overrides the system and misses a trade or an entry/exit point. There are a number of futures brokers who offer this service.

Advantages of System Trading

There are some definite emotional and psychological *advantages* to day trading. One is that you don't have to work every day. If you decide to skip a day or go on vacation, there are no positions—by its definition, day trading means that you close out your positions at the end of the day. Many day traders really like the feeling of not having to worry about what happens overnight and also the feeling of starting out each day with a clean slate. If that doesn't appeal to you, then don't consider being a day trader—and that's all right, too. Not everyone can trade every style. Day trading is a style that historically has been for only a few. The fact that it recently caught the media's and public's attention does not alter that fact—it's still apropos for only a few. Those few will succeed; the others will fail and reenter the "normal" job market.

Another advantage of system/day trading is that you don't have to do much work to get back up to speed after time off. If you're a fundamental stock analyst, for example, you'd have to find out what the company is doing and what its industry is doing, how interest rates are behaving, what the general market tone is like, and so on. A system trader, however, needs nothing more than the inputs to the system—which should easily be available from the newspaper or the trader's quote machine. Once the system inputs are in hand, the day trader is ready to go. No long background research is required to get up to speed.

There is a margin advantage to day trading as well: Most brokers require a smaller margin for day traders—sometimes as low as 50% of the exchange minimum margin for overnight positions. Of course, decreased margin (i.e., higher leverage) is a two-edged sword: losses hurt more, and gains are greater, percentagewise.

SYSTEMS EXAMPLES

There are two systems relevant to this discussion. One is a very short-term trading system—Treasury Notes vs. S&Ps—with holding periods of a day or two. The second system (oscillator system) is more of an intermediate-term system where holding periods can run as long as several weeks.

Treasury Notes Opposite S&Ps

A system that is designed to trade the S&Ps (or a similar vehicle) is based on the movement in the 10-Year Treasury Note futures (base symbol: TY). The theory behind this system is that the "bond market" shows the "true" direction of the stock market, and if there is a large discrepancy between T-Note movements and the movements of the S&P 500 futures, then we should trade the S&P futures—figuring that they will catch up to the T-Note futures. Larry Williams, who has designed similar systems to take advantage of these movements between the bond market and S&Ps, first introduced this idea to me.

System Entry Rules: Specifically, we look at how the T-Note futures have done over the past six days. If they are *up,* say, and S&P futures are *down* over the same six-day period, then we would *buy* S&P futures at the opening of the next day's trading. Conversely, if T-Notes have been *down* over the last six days, while S&P's have been *up,* then we would *short* the S&P futures at the opening of trading.

This system is based on trading the S&P 500 futures contract. You may use other vehicles to trade this system, such as

$OEX options, e-mini futures, Dow Jones futures or options, and so on, but the system *requires* the buy and sell points to be computed with the S&P 500 futures prices.

Those entry rules are well-defined. However, there must be well-defined exit rules as well. You must use stops that are in line with the volatility of the market, lest you be stopped out on a small "wiggle" on nearly every trade. Even a very profitable system will lose money if the stop is too tight. The stop must be placed at a wide enough level where random market noise won't affect the overall workings of the system. The stop points *could* be optimized with back-testing software, but as a general rule, with S&P futures at or above 1000 and with $VIX in the low-to-mid-20's, I use a stop of 5.00 points.

Actually the exit rules are composed of three parts:

a. Once the position is initially taken, set a stop at 5.00 points from the market's opening price (your theoretical entry price), *not* from your *actual* entry price. So if you bought the S&P futures at 1115.00 on the opening, you would place a stop with your broker to sell them at 1110.00.

b. *If a 5.00-point profit develops,* then begin to use a 5.00-point trailing stop. In this example, then, if the futures traded up to 1120 (after having bought them at 1115 on the opening), *then* a trailing stop of 5.00 points would be used. The next section describes a trailing stop order in greater detail.

c. If you are not stopped out by either rule 1 or 2, as the end of the trading day nears, you should reassess the *entry* rules again. If the entry rules are no longer valid (that is, if today's movements have placed the T-Notes and the S&Ps in "agreement" over the past six days), then exit the trade "market on close." If not—that is, if T-Notes and S&Ps are still divergent over the past six days—then hold your position into the next trading day, keeping the same stop orders in place.

The system is not necessarily a day-trading system, although it often terminates during or after a single day's trading. Table 4.1 shows the rules and Table 4.2 shows an example of this system. The trade in Table 4.2 is closed out after one day.

A one-point move in the S&Ps is worth $250 per point. Originally, a one-point move was $500, but the contract size was halved with prices and volatility increase in the late 1990s. So, a stop of 5.00 points means that you are risking $250 × 5 = $1,250 per trade, plus commissions and slippage.

What's **slippage?** That's the amount of extra money you lose when you enter or exit the market. Simplistically, let's say your system calls for you to buy one S&P at 1312.50, and you place a stop order above the market to do so. Later, the market moves higher and hits your stop. At that point, your order becomes a

Table 4.1 T-Bonds Trending Opposite S&Ps—Rules

Using *day session* closing prices, compare the T-bond front month futures closing prices with the closing prices six trading days ago. Make the same comparison for S&P front month futures. After analyzing the results, if you see that:

1. T-bonds have *risen* over the six days, and S&Ps have *fallen,* then *buy* S&Ps at the day session open.

2. T-bonds have *fallen* over the six days, and S&Ps have *risen,* then *sell* S&Ps at the day session open.

Stop yourself out as follows:

a. Use a 5.00-point intraday stop loss initially.

b. If a 5.00-point *profit* accrues, then chance the stop to be a 5.00-point *trailing* stop.

c. At the end of the day, if not stopped out, exit the trade if T-bonds and S&P's are in "agreement." Hold the position if T-bonds are still trending opposite S&Ps.

Table 4.2 T-Bonds Trending Opposite S&Ps—Example

	9/18 Close	9/26 Close	Change
US	115-15	115-24	+0.09
SP	957.80	953.20	−4.60

⇒ Buy S&P on OPEN of 9/29: 952.95

	9/19 Close	9/29 Close	Change
US	115-21	115-22	+0.01
SP	960.60	961.10	+0.50

Now the two are in synch, so sell the long S&Ps on close.

market order. So your floor broker buys one S&P at the market. Perhaps he has to pay 1312.70 to do so. The extra 20 cents (0.20) that you paid to enter the trade above the stop price is considered slippage on the way in. There will also be slippage on the way out. Twenty cents at $250 per point is slippage of $50. You can see that slippage can be a big part of things—probably much more expensive than commissions. When markets are volatile, the slippage increases. In fact, if you trade right after a major economic announcement such as a volatile unemployment report, you could face slippage of monstrous proportions. That's why it's sometimes a good idea to stand aside from any system trading when government reports are released—that applies to almost any futures contract.

Types of Stop Orders

The previous paragraph described the way a stop order works. There are *other* types of stop orders that can be used. For example, there is something called a *stop limit order.* In *that* case, you place a stop limit order to buy the S&P at 1312.50, say. When they rise up to your stop price, your order becomes a *limit order,* not a market order as in the previous paragraph. This could lead to better or worse results. If the S&Ps stabilize right after hitting your limit, then you will buy them at 1312.50, and therefore you will have *no* slippage entering the trade. However, if they keep right on going higher, you will not be "in" the trade, and it will be making money for those who used regular stop orders, while those who used stop *limit* orders are sitting on the sidelines, twiddling their thumbs. I use stop limit orders when slippage becomes too large.

However, upon exit of a trade, you should *never* use a stop limit order. The reasoning is simple. The exit stop is there to keep your losses limited. That is, the system designers have determined that once the market reaches the exit stop level, the system is not working for this particular trade, and it should be exited. If you use a stop limit order, there is a possibility that you will *not* exit the trade if your limit is not attained. Therefore, you could wind up losing a *vast* amount of money—far more than the 5.00 points that the system is designed for (plus slippage). Consider this example: Your entry point was 1312.50 for the S&Ps when you bought them. Therefore your sell stop would be placed at 1307.50. Suddenly, bad news arises (Iraq attacks Kuwait, or Greenspan rases interest rates, or you name it) and the market crumbles. It slashes right down through your limit and falls to 1290.00. If you had used a regular stop, you might have received a fill on your sell order at 1306.50—slippage of a whole point ($250) but at least you would be out. If you used a stop *limit* order, it is unlikely that your order would have been filled because the market was plunging. Therefore you would still be long in the futures when they finally settled down at 1290.00, a loss of 22.50 points or $5,625. In a system where the loss is designed to be $1,250 plus slippage, that's a *huge* and possibly irreversible mistake for you to make. So, *do not use stop limit orders for exiting a system trade.*

The previous example contained a subtlety that is important: *No matter at what price you actually enter the system, the stop must be placed 5.00 below the system entry price.* In this example, the system called for you to buy at 1312.50. If you paid

1312.70 because of slippage, that is *irrelevant* as far as determining where to place the stop. The stop is placed at 1307.50 because that's 5.00 below the system entry price of 1312.50.

Next, we must address the issue of a trailing stop, because that is what the system calls for. A **trailing stop** is one that moves *with* the futures position when it is making money but remains static if it begins to lose money. Let's once again use the same example. Suppose that we bought our futures at 1312.70, as above, which include the 20 cents for slippage. Also as shown above, our stop is originally placed at 1307.50, five points below the *opening* price. Now suppose that the S&P futures rise by 5.00 points to 1317.50—that is, we have a 5.00-point profit (unrealized). The *trailing stop* now needs to be used. It would initially be set at 1312.50—5.00 points below the current prices of 1317.50. If the market moves higher, the trailing stop would need to be raised, since it should always be 5.00 points below the *best* price your trade has reached so far.

If you are using a broker, you would call him and tell him to cancel the original stop at 1307.50 and instead to place a new stop at 1312.50. Later, if the market moves higher, you would cancel *that* stop and replace it with a higher stop. Obviously, you can't keep calling your broker every time the S&Ps rise another dime. That would require too much work from you and would drive your broker crazy. So you must use some judgment here— perhaps as a practical matter, only calling your broker if you are raising the price at least a point (1.00) or so. As long as you're watching the trading on your quote screen, you can always know yourself where the trailing stop is (theoretically) even if you haven't physically placed the order with your broker. If the S&Ps trade at the theoretical stop, you can always call your broker and sell your position at the market, while canceling whatever stop you had in there at the time.

Just to continue with our example describing trailing stops, suppose that the S&Ps subsequently trade down to or up to the following prices. Table 4.3 shows what you would do with your

Table 4.3 Trailing Stop Orders

S&Ps Move To	Your Stop Becomes
1318.00	1313.00 (as covered above).
1315.00	1313.00 (no change; the stop is never lowered for a long position).
1320.00	1315.00 (5.00 below the highest price reached so far).
1316.00	(again, no change in the stop when losing money).
1324.00	1319.00 (5.00 below the new highs).
1319.00	You're stopped out.

trailing stop order. Again, this assumes that you bought S&Ps at 1312.70 and set your stop initially at 1307.50.

In this example, you are eventually stopped out at 1319.00, or perhaps something slightly lower if there was slippage. You originally bought the futures at 1312.70, so your profit is 7.30 points, or $1,825.00, less slippage on the exit, less commissions. However, you can see that, at one point, with the S&Ps at 1324, you had a profit of 12.30 points, or $3,075. So you gave back a lot by waiting for your stop to be hit. Or did you Will, in this case you did, but what if the S&Ps had gone on to 1335? Then you would have been glad you stayed with the position instead of arbitrarily selling it out at 1324. So, stick with the system rules and don't try to countermand them.

The system designers should attempt to incorporate these things into the system—which eventually evolves as the stop price. Some systems may have targets. This one doesn't. So you will have occurrences like the one above, where the eventual profit seems small in comparison with the best profit you had at any time during the day. The trailing stop is designed to lock in a good chunk of that best profit, but obviously it can't lock in all of it.

Some traders will compromise a little, by trading several contracts (i.e., buy two or three S&Ps instead of just one), and then sell one out at the stop distance (after a profit of 5.00 points), holding the others in accordance with the system design. In this case, you'd sell one at 1317.50 (the entry stop, 1312.50, plus 5.00) and the other(s) at 1319.00 in accordance with the regular system. By increasing the number of contracts you trade initially, you increase your overall dollar risk if the position lost money and stopped you out immediately.

How Much Money Should I Allot?

In any type of trading, if you are undercapitalized, you will probably lose *all* of your money. You can see that you will need at least the initial margin, plus a dollar amount equal to the stop, plus commissions and slippage. Even with that, if you lose on your first two trades, your broker will ask for more margin. In reality, you should have an idea of the drawdown of the system before beginning to trade it. Then you should allot the initial margin plus the drawdown as your initial capital.

Table 4.4 gives the daily profits or losses for this system from 3/20/96 through 1/26/98. You can see that it only trades a few days per month. On the other days, the T-Notes and S&Ps are in "agreement" and there is no trade. This system has a drawdown of $16,254, as shown in Table 4.4. That drawdown was for the specific period of time shown in the chart. That figure was for trading *two* of the current-size S&P contracts. That is, the figures in Table 4.4 represent trades with a potential for risk of $500 per point (two contracts). So, for one contract, the drawdown would only be $8,127 or so.

In any case, returning to the question of how much money to start with, we want to allow the initial margin plus the drawdown. So, if your broker is charging $22,000 for the initial margin on an S&P contract, and the drawdown is $8,100, then you need $30,100 in your account to begin trading this system with just *one* contract! Many traders start out with far less capital and wind up losing most or all of it because they

Table 4.4 T-Bonds Trending Opposite S&Ps—Daily Profits

Date	Profit/Loss	Date	Profit/Loss	Date	Profit/Loss
3/20/96	553	11/1	−1,597	9/16	10,750
3/27	−3,600	12/4	403	9/25	−2,522
4/2	−600	12/5/96	−247	9/29	4,353
4/3	−250	1/10/97	−3,772	10/10	−2,522
4/18	550	1/13	1,050	10/13	1,850
4/24	2,500	1/14	−4,397	10/14	1,228
4/25	−1,697	1/20	353	10/21	6,453
4/30	200	1/23	6,278	10/24	−2,522
5/1	−850	2/24	−2,572	10/27	−2,522
5/2	5,328	2/26	5,003	10/28	−2,522
5/24	−1,097	3/10	−2,522	10/30	−2,522
6/6	4,453	3/11	1,778	11/3	6,078
6/10	1,250	3/12	3,678	11/5	−2,522
6/11	−97	3/13	6,703	11/11	928
6/12	853	3/24	4,228	11/12	−2,522
6/18	−2,150	3/25	−3,047	11/14	5,028
6/19	600	3/27	11,928	11/16	8,628
6/20	−925	4/10	928	12/1	−2,522
6/21	3,300	4/17	−872	12/12	−2,522
6/24	828	4/28	−3,272	12/15	2,578
7/17	2,850	5/14	1,753	12/16	3,078
7/18	4,825	5/20	−2,522	12/17	−2,522
7/19	−2,725	5/21	1,778	12/18	−2,522
7/22	−2,225	5/22	1,353	12/19	−2,522
7/23	−4,700	5/23	−2,522	12/22	−2,522
7/24	1,253	5/27	−2,522	12/23	−2,522
7/26–30	2,028	5/28	−547	12/24	−2,522
7/31	−2,372	5/29	2,523	12/26	−1,122
8/1	5,578	5/30	−2,522	12/29	6,378
8/14	−522	6/4	−525	12/31/97	−1,072
8/20	200	6/5	1,728	1/2/98	−1,122
8/21	975	6/6	8,228	1/9	−2,522
8/22	−2,925	6/24	7,528	1/12	10,478
8/23	1,500	7/2	−2,522	1/13	6,978
8/26	2,278	7/3	−5,022	1/14	1,878
9/9	−4,466	7/15	−2,522	1/15	−2,522
9/24	−547	8/4	−1,700	1/16	2,178
9/25	478	8/5	978	1/20	−2,522
10/1	1,978	8/6	−2,522	1/21	2,078
10/15	2,903	8/7	5,128	1/22	4,528
10/17	78	8/19	4,978	1/23	928
10/25	703	8/20	6,753	1/26	378
10/30	−2,600	8/26	−2,522		———
10/31	3,425	9/9	−2,522		84,907

130 trades.
Average profit: +$653.
Drawdowns: −13,331 (July–August '97).
        −16,254 (December '97).

are undercapitalized. Note: you might be able to halve the margin portion of the requirement if your broker only charges half for day trades. However, you would then have to be *absolutely* certain that you never hold a position overnight inadvertently. If you did, you would get a margin call, and if you didn't have the excess capital to deposit into the account to meet the margin call, you might find your account restricted.

Trading Vehicles

It was mentioned earlier that this system could be traded with other broad market instruments—other than the S&P 500 futures contract. This is not to say that the system applies to corn or Swiss francs. It does not. There may be similar systems that do, but it would be up to the reader to discover them, perhaps with the aid of system-testing software. Rather, since this system indicates the short-term movements of the S&P futures (and hence the broad stock market), then other broad stock market vehicles could be traded using this system. These would include the $OEX options, Dow Jones futures and options, and the S&P e-mini futures, to name a few.

If you are going to use the system to trade one of these other instruments, then your stops would become *mental* stops, in general. That is, you would put the limits in your quote machine based on the S&P futures' trading movements, as usual, but when the limit was hit, you would pick up the phone and buy or sell one of these other instruments instead of actually having a stop order the S&P pit.

For example, suppose you don't have a futures account and/or your broker is not registered to do futures business. Then I would recommend trading $OEX options with this system. To once again use the above example, you would set up your quote machine with a limit at 1312.50 (the buy point for the S&P futures). However, since you are trading the S&P futures themselves, there would *not* be a stop order on any exchange floor. Rather, when your limit blinks (or beeps, or whatever it does) on your machine, then you would call your broker and tell him to buy $OEX calls. You should probably trade relatively short-term $OEX calls because that's where the greatest liquidity is; and you should probably trade calls that are at least slightly in-the-money in order to minimize the vagaries of volatility changes on your position (time decay really isn't much of a problem since these will be day trades). One rather larger problem with $OEX options, though, is that the bid-asked spread is quite wide in comparison to that of the S&P futures. Hence slippage can be much larger.

If you *do* have a futures broker and a futures trading account, but worry that the risk in the S&P 500 futures is too large, you may want to consider trading the system with the S&P 500 e-mini futures. These are very similar to the S&P 500 futures, but the e-mini futures are only worth $50 per point— one-fifth the size of the "big" S&P futures. The e-mini futures are traded *electronically only*. Thus, to enter a trade you must call your broker to put in the order through an electronic terminal. Stop orders are not really allowed, per se, but most brokers will enter a *not held* stop order for you. That is, if you give your broker an order to buy the futures at 1312.50, *stop,* the broker will watch the futures trade, and when they trade at 1312.50, will put a market buy order into the electronic terminal. This might increase your slippage a little, but it might be worth the price if you really don't feel comfortable trading the bigger-sized S&P 500 regular futures.

The Oscillator—An Intermediate-Term System

The final trading system that is included in this section is a more intermediate-term one. In this system, positions are held for several days, or perhaps even a few weeks, as opposed to the day-trading philosophy of the previous two systems. This system is based on an exponential moving average of the net advances minus declines, daily, of the NYSE stocks. It is a simple computation (see Table 4.5) and only needs to be made once a day. To get started, though, you must know the value of the oscillator on a certain day because each successive day's value depends on knowing the previous day's value. Once you have that, then you can compute the oscillator value each day after that. There are a couple of ways to get the oscillator value. One is to subscribe to our daily service, *Daily Volume Alerts.* The oscillator value is published there each day. Failing that, you can e-mail us at info@optionstrategist.com and ask us for the current value, which we will be glad to supply to you.

Since this is an intermediate-term system, we recommend using *options* to trade it. Many traders have trouble deciding whether to trade options or the underlying in certain situations. One general rule of thumb is this: *The longer-term the system, the more one should lean toward trading options.* For example, in a day-trading system, we would *not* recommend trading options. There is far less slippage and more accurate use of stops

---

Table 4.5   A Short- and Intermediate-Term Trading Indicator

Computation

Let M = Current exponential moving average

"New" M = 0.9 * M + 0.1 * (Today's advances – declines)

Example:	M =	100
	Advances =	1,200
	Declines =	900
Then:	New M =	120

Market is overbought when M > 200

Market is oversold when M < –200

Action

1. Sell signal: when M falls below 180 after having been overbought.
2. Buy signal: when M rises above –180 after having been oversold.
3. Stop yourself if signal goes on alert again; for example, if on a sell and M rises above 200 or if on a buy and M falls below –200.

with the underlying in a short-term trading situation such as day trading. Moreover, you know that your stop is tight and losses will be small, hopefully.

However, as your systems extend farther out in time, you acquire more risk. For example, in *this* system, we are risking 2% of the price of $OEX (or $SPX if you are trading futures). With futures prices near 1300, a 2% move would be 26 points, or $6,500 for one contract. Almost certainly, an $OEX at-the-money option is going to cost far less than 65 points. So, for the intermediate-term, an option is probably a better choice than is trading the underlying. The basic reason for this is that an intermediate-term system, by nature, is looking to make big gains and thus it must use relatively large stops in order to avoid getting stopped out too soon before the big gains have a chance to be made.

The oscillator system is a good one, and it has a fairly long track record. As you become familiar with it, you may be able to make some adjustments in your positions as time goes by. For example, when the oscillator becomes extremely overbought or oversold—even though it has not given a buy signal or sell signal by the system's definition—a sharp, short-term move may be about to occur in the market. These most often occur on the downside. There have been several occasions on which the oscillator has dipped below −400. Those are the types that result in a short, sharp rally. However, it is quite possible that such a rally does not bring the oscillator all the way up to a buy signal.

It is a *general* rule of thumb that the more deeply oversold the oscillator gets, the better the ensuing intermediate-term rally will be. This is especially true if the oscillator falls below −500 before a buy signal is given. The most extreme reading ever was −967 in September 1998. It took another month before the intermediate-term buy signal took effect, but then the market shot significantly higher, with the broad market rallying nearly 50% in the next six or seven months.

Table 4.6 An Intermediate-Term System Using an Oscillator Indicator

1. Initial stop = 2% of OEX.
2. Take partial profits on one-third of your position if OEX moves 2% in your favor, and at that time begin to use a 2% *trailing* stop.
3. Take profits on another one-third of your original position if OEX rises another 2% (4% from the initial price).

Year	Signals Profitable	Net Result in OEX Points
1984	5 of 6	+15.7
1985	6 of 7	+35.4
1986	5 of 5	+35.5
1987	5 of 9	+8.8
1988	4 of 8	−2.8
1989	2 of 5	−4.3
1990	4 of 7	+15.0
1991	5 of 5	+58.3
1992	4 of 4	+41.7
1993	4 of 5	+28.3
1994	6 of 12	+56.3
1995	3 of 9	−15.7
1996	7 of 11	+34.7
1997	9 of 12	+160.7
1998	10 of 15	+85.2
1999	5 of 10	+40.0
2000	5 of 10	+72.8
2001	6 of 9	+121.7
Totals	95 of 149 (64%)	+787.3

Maximum gain:	38.6 points
Maximum loss:	18.3 points
Average trade:	+5.28 points
Longest holding period:	155 calendar days
Average holding period:	24 days

Can use S&P futures or options in this system.

Note: $OEX split 2-for-1 on 11/24/97.

Overall, this is an easy indicator to keep track of, and its track record shows that it is worthwhile to do so. A simple system using this indicator is summarized in Table 4.6.

OPTION EXPIRATION AND ITS EFFECTS ON THE BROAD STOCK MARKET

The stock market has been quite volatile on many option expiration days during the year since index option trading was invented. What many people do *not* understand, however, is *why* index futures and option expiration make the stock market move. There is a direct cause and effect, as you will see. Furthermore, the stock market doesn't just move *because* it's expiration day or expiration week. No, there must be some significant open interest in the futures and options in order to create the potential for market movement.

First, let's understand *what* makes the market move. Then we'll concentrate on finding out how to identify expirations in which there is a large potential for the market to move. You will see that, depending on how aggressive index arbitrageurs are, the stock market can experience serious movements from as far as a week prior to expiration to the period immediately following expiration day itself.

Index Arbitrage

Index arbitrage is what makes the market move at or near expiration. The following scenario describes how index arbitrage positions can be built up to levels that are large enough to cause the entire stock market to move. Suppose that the market is rising strongly over a few months' time. In that case, public customers who bought $OEX options would find themselves with nicely profitable positions. Moreover, those long calls would be heavily in-the-money by the time expiration was drawing nigh. So, the public usually sells these expensive calls (perhaps rolling to other, less expensive contracts). Thus, a number of calls with prices of 30, 40, or even higher are sold. The only traders who will buy these calls are market makers and arbs, for no one else is usually interested in purchasing such high-priced inventory.

Arbs and market makers, however, are not sanguine about owning such high-priced inventory either, at least not without hedging it. So they sell short the appropriate quantity of the 100 stocks that make up the $OEX index in order to hedge their long call position. As time progresses and expiration draws nearer and nearer, most of the $OEX in-the-money calls in the series that is about to expire fall into the hands of these arbs. So, going into expiration, the arbs have a position that consists of lots of long $OEX calls hedged by the appropriate amount of short stock. The action of acquiring these arbitrage positions doesn't affect the stock market much at all. However, the unwinding of these positions can have a large influence on the market.

To see why this is true, let's assume that the arbs unwind their entire $OEX position at the close of trading on expiration Friday (the third Friday of the expiration month). In reality, they may dispose of part of their position in other manners, but to illustrate our point, we will assume they hold their positions until expiration and unwind them then. At the end of trading on expiration Friday, the arbs exercise their long $OEX calls. $OEX calls—and, in fact, all index options—exercise for *cash*, not for stock as an IBM call would. That is, when the index contracts were originally designed, it was decided that it would be too cumbersome to expect a public customer who exercised one $OEX contract to receive 100 odd lots of different stocks. So the contracts settle for cash in the amount of the index price less the strike price.

Remember, though, that the arb has a two-sided position— long $OEX calls *and* short the appropriate stocks. So, to completely unwind this position, the arb buys back all the short stock at the close of trading on Friday with market-on-close orders. By definition, then, since he is actually getting the last sale price of each of the 100 stocks, he also gets the same last sale when he exercises his long $OEX calls for cash. Thus, the arbitrage is removed at parity—there is no error factor or slippage.

But what has happened here? Many stocks were bought market on close. That makes the stock market go up. Thus, we have now identified exactly how index option expiration can have an effect on the stock market itself. Very similar strategies apply to index futures and index futures options as well. The largest contract in the futures arena is the S&P 500 futures contract.

As the years have gone by, certain procedures have been instituted by the NYSE in order to mitigate the problems associated with unwanted stock market fluctuations on expiration day. One is that market-on-close orders must *all* be entered by at least 30 minutes before the close of trading. This gives other traders a chance to react to the perhaps abnormal buy (or sell) imbalances that the index arb creates. More and more professional traders have come to understand how the index arb works, so if they have some stock to sell, for whatever reason, when they see that there is a lot of stock to buy market-on-close on expiration day, they will sell into the buy orders because they can be assured of getting a reasonably good price.

Finally, note that at some expirations, the whole process may be reversed, and there might be *sell* programs entering the market on expiration day. These would occur when the market is declining as expiration draws near, and holders of long, in-the-money puts sell them to take profits or to roll them. Once again, these deeply in-the-money options (puts, in this case) fall into the hands of arbs and market makers. In order to hedge long puts, the arbs will *buy stock* in the appropriate ratio. At expiration, then, to unwind their positions, they exercise the long puts (for cash, remember) and *sell* their stocks. Thus, this form of arbitrage activity will force the stock market down at the end of the day on expiration Friday.

During the bull market in recent years, there have been many expirations where we saw buy programs because the bull market created in-the-money calls—and the first example showed how that creates arbitrage buy programs on expiration day. Conversely, there have only been a few expirations where sell programs were prevalent.

Another procedure instituted by the NYSE and the Chicago Mercantile Exchange—the exchange where the S&P 500 futures are traded—is that the S&P contracts (and most other stock index contracts) expire on the *morning* of expiration Friday. The expiration value of the S&P 500 Index is determined by using the *opening* trade on Friday morning of each of the 500 stocks in the S&P 500. Thus, the arbs remove these contracts by executing *market on open* orders. This procedure was initiated because specialists felt that it would be easier to handle big blocks of stocks from the market-on-open orders if they had some time during the morning to work on it, rather than having to take on a big block of stock right at the close of trading on Friday and then having to hold it over the weekend.

Open Interest

So now that we know *how* arb programs affect the market, it makes sense to see if we can tell *when* these programs will come into effect. As expiration nears, we want to know if we should expect buy programs, sell programs, or nothing at all. As stated earlier, arb programs are engineered with the S&P 500 futures and futures options, too. However, it is very difficult to discern what the arbs are *really* going to do with their futures because one cannot tell if arbs are holding long or short futures against their stocks. Hence, for predictability, $OEX options are much easier to use.

What you need to observe is the open interest of the $OEX in-the-money options. **Open interest** is merely the number of contracts that exist—that have been opened by traders and not

yet closed. It is reported for each option each day by the exchanges and the Option Clearing Corporation. The figures are
in the newspaper and on quote systems on the Internet and elsewhere. So, if we monitor the open interest as expiration day approaches, we can get a pretty good idea as to whether or not
there will be arbitrage buy or sell programs.

The following example is more typical of actual situations
where the market has oscillated back and forth and there are
both in-the-money calls and in-the-money puts heading into expiration week. The process is simple: For each strike, merely
calculate the *total* open interest of all calls with lower strike
prices, and also calculate the total open interest all puts with
higher strike prices. Then subtract the two: Total-in-the-money
call open interest minus total in-the-money put open interest. If
the resulting figure is greater that +40,000 contracts, buy programs are feasible and are probably large enough to move the
market. On the other hand, if the resulting figure is *less than*
−40,000, then sell programs can be expected at expiration.

Table 4.7 shows an example of this approach. Suppose that
OEX closed at 500.93 on some day during expiration week, prior
to expiration Friday. The leftmost column in the table shows the
applicable striking prices that are near OEX's price. The next
two columns, under the heading Raw Open Interest shows the
open interest of the calls and puts at each one of those strikes.
Next, under the column heading Running Sum, the call open interest is summed—starting from the lower strike and summing
toward the higher strikes. Similarly, the put open interest is
summed, starting from the higher strikes and working down to
the lowest strikes. Finally, the running sum of the put open interest is subtracted from the running sum of the call open interest to produce the Net Difference.

Whenever the absolute value of the net difference is greater
than 40,000 contracts, it is probably that buy or sell programs
will be large enough to have an influence on the stock market on
expiration day or on the days immediately preceding expiration.

Table 4.7 Cumulative Open Interest

| | OEX Close: 500.93 | | | | |
| | Raw Open Interest | | Running Sum | | Net |
Strike	Calls	Puts	Calls	Puts	Difference
up through 480	12,000		12,000		
485	4,000	40,000	16,000	108,000	−92,000
490	8,000	30,000	24,000	68,000	44,000 . . . Sell
495	17,000	20,000	41,000	38,000	3,000
500	30,000	10,000	71,000	18,000	53,000 . . . Buy
505	40,000	5,000	111,000	8,000	103,000
510	50,000	2,000	161,000	3,000	158,000
515	35,000	500	196,000	1,000	195,000
down through 520		500			

In Table 4.7, that means that at 490 and below there would be sell programs at expiration because the net differential is −40,000 or less. Conversely, if $OEX is above 500 at expiration, we would expect arbitrage buy programs because the net differential is greater than +40,000 contracts. If $OEX is between 490 and 500 at expiration, then we would not expect arbitrage programs to have a significant effect on the stock market on this expiration day.

Formulate a Strategy

Once you know what to expect from the arbs and—more important—at what prices to expect it, it is much easier to formulate a strategy as to how to approach trading near expiration. Remember, once again, that these examples deal with $OEX options. Although similar calculations can be made for $SPX options and S&P futures options, the fact that those products can be hedged by the futures makes it much more difficult to predict what the arbs are going to do. But, for $OEX, we have a pretty good idea. You should be aware that this is *not* an exact science, for it is always possible that the arbs will roll their options out to a later expiration month, or they may decide to exercise them early—before the last Friday—so the calculations of open interest accumulation could change. It is best to recalculate these figures each day for the five to seven days preceding expiration, in order to keep current.

Many expirations, your figures will show that there is really very little chance of $OEX index option arbitrage affecting the stock market. However, when there *is* a good chance, you can use the hedged strategy on expiration Friday itself, or be prepared for some "game playing" earlier in expiration week. On expiration Friday itself, the $OEX arbs will unwind at the end of trading, and you can decide to do one of two things: (1) try to buy calls if you think the arbs are going to engineer buy programs (or buy puts if they're going to sell), or (2) adopt a hedged strategy. The first strategy is quite risky, from both the viewpoint of timing (it's probably best to wait until late in the day to buy options if you're going to use this aggressive tactic) as well as from the viewpoint that other larger institutional players may enter the market to "meet" the arbs market on close orders and negate the arbs' impact on the marketplace. The second, hedged, strategy is probably a better choice, for in it one buys 5 $OEX expiring in-the-money options—being very careful to spend as little as possible for time value premiums—and hedges it by selling one S&P 500 *futures* contract. The idea here is that you don't care so much about the timing of your entry point on expiration day, nor do you care if institutions arrive to meet the arbs market on close orders. All you want is for $OEX to outperform $SPX on that day, and since the arbs are concentrating their activity in *exactly* the 100 $OEX stocks, that should happen. Even though all of those 100 stocks are also in the $SPX, the effect of arb programs will be more dramatic on the $OEX than on $SPX. Let's use a simple example:

You expect arbitrage buy programs, and on September expiration Friday, $OEX is trading at 650, while the *December* S&P 500 futures are trading at 1310.00 (the *September* futures will have already expired on Friday *morning*). After the market opens on Friday, you begin to monitor the time value premium of the OEX September 640 calls. Finally, you notice that, with $OEX at 650.03, the Sept 640 calls are offered at 10½. Thus the time value premium is 0.47 (640 + 10.50 − 650.03). So you buy 5 OEX Sept 640 calls and sell one S&P 500 futures contract at 1310.00. Now, you sit back and wait for the close of trading. The following table shows how the prices might look at various times near the close:

Time	$OEX	$SPX	December S&P Future
3:30 P.M.	651.00	1,302.00	1,312.00
3:45 P.M.	651.50	1,303.00	1,313.00[1]
3:55 P.M.	652.00	1,303.20	1,313.20[2]
4:00 P.M.	653.00	1,303.70	1,313.70
4:05 P.M.	654.50	1,305.00	1,315.00

[1] Things are staying "in line."
[2] $OEX is beginning to forge ahead.

Not much usually happens after 4:05 P.M., for all the market on close orders have usually been reported by then. Normally, there is a 2-to-1 relationship between $SPX and $OEX. However, you can see in the above table, that $OEX—after 3:45 P.M.—move up 3.00 points, while $SPX only rose by 2.00 (usually 3 points in $OEX would result in 6 points in $SPX). So, how did our position do? The long Sept 640 calls can be exercised for their closing value of 14.50 (654.50 − 640.00, the strike price). That's a gain of 4 points each on five contracts for a total gain of $2,000. Meanwhile, the futures would be bought back at 1315.00 for a *loss* of five points or $1,250 loss. Overall a gain of $750, less commissions, for one day's work with a nicely hedged position.

In actuality, there might be a couple of opportunities for the hedged position to perform even better. One is that the futures might actually lose a little bit of premium near the close. This might allow the hedged trader to buy them back at slightly lower prices. The other is that the hedged position has an open end on it. In this example, we were short futures and long Sept 640 calls. What if something completely unusual happened and $OEX fell below 640? The hedged position could make a *lot* of money because the short futures would keep generating profits in that case, while the long calls could only fall to zero.

Some hedged traders—the more aggressive ones—might even stay short the futures over the weekend, after they exercise their long $OEX calls on Friday night. As shown in Table 4.8, there is often a post-expiration effect in which the market

Table 4.8 Post-Expiration Effect

If there are buy or sell programs during expiration week, the next week normally sees a market reversal.

Time Period	Number of Expirations	Number of Times Market Reversed
Monthly expirations		
All expirations	152	121 (80%)
After 1/1/85	130	103 (79%)
After 1/1/90	71	53 (75%)
Quarterly expirations		
All quarterly	54	42 (78%)
After 1/1/85	46	36 (78%)
After 1/1/90	26	18 (70%)

On Friday's close of expiration week, take a position *opposite* to the programs that occurred:

1. Use an *intraday* stop.
2. Take partial profits on *intraday* moves in your favor.
3. Close everything (if not stopped) at the following Friday's close.

has a reaction in the opposite direction of the arbs' Friday programs. That is, if the arbs bought stock heavily on Friday night, forcing the market suddenly higher, then there is often a sell off on Monday (morning). If you stayed short your S&P futures over the weekend, then you would cover them Monday morning.

This might also be a good place to say something about margin: the current margin rules require that *both* sides of this hedge be margined independently. That is, one would have to pay for the five calls in full ($5,250 in the earlier example, where five were bought at a price of 10½), *plus* the $S&Ps would have to be margined ($11,000 or so for a day trade). That's a fairly hefty margin requirement—and it's preposterous because there certainly isn't that kind of risk associated with the position. If the exchanges ever get together and agree on cross-margins for $OEX and S&Ps, then the margin requirements would drop substantially for this strategy.

SHORT-TERM TRADING

So far, we have mostly been discussing directional, short-term trading (except for the hedged position just described). This type of trading is the most taxing on any trader, and it requires a large amount of self-discipline to operate properly. The items listed in Table 4.9 are important to any short-term trader. Use the underlying for day trading; use options for longer horizons. The advantages to using the underlying are significant and should not be ignored—especially if the options are overpriced.

One thing that every trader of $OEX options and/or S&P futures—or any other broad-based index product, for that matter—should understand *very well* is the concept of *fair value of the S&P 500 futures contract*. This is *extremely* important for the short-term trader to keep an eye on.

Table 4.9 Guidelines for Short-Term Trading

1. The underlying may be better than the options.
2. Advantages to using underlying:
   a. Liquidity
   b. Tighter markets
   c. Stop orders
3. Advantages to using options:
   a. Less capital (Leverage)
   b. Possible theoretical advantage

Fair Value of S&P Futures Contracts

There is a mathematical formula (actually, it's just arithmetic) for determining the fair value of any futures contract. For the S&Ps the formula is listed in Table 4.10. It seems somewhat simple until you realize that it requires knowing the present worth of the dividends of *each* of the 500 stocks that make up the S&P 500 Index. Not only do you need to know the *amount* of the impending dividend payments between today's date and the

Table 4.10 Determining Futures Index Fair Value

Characteristics
- Changes daily.
- Affects OEX option prices.
- Mandatory knowledge for OEX traders.
- Affects when and where buy and sell programs occur.

*Computation**

   Fair values of futures = SPOT $\times (1 + r)^1 - pw(\text{DIVS})$

where r = short-term interest rate
         t = time in years
$pw(\text{DIVS})$ = present worth of all dividends

*Best to get from TV or a service.

expiration date of the futures, but you must also know the *ex-dividend dates* in order to accurately compute the present worth of such dividends. Even if you had access to all of this information, it would be extremely difficult for an individual to record it and compute it. Realistically, it can only be done by computer—and most likely by *someone else's* computer at that.

Fortunately, the fair value has become widely available, thanks to the cable television station, CNBC. Mark Haynes, one of their top moderators, spent the time to understand the concept of fair value, and he was influential in getting input right on the ticker. So, when you watch CNBC and see the "Market Summary" go across the bottom of the screen, you will notice that it shows the Dow, the $SPX, the premium of the futures ($PREM), and the fair value, which they denote as "FV." Let's spend some time to define these terms and to see how to interpret them.

The **premium of futures** is the difference between the futures contract and the cash index ($SPX) itself. The term *cash* is also referred to as **spot** upon occasion. *Fair value* is usually stated in such a way that it can be compared to premium. If premium is substantially greater than fair value, then the futures are "expensive" and you can expect arbitrage buy programs to enter the market shortly thereafter. In this case, the arbs would *buy* stocks and *sell* futures in their arbitrage transaction. That would cause the market to rise. Conversely, if premium is too far below fair value, then the futures are "cheap" and the arbs will *buy* futures and *sell* stocks. In *that* case, the arbs action will force the market down because they are selling stocks. Look at the following example:

Suppose $SPX = 1300.00 and the Dec futures are trading at 1315.00

Then the premium would be 15.00 (1315.00 − 1300.00).

Furthermore, suppose that fair value, as gleaned from CNBC or some other source, is 11.80. Thus, the premium of

15.00 is quite a bit higher than the fair value of 11.80. Whenever premium differs from fair value by at least 2.00 points in either direction, arbitrage programs are possible. Therefore, we would expect arbitrage buy programs to enter the market shortly.

What is *more* important to recognize, though, is that $OEX market makers use the S&P futures to hedge their positions, and market makers of *all* index options pay close attention to the premium in the S&P futures. Hence, if the futures are expensive—premium is well above fair value—then *calls will be expensive and puts will be cheap.* So, if you are buying $OEX call options when the S&P futures are expensive, then you are overpaying for those $OEX calls. Hence, you might buy your calls, after which you see $OEX move higher by a point or so, *but your calls are unchanged!* Ever happen to you? Of course it has. What *really* happened was that you bought $OEX calls when the market makers had already figured in a rise in the price of $OEX because of the "expensiveness" of the futures. Hence, they had already discounted that one point move higher in $OEX because they knew arb buy programs were going to come into the market. Therefore, the option you bought was already priced as if $OEX had gone up a point. So, when in fact $OEX *did* go up a point, you made no money.

So, if you are trading $OEX or $SPX options—perhaps even the $DJX options—you must pay attention to the premium of the futures as compared to its fair value. If the futures are overpriced and you want to buy calls, perhaps it is best to stand aside for a few minutes until the futures premium returns to levels that are closer to fair value. Conversely, if you want to buy calls when the futures are cheap—the futures premium is below fair value by 2.00 points or more—then you are getting a "bargain" and you should enter your order immediately.

Let's complete this discussion by noting how $OEX put buyers should approach the situation. If you are thinking of buying puts, and you see that the futures premium is cheap, then the puts will be expensive. That is, the market makers know the futures are cheap, which means arb programs will force the market *down*. In that case, you—as a put buyer—should wait until the futures premium returns to values more in line with fair value before buying your puts. Finally, if you are a put buyer and you see that the futures are expensive, then your puts will be cheap, and you should step in to buy right away.

SUMMARY

This is the conclusion of the discussion of outright option purchases—directional trading. An important strategy for short-term traders is to set a stop before entering a position—and adhere to it. Moreover, take some partial profits if you are fortunate to attain them, and when you do, raise your stops to lock in further profits. Also, option traders *must* use a model to determine if options are expensive or cheap. It's okay to buy an overpriced option, but you should know that you are doing so when you do it.

The number one rule of option trading—or any type of investing for that matter—is *be comfortable with the strategies that you are using*. There are lots of ways of investing—day trading, position trading, option trading, stock trading, futures trading, and so on. However, not all are suitable for all traders. Despite what anyone else says about the "best" strategy, you should not use it if you find that you can't sleep at night with the positions that the strategy dictates. For example, you may have read about traders making money by selling naked options. However, if you find that such a strategy causes you a lot of worry and preoccupies your thoughts inordinately, then that strategy is not for you. If you find that buying option spreads drives you crazy because every trade has a losing side (and a winning one, too, hopefully), then perhaps

Table 4.11 Option Trading Philosophy

1. Be comfortable.
   Option buyers lose money daily to time decay.
   Naked option sellers have unlimited risk.
   Hedgers have limited profit potential.
   Speculators have large percentage risks.
2. Know the relative price of an option before you buy or sell it.
   Use a model.
3. Be flexible.
   Trade all markets.
4. Be patient.
   Beware market orders (except in OEX).
5. Always use follow-up strategies.
   Mental stops.
   Actual stops.
   Change stops as time passes.
   Take partial profits.

outright option buying is best for you. So, before you try a new strategy, think how it will affect you. See Table 4.11 for a summary of the option trading philosophy.

REVIEW QUESTIONS: SYSTEM TRADING

1. Identify any statements that are true regarding trading *systems*.

   a. Only a handful of trading systems actually make money.

   b. Trading systems only pertain to futures, not stocks.

   c. Only real-time traders can effectively use trading systems.

   d. Trading systems are most effective for day traders.

2. Drawdown is:

   a. The maximum amount of margin you can expect to have to place in a position.

   b. The difference between initial margin and maintenance margin for a futures position.

   c. The term to describe the worst period of performance of a particular trading system.

   d. The difference between fair value and premium for a futures contract.

3. When evaluating the performance of trading systems, which would be important (include all that apply)?

   a. The maximum investment required.

   b. The percentage of trades that are profitable.

   c. The amount of profits made.

   d. The drawdown.

4. If you don't have a futures trading account but want to follow an S&P futures trading system, identify any of the following statements that are true.

   a. You could trade $OEX options when the S&P futures systems give its signals.

   b. You really can't use this system without a futures account.

   c. You could trade Microsoft stock options when the system gives its signals, because MSFT has the heaviest weighting of any stock in the S&P 500.

   d. You could trade the Dow Jones futures options, because they can be done in a stock account.

5. Which of the following indices probably does not track well with the others?

   a. S&P 100 Index.

   b. S&P 500 Index.

  c. Dow Jones 30 Industrials.

  d. Russell 2000 Index.

6. Identify all true statements among the following, regarding exponential and simple moving averages:

  a. A simple moving average only includes prices for a fixed number of past trading days.

  b. An exponential moving average includes *all* past prices.

  c. To calculate the exponential moving average requires keeping more data on hand each day than would be necessary to calculate the simple moving average.

  d. More sophisticated trading systems employ exponential rather than simple moving averages.

7. Match the timing indicator in the left-hand column with the "best" trading vehicle to use, on the right:

  a. Day trading system

  b. One-to-two week system

  c. Three-month system

  d. Long-term (one year) system

  (1) $OEX out-of-the money option.

  (2) S&P futures.

  (3) $OEX in-the-money option.

  (4) $OEX at-the-money option.

8. Why does option expiration affect the stock market?

  a. Because the public is unwinding their positions on the last trading day.

  b. Because large brokers know in advance which way the market is going to move that day.

  c. Because market makers want their short options to expire worthless.

  d. Because arbitrageurs are unwinding their positions on the last trading day.

9. In determining if index options might have an effect on expiration day, note any of the following that you would use.

   a. $OEX in-the-money call volume.

   b. $OEX in-the-money put open interest.

   c. $OEX LEAPS open interest.

   d. The open interest of S&P futures contracts.

10. If you know that index arbs are net long $OEX in-the-money calls on expiration day, what would it mean?

    a. We won't know until we know what their put position is as well.

    b. We won't know until we determine their position in the underlying stocks.

    c. We won't know until we know what their position is in the futures.

    d. We can expect arbitrage buy programs at the close of trading on expiration day.

11. Why can $OEX arb programs have an end-of-day effect on the market in the last few days *before* expiration, but $SPX option arb programs cannot?

    a. Because open interest is not reported for $SPX options.

    b. Because $SPX options are European style options.

    c. Because $OEX options are European style options.

    d. Because there is no such thing as an $OEX futures contract.

12. Suppose that we are given the following data as an option expiration approaches: open interest of all $OEX calls with strikes equal to or less than 670 is 82,512 contracts. Furthermore, open interest of all $OEX puts with strikes equal to or *greater* than is 670 is 12,293 contracts. What can we deduce from this?

    a. There will be arb sell programs if $OEX is below 670 at expiration.

b. There will be arb buy programs if $OEX is below 670 at expiration.

c. There will be arb sell programs if $OEX is above 670 at expiration.

d. There will be arb buy programs if $OEX is above 670 at expiration.

13. After a particularly strong expiration Friday spate of arb buy programs, why would the market tend to decline on the following Monday? Mark all that apply.

a. The buying was substantially artificial and that buying power is no longer present on Monday.

b. Arbs are reestablishing their positions for the next expiration.

c. Traders notice the higher prices after Friday's close of trading or in the weekend newspapers and that increases the number of sellers on Monday morning.

d. Arb buy programs are a contrarian sell signal for the broad market.

14. Given the following prices:

$SPX cash index: 1331.00.

S&P Dec futures: 1345.00.

Fair value: 13.00.

Which of the following is (are) true?

a. The futures premium is 14.00.

b. The futures premium is 1.00.

c. The futures premium is 1344.00.

d. The futures premium is −1.00.

15. Again using the prices from the above example, explain what arbitrage activity they would instigate, if any, and explain why you have answered in this manner.

16. What makes it necessary to use a computer to calculate the fair value of the S&P 500 futures contract?

   a. The fact that interest rates fluctuate frequently during the life of the futures contract.

   b. The compounding effect of interest rates.

   c. The myriad of option expiration dates.

   d. The dividends on the underlying stocks.

17. When deciding whether to use the underlying or its options for a short-term trade of 1 to 3 days, which of the following would be the best reason for using the *options* instead of the underlying futures or stock?

   a. Liquidity.

   b. The options offer leverage.

   c. The options are trading with a low implied volatility.

   d. Stop orders work better with options.

18. Mark all of the following that would be examples of trailing stops.

   a. The 20-day simple moving average.

   b. The lowest daily price low attained since the position was established.

   c. The 90% exponential moving average.

   d. The highest daily price low attained since the position was established.

19. Which statement is "most" true?

   a. All option traders should use a model to evaluate any option before trading it.

   b. Models are only used by advanced traders.

   c. Only beginners need models, because advanced traders can evaluate option prices in their heads.

   d. Models cannot be relied upon, because they don't depict the real world of trading.

20. What is the most important rule of investing?

   a. Find someone who has a profitable system and follow it to the letter.

   b. Design your own trading system, so that you fully understand how it works.

   c. Be comfortable with the type of trading that you are engaging in.

   d. Buy and hold is the single best strategy available.

5

PROTECTING A STOCK PORTFOLIO

LEARNING OBJECTIVES

The material in this chapter helps you to:

- Decide when to use index options as portfolio protection rather than put options against individual stocks.
- Reduce the cost of portfolio protection.
- Understand why you would use OEX or SPX indices for a broad-based portfolio but use puts on a sector index for a more specific portfolio.
- Know when it is more profitable to protect your portfolio with puts against each stock you own.

The term *portfolio protection* isn't always met with pleasantries on Wall Street. It gained notoriety during the Crash of 1987 because it was the name that was associated with a strategy that not only failed but, some feel, contributed heavily to the market's crash. At that time, a group of professors had designed a "synthetic" futures selling program. To protect a portfolio against a loss of 10%, say, you would sell a certain number of futures against the portfolio at current prices. Then, if prices fell, more futures would be sold until, eventually, the entire portfolio would be hedged by futures and their average sale price would protect the portfolio—holding losses to only 10% as the market declined. In theory, it worked. In practice, it didn't, because the sales couldn't be made in a timely manner when the market was crashing. In fact, when the market actually began to crash, practitioners of this theory finally regurgitated everything they had to sell, thereby, exacerbating the biggest single day decline (in percentage terms) in market history.

While this particular form of portfolio insurance doesn't really have many adherents any more, the use of futures as protection for a portfolio is still theoretically useful. However, today portfolio protection is usually accomplished with options rather than futures. We discuss protection strategies in this chapter.

OPTIONS VERSUS FUTURES AS PORTFOLIO PROTECTION

Selling futures against stocks removes not only the downside risk but also the upside profit potential. That is, once the futures are in place, no matter which way the market moves, the only profits or losses that will be generated are those that result from the stock portfolio performing in a slightly different manner than the index underlying the futures contract (generally the S&P 500). This differential in performance is called the **tracking error.** An approach such as this might be acceptable for a fund manager who wants to be only x% invested in the stock market; the futures offer a quick way to liquidate that much of the portfolio without spending a great deal on commissions and tying up brokers and manpower entering sell orders. Just one simple order in the futures will suffice instead.

However, for the individual trader or smaller portfolio manager, such a macro approach is not generally viable. Rather, the trader or manager would like to keep more control over the individual stocks in the portfolio and would probably *not* want to use the sale of futures to hedge the long stock portfolio. The concept now is to buy put options against individual stocks, or to buy index options to hedge an entire portfolio. In this way the put acts much like an insurance policy—expiring worthless if not used during its lifetime, but providing valuable protection should the market take a precipitous fall.

PUT OPTIONS AS INSURANCE

With the current option method, you buy put options in a proper ratio against your portfolio as insurance. In this manner, the "cost" of the insurance (what you pay for the puts) is known in advance. There will be no panicking later if the market starts to crash. Moreover, the manager can choose where protection will begin by selecting the striking price of the purchased option.

The original (circa 1987) form of portfolio insurance supposedly had the advantage that the portfolio manager was *collecting* premium in the form of futures sales rather than expending it in the form of buying options. However, that argument doesn't seem to hold water any more with most portfolio managers, who were burned so badly in 1987. But it *does* point out a real problem with buying options for insurance—it's expensive to do so. If you are using $OEX or $SPX put options, it costs about 7% of your portfolio value, annually, to protect it against a 10% loss. That is, if you are buying puts that are 10% out-of-the-money, your stocks will have to earn 7% over the next year just to break even. That is the cost of buying put options as insurance. It is usually considered to be too great of a cost by most individuals and by many portfolio managers as well. It is for that reason that not too many people actually go through with the purchase of options as insurance, even though many go through the exercise of determining what the cost will be for them to hedge themselves.

Not only is the cost somewhat prohibitive, but there is another problem with portfolio insurance—the amount of insurance acquired is static, but the value of your portfolio is not. That is, once you buy the puts, you have locked in the strike price at which the insurance takes effect. However, if the market rallies strongly while you have this insurance in place, eventually your insurance will be very far below the present value of your portfolio. You might have started out with the options 10% out-of-the-money, but after a substantial market rally, they might then be 60% or more out-of-the-money. That is, your insurance would "kick in" at a price so far below the current market value of your portfolio that it doesn't really do you any good. If you want to retain protection, your only recourse is to buy more insurance at higher prices. That would raise the cost of insurance well above the 7% annual level—a cost that was already considered somewhat prohibitive.

The advantage of using index options is that you can protect an entire portfolio of stocks with an index or sector option. This is the easiest method of protection because you only need to place a single order to acquire the protection. Whereas, if individual stock options are used, you have to place as many orders as you have stocks. This could be a tedious process.

Reducing the Cost of Protection

For some of the reasons just stated, many people don't buy insurance against their portfolio, or if they do, they try to mitigate the cost somehow. One way to reduce the cost of the puts bought as insurance against stocks is to simultaneously sell some out-of-the-money calls. This can be done either with index calls or with individual equity options against the stocks that are in the portfolio.

If you sell index calls as a means of reducing the cost of index puts purchased as insurance, then they would be considered naked calls for margin purposes. That is generally something of a formality since the loan value of the stocks in the portfolio would provide more than enough collateral (assuming that they weren't already margined for some other purpose) to satisfy the margin requirements for selling the index calls. In theory, the portfolio's value would appreciate if the market rose—especially if the proper calculations were done (more about that later). The rise in the portfolio's value in that case would offset any loss the naked index calls might incur if the index rose above the strike prices of those calls.

On the other hand, if individual equity options are used to protect stocks, then any calls sold to reduce the cost of puts purchased would be *covered* calls. This strategy is called a **collar**—when an individual owns a stock and simultaneously buys puts and sells calls on that stock. It behaves just like a bull spread; there is limited risk below the striking price of the put that is owned, and there is limited profit potential at the striking price of the call that is written.

In the interest of presenting both sides of the case, the sale of any such calls will put a lid on the portfolio. That is, if the underlying stocks rally strongly, they can appreciate only so much. Once they reach the equivalent of the strike price of the written calls, no more gain is possible. Thus, it is possible that one who buys insurance and tries to reduce its cost by selling out-of-the-money calls could wind up *severely* limiting returns during a large rally.

INDEX OPTIONS AS INSURANCE

If you owned a portfolio of stocks that were the exact makeup of the S&P 500 or the OEX (S&P 100) indices, then you could easily compute the number of options or futures that would be required to hedge your position. However, no individual investors and a few institutional investors are in this position. Rather you usually have a portfolio of stocks that bear little resemblance to the indices themselves. In order to hedge this portfolio, you have to use the options or futures that are listed—ones that don't exactly match the makeup of your portfolio. So you must try to select an index that will perform more or less like your portfolio of stocks if you want to use index puts as protection. If the portfolio is broad-based, then OEX or SPX will suffice. If the portfolio is more specific, you may be better served by using puts on a sector index.

It's a simple matter to calculate your portfolio's actual net worth, but when you are attempting to use index puts as protection—assuming you don't own *exactly* the stocks that make up the index—then you must first calculate the *adjusted* net worth of your portfolio. In order to do this, it is necessary to use a factor that we call **relative beta.** We will define relative beta later, but for now suffice it to say that it is a measure of how each stock in the portfolio in question relates to the index that you are using as a hedge. Simply stated, if the relative beta is 2.0, then the stock in question moves twice as fast as the index in question. The video explains this concept for a simple portfolio involving three stocks.

The adjusted volatility is a fairly simple computation that uses the historical volatility of the stocks in question and compares it to the historical volatility of the index whose puts are being used for the hedge. So, for example, assume you own the GOGO stock mentioned in the video and it has a historical, or statistical, volatility of 60%. Further, assume you are planning to use $OEX puts to hedge the GOGO stock, and $OEX historical volatility is 15%. Then the adjusted volatility of GOGO stock is 4.0 (60 divided by 15). Consequently if you owned $80,000 worth of GOGO stock, you would need to hedge it with $320,000 worth of $OEX. The $320,000 figure is arrived at by taking the actual market value of the GOGO stock in the portfolio ($80,000) and multiplying it by the adjusted volatility for GOGO.

This procedure is repeated for each stock in the portfolio in order to determine a total adjusted dollar volatility of the portfolio. See Table 5.1 for an example of determining portfolio

Table 5.1 Protecting a Stock Portfolio Using Index or Sector Options

1. Determine a portfolio's beta:
   Must know the index volatility.

2. Use $OEX or $SPX (broad-based indices) as protection:
   Assume market volatility = 15%

$$\text{Adjusted volatility} = \frac{\text{Stock's volatility}}{\text{Market volatility}}$$

Stock	Quantity Owned	Price	Beta or Adjusted Volatility	Volatility	Volatility Dollars
GOGO	2,000	80	60%	4.0	$ 640,000
UTIL	5,000	70	12	0.8	280,000
OIL	2,000	55	30	2.0	220,000
					$1,140,000

Actual portfolio value: $620,000

Thus, you must hedge $1,140,000 of $OEX because your portfolio is more volatile than the market.

3. Use a sector index instead. For example, $SOX volatility = 30%, then beta vis-a-vis $SOX is different (half, in this case).

volatility. Once that amount is determined, you can select the strike price of the option to use as insurance (this decision is a personal matter, but generally one chooses something that is about 10% out of the money). Having done that, you can then determine the *number* of puts to buy. Furthermore, using the market price of those puts, you can then compute the *total cost* of insurance—either in actual dollar terms, or in percentage terms. This is where you arrive at a figure that usually indicates the cost of insurance is something in the 7% range (annually).

In Table 5.2, a specific example is shown. In this particular case, we use $OEX LEAPS (long-term) options to hedge a portfolio of stocks. It is generally—but not always—more efficient to use longer-term puts as a hedge, since they don't have as much time value premium as a series of short-term puts purchased

Table 5.2 Insurance Using Index Options

OEX LEAPS: OAX, OBX, OCX, OLX = ⅕ of OEX
Assume OEX = 460 so OLX = 92

$$\text{Number of puts to buy} = \frac{\text{Votality \$}}{(\text{Strike price} \times \text{Shares per option})}$$

Number of Puts to Buy

Strike	OLX '98	OBX '99
85	134	134

Example Prices

Strike	OLX	OBX
85	4½	6

Cost as a Percentage of Portfolio

Strike	OLX	OBX
85	5.3%	7.1%

Problems

1. Equity options may be cheaper.
2. Index options expensive.
3. Protection is not dynamic: tracking error.

---

over the course of a year. $OEX LEAPS have symbols such as OLX, OAX, OBX, and OCX—each one depicting a different expiration year for the puts. In addition, these are options on the $OEX Index *divided by 5*. (It used to be OEX divided by 10 until $OEX split 2-for-1 a couple of years ago.) As shown in Table 5.2, the cost of hedging through December 1998 (using the OLX options) is 5.3% of the portfolio, while the cost of hedging through December 1999 (using the OBX options) is 7.1% of the portfolio. Hence the *annualized* cost is cheaper with the longer-term OBX put options.

We alluded earlier to the fact that your portfolio may not perform exactly like the index that you have selected to hedge it with. For example, suppose you have used $OEX options to hedge your portfolio, planning on limiting your losses to a 10% decline. Furthermore, assume that adjusted volatility calculations have shown that your portfolio behaves just about like $OEX does; that, is your beta was about 1.0. After you buy your insurance, the market begins to fall. Several months later, your portfolio is down 28%, but the $OEX index is only down 20%. This is not good. Not only did you lose the 10% before your insurance began to work, but you have lost another 8% because your portfolio went down faster than $OEX did. This difference in performance is tracking error and is an unavoidable consequence of using index options to hedge a broad portfolio: unless you own the *exact* stocks that make up the index; then there will be a difference in performance between your portfolio and that index. Hopefully, this difference will be small, but there is no way to know for sure.

There are two ways around tracking error. One would be to buy puts on the individual stocks in your portfolio. In that way, there would be no tracking error at all. However, when you do that, you give up the ease of use of index options—which may be large in the case of a large portfolio that includes many different stocks. There may be a middle ground—the sector index. A **sector index** is, as the name implies, an index whose stocks belong to a certain sector. There are many of them—gold and silver sector, oil and gas sector, forest and paper products sector, and so forth. Many of these sector indices have listed options, too. The same sorts of computations that were done with $OEX options (above, and in the video) can be done with the sector index in order to determine how many puts to buy to hedge your portfolio. However, instead of using 15% as the index volatility, you would use the historical volatility of that particular sector index in your calculations.

For example, suppose you have a portfolio that is largely composed of Internet stocks. Perhaps you are employed in that industry and you acquired companies with which you were familiar. Or perhaps you just were trying to ride the tidal wave that was sweeping them higher at some point in time. In any case, suppose your portfolio is very skewed toward those stocks, which you'd prefer not to sell because of tax reasons. However, you are leery of a market downturn—especially in this sector—and you'd like to buy some protection.

You are quite sure that using $OEX options to hedge this portfolio won't work well, because there has been very little correlation between the $OEX index and the performance of Internet stocks over the past few years. There are several Internet sector indices. Let's say you decide to use the Street.com index (symbol: $DOT). Assume its historical volatility is 50%—quite a bit different from $OEX, which is about 15%. Suppose you owned 1,000 shares of Flyer.com, priced at $140, with its own historical volatility of 100%. Then its beta would be 2.0 (100% divided by the $DOT's 50%), and the adjusted volatility dollars would be $280,000 (1,000 shares times its price of $140 times the beta of 2.0).

You would make similar calculations for your entire portfolio, and arrive at how many puts to buy. Furthermore, you would know what the cost of your insurance would be.

Individual Stock Options as Insurance

Many investors looking to buy insurance are put off by the high cost of insurance based on index options, so they investigate the more tedious procedure of buying puts against each stock they own. Once again, the total cost of those puts can be added together, and a cost of insurance—stated as a percentage of the portfolio's value—can be computed. This isn't necessarily going to be cheap, but it might be a little cheaper than index option insurance would be. The reason is that there is an ever-present demand for index option insurance, and so the out-of-the-money puts tend to be somewhat overpriced. That is not the case with individual equity put options.

Nevertheless, buying individual stock puts can still be an expensive proposition. Moreover, the individual investor might not have enough extra cash around to pay for such puts and might be reluctant to sell some stocks in order to purchase the puts. It is at about this time that the investor begins to toy with the idea of selling calls in order to pay for the puts. As mentioned earlier, this strategy of selling out-of-the money calls to finance the purchase of out-of-the-money puts is called a **collar.** If the proceeds from the call completely cover the cost of the put, it's called a **zero cost collar.** The strategy can be applied in many ways. If an equal number of calls and puts are traded, the resulting position is like a vertical bull spread—limited risk and limited profit potential. Many investors, however, are unwilling to give away their entire upside, so they endeavor to fiddle with the strike prices so that they can buy enough puts to hedge all of their stocks but need to sell only a smaller quantity of calls to cover the cost. In *that* scenario, there is still *some* upside profit potential if the stock should rise dramatically in price—to levels above the strike price of the written call. Any of these forms of insurance is quite acceptable as long as you understand that you are giving away some of your upside profit potential when you sell the calls.

In fact, many fairly novice option traders think that they will sell calls against their stocks in order to gain additional income. This concept has been around the "Street" since options were first listed. It sounds so good, but you must realize that *there is no free lunch on Wall Street.* Everything is arbitraged; everything has its counterbalance between risk and reward. That's why if someone is promising you 50% annual gains, you know they're lying if they say risk is small. Investments just don't work that way. So it is with writing call options for income—whether that income is to be spent or to be used to buy puts as insurance. You are giving something away to get that income: namely, some of the upside profit potential of your stocks.

Therefore, if you sell calls against stock that you have no intention of selling, you are selling naked calls. Many option traders, especially novice ones, don't understand this concept until they are in its throes—and that's often too late. I have seen many lawsuits brought against well-meaning advisors who talked an elderly couple into writing calls against their long-term, sizeable holding in a blue chip stock. These advisors usually explain that the calls will provide income and that they can be rolled higher in case the stock rises in price. But if the stock's price rise is dramatic enough—and it certainly has been for many blue chips in the 1990s—then there just isn't enough room to keep rolling up for credits. Eventually, debits are incurred, and some of the stock will have to be sold to pay for those debits. That's about the time that the elderly couple realizes that something has gone wrong and reaches for the Yellow Pages to find a lawyer.

Meanwhile, the advisor has been sweating it out—sleepless nights, pains in the stomach, hoping against hope that the stock will just drop in price for one expiration cycle so the calls will expire worthless, thus relieving the pressure. The advisor has *exactly* the same feelings that a naked call seller has when the underlying stock begins to rise quickly against him. Not pleasant ones. These things can happen to a well-meaning advisor, too, such as a nephew who is going to write calls against Aunt Mary's lifelong holding of General Electric stock in order to generate some additional income for her. Once things begin to go awry, there is no way that the nephew is going to be able to explain to Aunt Mary why she has to sell some of the stock that poor old Uncle Ed spent a lifetime accumulating.

The point to be learned—and one that must be explained to the stock owner in great detail in advance—is that *if calls are written against any stock, there may come a time at which the stock has to be sold.* The stock owner must not enter into the strategy if he or she is unwilling to sell the stock.

SUMMARY

Stock owners today generally choose to protect their portfolios with options rather than futures. When protecting the value of a portfolio, it is important to make sure that the cost of the insurance is not counterproductive and that the protection itself does not actually prevent your making a profit. Portfolios can be protected by using index or sector options or individual stock options. While the latter method is more time consuming, it may be more cost effective. If you protect your portfolio by selling individual calls to pay for puts, you must be willing to sell the stock the calls are written on.

REVIEW QUESTIONS: PROTECTING A STOCK PORTFOLIO

1. A money manager owns a sizable, diverse portfolio of large-cap stocks. What listed derivative would she most likely use as insurance for her portfolio?

   a. S&P Index futures.

   b. Sector options.

   c. S&P Index options.

   d. Individual stock options.

2. When using index derivatives as insurance, why is it necessary to compute the adjusted market volatility, or beta, of the portfolio?

3. You are considering using either $SPX options or value line ($VLE) (a small-cap index) options to hedge your portfolio, which consists almost completely of small-cap stocks. You know that the historical volatility of $SPX is 15% and the historical volatility of $VLE is 20%. Furthermore, you have determined that it would take 60 SPX puts to properly hedge your portfolio, using a strike price of 1300. How many VLE puts would be required, also using a strike price of 1300 for that index?

   a. 45.

   b. 75.

   c. 60.

   d. Can't be determined from the information given.

4. What are the problems with using dynamic insurance—insurance that is purchased only as prices begin to fall? This was the type of portfolio insurance used during the Crash of 1987. Choose all that apply.

   a. The cost of insurance may skyrocket just when you need to purchase it.

   b. The market might fall so fast that you can't buy as much insurance as you need.

   c. You can't accurately estimate what your cost of insurance will be.

   d. The exchanges might halt trading, and therefore you couldn't buy insurance.

5. If the adjusted volatility worth of your portfolio is $1,000,000, and the beta, or adjusted volatility, is 2.0, how much is your portfolio actually worth?

   a. $2,000,000.

   b. $500,000.

   c. $1,000,000.

   d. Can't be determined from the information given.

6. A money manager manages a portfolio worth $5,000,000, and through various calculations, determines that the adjusted volatility worth of his portfolio is $12,000,000. He is going to hedge by buying the SPX Dec 1000 puts. How many puts should he buy?

   a. 1,200.

   b. 500.

   c. 120.

   d. 50.

7. Continuing with the same facts from Question 6, if the SPX Dec 1000 puts can be bought at 25, what will the cost of his insurance be as a percentage of his portfolio?

   a. 2.5%.

   b. 3.0%.

   c. 5.0%.

   d. 6.0%.

8. Index options normally trade with implied volatilities that are much less than those of individual stock options. Yet, it was stated that equity options may be cheaper insurance than using index options. How can that be? Explain.

9. What is tracking error?

   a. The difference in the profit of your portfolio and the loss in an insurance product you bought.

   b. The difference in the loss of your portfolio and the gain in an insurance product you bought.

   c. The difference in performance between your portfolio and an index used to insure it.

   d. The difference between realized gains and unrealized gains in your portfolio.

10. The collar is an insurance strategy. It uses which type of option? Mark all that apply.

    a. Stock options.

    b. Index options.

    c. Futures options.

    d. Over-the-counter options.

11. A zero-cost collar is (mark all that apply):

    a. Constructed by selling enough puts to counter the cost of the calls purchased.

   b. One where there is no downside risk—the position is
      fully insured.

   c. Similar to a vertical bear spread.

   d. Constructed by selling enough calls to counter the cost of
      the puts purchased.

12. Explain why selling covered calls against stock that you
    have no intention of selling is essentially the same as writ-
    ing naked calls on that stock.

6

TRADING VOLATILITY

LEARNING OBJECTIVES

The material in this chapter helps you to:

- Recognize volatility abnormalities and use them in profitable trading strategies.
- Understand and use the measures of option price change ("greeks").
- Read and interpret price distributions.
- Decide on the appropriate strategy when volatility is skewed either in the positive or the negative direction.
- Know when to use ratio spreads and backspreads.

Volatility trading should appeal to more sophisticated derivatives traders because, in theory, trading volatility does not involve predicting the price or direction of movement of the underlying instrument. Instead, it means, essentially, to *first* look at the pricing structure of the options—at the *implied volatility*—and then, if abnormalities are identified, to attempt to establish strategies that could profit if the options return to a more normal value. Simply put, a volatility trader tries to either (1) find cheap options and buy them or (2) find expensive options and sell them. Typically, a volatility trader establishes positions that are somewhat neutral initially, so that profitability emphasis is on the option price structure rather than on the movement of the underlying stock. This chapter shows you how to use volatility to your advantage.

NEUTRALITY

This neutrality is usually identified by using the deltas of the options involved to create a delta neutral position. In practice, any neutrality most likely disappears quickly, and you are forced to make some decisions about your positions based on the movement of the underlying instrument anyway, but at least it *starts out* as neutral. That may be true, but you must understand one thing: *It is certain that you will have to predict something in order to profit, for only market makers and arbitrageurs can construct totally risk-free positions that exceed the risk-free rate of return, after commissions.* Moreover, even if a position is neutral initially, it is likely that the passage of time or a significant change in the price of the underlying will introduce some price risk into the position.

The price of an option is determined by the stock price, striking price, time to expiration, risk-free interest rate (0% for futures options), volatility, and dividends (stock and index options). Volatility is the only unknown factor. The "greeks," delta, theta, vega, rho, and gamma, are all measures of how much an option's price changes when the various factors change. For example, **delta** is how much the option's price changes when the stock price changes. This is a term that is known to many option traders. Delta ranges between 0.00 (for a deeply out-of-the-money option) to 1.00 (for a deeply in-the-money option). An at-the-money option typically has a delta of slightly *more than* 0.50.

The **theta** of an option describes the time decay—that is, how much the option price changes when one day's time passes. Theta is usually described as a negative number to show that it has a negative, or inverse, effect on the option price. A theta of −0.05 would indicate that an option is losing a nickel of value every day that passes.

Vega is not a greek letter, although it sounds like it should be. It describes how much the option price changes when volatility moves up or down by 1 percentage point. That is, if implied volatility is currently 32% and vega is 0.25, then an option's price would increase by ¼ point if implied volatility moved up to 33%.

When interest rates change, that also affects the price of an option, although it is usually a very small effect. **Rho** is the amount of change that an increase in the risk-free interest rate would have on the option.

Finally, **gamma** is the delta of the delta. That is, how much the delta of the option changes when the stock changes in price by a point. For example, suppose we knew these statistics:

Stock Price	Option Price	Delta
50	5	0.50
51	5½	0.53

When the stock moved up from 50 to 51, the option's price increases by the amount of the delta, which was one-half. In addition, since the stock is a little higher, the delta itself will now have increased, from 0.50 to 0.53. Thus the gamma is 0.03—the amount by which the delta increased. We will talk more about gamma and its usages later.

So, not only are the factors that determine an option's price important, but so are the *changes* in those factors. For those familiar with mathematics, these changes are really the partial derivatives of the option model with respect to each of the determining factors. For example, delta is the first partial derivative of the option model with respect to stock price.

VOLATILITY AS STRATEGIC INDICATOR

Volatility trading has gained acceptance among more sophisticated traders—or at least those who are willing to take a mathematical approach to option trading. This is because volatility is really what earmarks the only *variable* having to do with the price of an option. All the other factors regarding option price are fixed. As listed previously, the factors that make up the price of an option are stock price, striking price, time to expiration, risk-free interest rate, dividends (for stock and index options), and volatility. At any point in time, we know for a certainty what five of these six items are; the one thing we don't know is *implied volatility*. Hence the only thing that a "theoretical" option trader *can* trade is (implied) volatility. Unfortunately, there is no way to *directly* trade volatility—so one can only attempt to buy cheap options and sell expensive ones and then worry about how the other factors influence the profitability of his position.

Imagine, if you will, that you have found a stock that routinely traded in a fixed range. It would then be a fairly simple matter to buy it when it was near the low end of that range, and to then sell it when it was at the top of the range. In fact, you might even decide to sell it short near the top of the range, figuring you could cover it when it got back to the bottom of the range. Occasionally, you are able to find stocks like this, although they are rather few and far between.

However, in many, many instances, volatility exhibits this exact type of behavior. If you look at the history of volatility in many issues, you will find that it trades in a range. This is true for futures contracts, indices, and stocks. Even something as seemingly volatile as Microsoft, whose stock rose from about 12 to 106 during the 1990s, fits this pattern: its implied volatility never deviated outside of a range between 26% and 50%, and most of the time was in a much tighter range: 30% to 45%. Of course, there are times when the volatility of anything can break out to previously unheard-of levels. The stock market in 1987 was a classic example. Also, volatility can go into a slumber as well, trading below historical norms. Gold in 1994 to 1995 was an example of this, as historical volatility fell to the 6% level, when it normally traded about 12%.

Despite these occasional anomalies, volatility seems to have more predictability than prices do. Mathematical and statistical measures bear this out as well—the deviation of volatilities is much smaller than the deviation of prices, in general.

You should recall that there are two types of volatility—implied and historical. The historical volatility can be looked at over any set of past data that you desire, with 10-day, 20-day, 50-day, and 100-day being very common measures. *Implied volatility,* on the other hand, is the volatility that the options are displaying. Implied volatility is an attempt by traders and market makers to assess the *future* volatility of the underlying instrument. Thus, implied volatility and historical volatility may differ at times. Which one should you use if you are going to trade volatility?

There is some debate about this. One certain thing is that historical and implied volatility converge at the end of an option's life. However, prior to that time, there is no assurance that they will actually converge. An overpriced option might stay that way for a long time—especially if there is some reason to suspect that corporate news regarding new products, takeovers, or earnings might be in the offing. Cheap options might be more trustworthy in that there is very little insider information that can foretell that a stock will be stagnant for any lengthy period of time.

So, it is often the case that the better measure is to compare implied volatility to past measure of implied volatility. That may point out some serious discrepancies that can be traded by the volatility trader. In this case, we would say that the *prediction* of volatility might be wrong. That is, implied volatility—which is a prediction by the option market of how volatile the underlying is going to be during the life of the option—is significantly different from past readings of implied volatility. That might present a trading opportunity.

The second way in which volatility might be wrong is if there is a skew in implied volatility of the individual options. That is, the individual options have significantly different implied volatilities. Such a situation often presents the volatility trader with a spreading opportunity because, in reality, the actual distribution of prices that a stock, index, or futures contract adheres to is most likely *not* a skewed distribution.

VOLATILITY SKEW

Certain markets have a volatility skew almost continual—metals and grain options, for example, and OEX and S&P 500 options since the crash of 1987. Others have a skew that appears occasionally. When we talk about a volatility skew, we are describing a group of options that has a *pattern* of differing volatilities, not just a few scattered different volatilities. In fact, for options on *any* stock, future, or index, there will be slight discrepancies between the various options of different striking prices and expiration dates. However, in a volatility skew situation, we expect to see rather large discrepancies between the implied volatilities of individual options—especially those with the same expiration date—and there is usually a pattern to those discrepancies.

The examples in Table 6.1 describe two markets that have volatility skews. The one shows the type of volatility skew that has existed in OEX and S&P 500 options—and many other broad-based index options—since the crash of 1987. This data is very typical of the skew that has lasted for over eight years.

Note that we have not labeled the options in Table 6.1 as puts or calls. That is because a put and a call with the same striking

Table 6.1 Volatility Skewing

Soybean Volatility Skewing July Beans: 744		OEX Implied Volatility Skewing OEX: 630	
Strike	Implied	Strike	Implied
700	12.2	600	23.9
725	13.9	610	21.7
750	15.1	620	19.4
775	16.5	625	17.1
800	17.7	630	14.9
825	19.7	635	13.6
850	20.9	640	11.7
900	24.1	645	11.3
Forward skew		Reverse skew	

Note: Calls and puts at the same strike must have the same implied volatility unless there is no arbitrage capability.

price and expiration date must have the same implied volatility, or else there will be a riskless arbitrage available.

In the OEX volatility skew, note that the lower strikes have the highest implied volatility. This is called a *reverse* volatility skew. It is sometimes caused by bearish expectations for the underlying, but that is usually a short-term event. For example, when a commodity undergoes a sharp decline, the reverse volatility skew will appear and last until the market stabilizes.

However, the fact that the reverse skew has existed for so long in broad-based options is reflective of more fundamental factors. After the crash of 1987 and the losses that traders and brokerage firms suffered, the margin requirements for selling naked options were raised. Some firms even refused to let customers sell naked options at all. This lessened the supply of sellers. In addition, money managers have turned to the purchase of index puts as a means of insuring their stock portfolios against losses. This is an increase in demand for puts, especially out-of-the-money puts. Thus, we have a simultaneous increase in demand and reduction in supply. This is what has caused the options with lower strikes to have increased implied volatilities.

In addition, money managers also sometimes sell out-of-the-money calls as a means of financing the purchase of their put insurance. We have previously described this strategy as the *collar*. This action exerts extra selling pressure on out-of-the-money calls, and that accounts for some of the skew in the upper strikes, where there is low implied volatility.

A *forward* volatility skew has the opposite look from the reverse skew, as one might expect. It typically appears in various futures option markets—especially in the grain option markets, although it is often prevalent in the metals option markets, too. It is less frequent in coffee, cocoa, orange juice, and sugar but does appear in those markets with some frequency.

The soybean options shown in Table 6.1 are an example of a *forward* skew. Notice that in a *forward* skew, the volatilities increase at higher striking prices. The forward skew tends to appear in markets where expectations of upward price movements are overly optimistic. This does not mean that everyone is necessarily bullish, but that they are afraid that a very large upward move, perhaps several limit up days, could occur and seriously damage the naked option seller of out-of-the-money calls.

Occasionally, you will see *both* types of skews at the same time, emanating from the striking price in both directions. This is rather rare, but it has been seen in the metals markets at times.

Price Distributions

Before getting into the specifics of trading the volatility skew, let's discuss stock price distributions for a minute. Stock and commodity price movements are often described by mathematicians as adhering to standard statistical distributions. The most common type of *statistical* distribution is the normal distribution. This is familiar to many people who have never taken a statistics course. In Figure 6.1 the upper left graph is a graph of the normal distribution. The center of the graph is where the average member of the population resides. That is, most of the people are near the average, and very few are way above or way below the average. The normal distribution is used in many ways to describe the total population: results of IQ tests or average adult height, for example. In the normal distribution, results can be

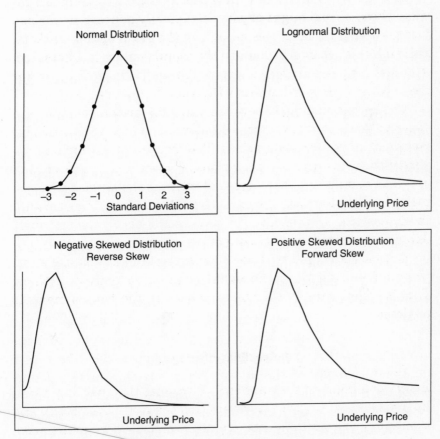

Figure 6.1 Price distributions illustrated.

infinitely above or below the average. Thus, this is not useful for describing stock price movements, since stock prices can rise to infinity, but can only fall to zero.

Thus, another statistical distribution is generally used to describe stock price movements. It is called the *lognormal distribution,* and it is pictured in the top right graph in Figure 6.1. The height of the curve at various points essentially represents the probability of stock prices being at those levels. The highest point on the curve is right at the average—reflecting the fact that most results are near that price, as they are with the normal distribution. Or, in terms of stock prices, if the average is defined as today's price, then most of the time a stock will be relatively near the average after some period of time. The **lognormal distribution** allows that stock prices could rise infinitely—although with great rarity—but cannot fall below zero.

Mathematicians have spent a great deal of time trying to accurately define the actual distribution of stock price movements, and there is some disagreement over what that distribution really is. However, the lognormal distribution is generally accepted as a reasonable approximation of the way that prices move. Those prices don't have to be just stock prices, either. They could be futures prices, index prices, or interest rates.

However, when a skew is present, the skew is projecting a *different* sort of distribution for prices. The bottom right graph in Figure 6.1 depicts the forward skew, such as we see in the grains and metals. Compare it to the graph of the lognormal distribution. You can see that this one has a distinctly different shape: the right-hand side of the graph is up in the air, indicating that this skewed distribution implies that there is a far greater chance of the underlying rising by a huge amount. Also, on the left side of the graph, the skewed distribution is squashed down, indicating that there is far less probability of the underlying falling in price than the lognormal distribution would indicate.

The *reverse* volatility skew is shown in the bottom left graph. Note that it is also different from the regular lognormal distribution. In this case, however, the left-hand side of the graph is lifted higher, indicating that the probability of prices dropping is greater than the lognormal distribution implies that it is. Similarly, the graph flattens out on the right-hand side, which means that it is insinuating that prices will not rise as much as the lognormal distribution says they will.

Most traders feel that skewed volatilities are *not* the correct picture of the way markets move. Therefore, when we find significant volatility skewing in a particular group of options, examples shown in Table 6.2, we have a good trading opportunity. A neutral option spread position can be established that has a statistical advantage because the two options have differing implied volatilities.

The best place to look for this volatility skewing is in the options with the same expiration date, as shown in the previous tables of OEX and corn options. The reason that we prefer using options with the same expiration date as the basis of volatility skew trading is that, even if the skew does not disappear by expiration, the very fact that the options must go to

Table 6.2 Markets that Often Display a Volatility Skew

Forward	Reverse	Dual
Corn	S&P	Gold
Wheat	OEX	Silver
Soybeans	Other stock market indices (illiquid)	
Other grains (bean oil, meal)	*Some* fast-declining markets (T-bonds, oil, cattle)	
Orange juice		
Coffee		
Any fast-rising market (oil products in '96)		

parity at expiration means that they will then have behaved in a manner similar to the underlying instrument—that is, they will have adhered to the lognormal distribution, not to the skewed distribution.

What we want to accomplish by trading the volatility skew is to capture the implied volatility differential between the two options in question, without being overly exposed to price movements by the underlying instrument. You *could* use the simple bull or bear spreads. Bull spreads would be used in *forward* skew situations. That is, you would buy a call with a lower strike price and sell a call with a higher strike price. Since there is a forward skew, this means that you are buying a call with a lower implied volatility than that of the one you are selling. This is a nice theoretical advantage. Conversely, in *reverse* skewing situations (OEX, SPX, and other indices), a bear spread would work best: buying a put with a higher strike, say, and selling a put with a lower strike. Again that means you are buying an option with a lower implied volatility than the one you are selling. The problem with these vertical spread strategies is that they are dependent on a favorable move by the underlying in order to produce profits. There is nothing wrong with that, but some volatility traders prefer to trade the volatility skew with a more neutral strategy—one in which it is not necessary to predict whether the underlying is going to rise or fall. Accordingly, they feel that the best strategies are vertical spread strategies: ratio writes or backspreads.

TRADING THE FORWARD (POSITIVE) SKEW

When the volatility skew is *positive,* as it is with grain options, then it is the *call* ratio spread or the *put* backspread that is the preferred strategy. The reason that these are two chosen strategies is because, in each one, the trader is buying options with a lower striking price and selling options with a higher striking price. Since the higher strikes have the inflated volatility in a positive volatility skew, these strategies offer a statistical advantage. This advantage arises from the fact that the trader is buying the cheap option(s) and selling the relatively expensive option(s) simultaneously, on the same underlying. These strategies will be described in more detail in the following pages.

The general way to choose between the two strategies is this: If implied volatilities are low with respect to where they have been in the past, then we want to establish the backspread. On the other hand, if implied volatilities are currently high with respect to where they've been in the past, then we'd want to establish a ratio spread. The reasoning behind these choices centers on whether the position is net long or net short options. The backspread is net *long* options, so we want to establish it when implied volatility is low—as would be the case in any option buying strategy. Conversely, if the options are expensive, then we might select the ratio spread as the preferred strategy because it is net *short* options; there are naked options in this type of spread.

When you trade the volatility skew in this manner, you have several ways in which you can profit. First, you would profit almost immediately if the volatility skew disappeared, because your options would then have the implied volatility. That is a rather rare occurrence, but it sometimes does happen. Second, you would profit if the underlying were within your profit range at expiration, and third, you could profit if implied volatilities move in your favor (i.e., higher if you own the backspread or lower if you have the call ratio spread in place).

The Ratio Spread

A ratio spread is a strategy that employs either all calls or all puts—using different strikes, of course—and is one in which the trader sells more options than he or she buys. Thus, the strategy has naked options. As such, it might not be suitable for all

XYZ Common: 98			
Option	Price	Delta	Implied
90 call	12	0.90	30%
100 call	5.5	0.45	35%

Delta neutral = 0.90/0.45 = 2.00

Buy one 90 call and sell two 100 calls (1 point debit: 2 x 5½ − 12)

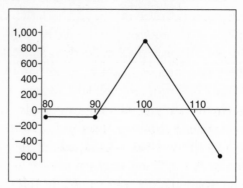

Maximum profit always at strike of short option.

Maximum profit = (Difference in strikes × Number long options) − Initial debit = (10 × 1) − 1 = 9

Upside B/E = Short strike + (Maximum profit/number naked options) = 100 + (9/1) = 109

Figure 6.2   Neutral trading—ratio spread.

traders. There is generally limited risk on one side of the spread (the side that does not have a naked option written) and *unlimited* risk on the other side (the side that *does* have the naked options). Typically, such a spread is established to be delta neutral to begin with—meaning that the spreader does not care which way the stock moves initially. Of course, once the position is in place, the spreader will have some bias as to where he or she wants the underlying to go.

The information in Figure 6.2 depicts a ratio spread. It is a generic example, using call options. This is the type of spread that we would use to trade the forward volatility skew, although it is far more likely that we could find a forward skew in futures options than in stock options. Nevertheless, this example is useful in describing the general capabilities of the call ratio spread position. Look at the following example:

With XYZ stock at 98, we are considering the initiation of a call ratio spread using the October 90 call and the October 100 call. The details of the call options are shown below and are in Figure 6.2 as well:

Option	Option Price	Delta	Implied Volatility
October 90 call	12.00	0.90	30%
October 100 call	5.50	0.45	35

The way to construct a delta neutral spread is to divide the deltas of the two options involved. This will tell you how many to sell for each one you buy. In this case, the delta neutral ratio is 2.0 (0.90 divided by 0.45). Thus we want to by one Oct 90 call and sell *two* (2.0) Oct 100 calls. If we do this, we will have an initial debit in the position, for the option we buy costs 12 points and the two we sell—at 5½ points each—only bring in 11 points. Thus, our debit is one point plus commissions.

If the underlying XYZ stock drops and is below 90 at expiration, all of the calls will expire worthless and our loss will equal the initial debit or credit of the position—a one point debit, plus commissions, in this example.

The maximum profit of a ratio spread always occurs at the strike price of the written calls. In this example that would be at a price of 100 for XYZ at expiration. There is a simple formula that you can use to determine what that maximum profit would be:

$$\text{Maximum profit} = \left(\frac{\text{Difference in strikes} \times \text{Number}}{\text{of long options}} \right) - \text{Initial debt}$$

In this example, then, the maximum profit would be

$$\left[(100 - 0) \times (1) \right] - 1 = 9$$

This means that if XYZ were exactly at 100 at expiration—
which means that the short options expired worthless and the
long option was worth 10—then the *net overall* profit would be 9
points, less commissions.

The risk in a ratio spread is greatest if the underlying moves
through the breakeven point, at which time the short naked op-
tion(s) in the spread can subject the spreader to unlimited, or at
least very large, losses.

The breakeven point for a call ratio spread can be computed
with a simple formula:

$$\text{Upside breakeven point} = \text{Strike price of naked options} + \left(\frac{\text{Maximum profit}}{\text{Number of naked calls}} \right)$$

In this example, that would mean the upside breakeven point is:

$$\text{Upside breakeven point} = 100 + \left(\frac{9}{1} \right) = 109$$

The profit graph of this call ratio spread is shown in
Figure 6.2.

Hence, at expiration, this spread will make money if the underlying is between 91 and 109. But, if XYZ rises above 109,
large losses are possible. In that case, the spreader needs to take
some defensive action in order to prevent a very large loss from
occurring. That action could be any of the following:

1. Buy the proper number of shares of underlying stock to
   cover the naked calls.

2. Buy back the naked calls.

3. Roll the naked calls up to a higher strike price.

All three have their pluses and minuses, but *something* must
be done. When writing naked options, it is *imperative* that you

Table 6.3 Volatility Skew Example: May Silver Futures Options

				May Futures: 615						
Strike	Call	VTY	Delta	Gamma	Theta	Vega	Put	Putdel	CVOL	PVOL
575	57.00	31.3	0.71	0.40	0.20	0.95	24.00	−0.29	3	5
600	43.00	32.3	0.60	0.44	0.24	1.07	37.00	−0.40	8	2
625	35.00	(36.0)	(0.49)	0.40	0.27	1.10	44.88 E	−0.51	39	0
650	27.00	37.5	0.40	0.38	0.27	1.07	61.58 E	−0.60	12	0
675	21.00	39.0	0.33	0.34	0.27	1.00	83.20	−0.67	35	1
700	15.00	(38.8)	(0.25)	0.30	0.23	0.89	103.70	−0.75	17	1
725	12.00	40.6	0.21	0.26	0.22	0.79	125.00	−0.79	26	1
750	10.00	42.7	0.17	0.22	0.21	0.71	143.39 E	−0.83	90	0
775	7.50	43.2	0.14	0.18	0.18	0.61	167.00	−0.86	1	1
800	6.00	44.4	0.11	0.15	0.16	0.53	191.30	−0.89	2	1

take defensive action if the underlying moves far enough to make the naked option an in-the-money option.

An example of a ratio spread possibility in silver options—in which the forward skew was quite steep at the time—is shown in Table 6.3. Note that the May futures were trading at 615 when these options prices existed. The column marked VTY is the implied volatility of these options on the day that the prices were extracted from. The pertinent options that might be used in a call ratio spread were:

Option	Price	Implied Volatility	Delta
May 625 call	35.0	36.0%	0.49
May 700 call	15.0	38.8	0.25

As in the previous theoretical example, the implied volatilities are skewed, so that a spread that involves buying the May 625 call and selling the May 700 call has a theoretical advantage. Since the deltas are approximately in the ratio of 2-to-1, one would by 1 May 625 call and sell 2 May 700 calls in such a spread. This would incur a small debit:

$$\text{Debit} = (2 \times 15) - 35 = 5 \text{ cent debit}$$

Since silver options are worth $50 per cent, the five-cent debit represents a *dollar* debit of $250. That is the downside risk of this spread, plus commissions.

Again using the formula from Figure 6.2, we can determine:

$$\underset{\text{profit}}{\text{Maximum}} = (75 \times 1) - 5 = 70 \text{ cents (which is } \$3,500)$$

$$\underset{\text{breakeven point}}{\text{Upside}} = 700 + \left(\frac{70}{1}\right) = 770$$

This seems like an attractive spread, then. If May silver is between about 630 and 770 at expiration, some profits will result. There is a small potential loss if May silver is below 625 ($250 plus commissions). The only significant risk is if May silver rises above 770 before expiration—155 cents above the current price of 615. While there is certainly some probability that such a price rise could occur, it is unlikely. We will see later on how some fairly strict probability criteria could be used to determine just how likely such a move might be.

The Backspread

The second strategy that we described for buying volatility when a forward volatility skew exists is the backspread. The profit graph shown in Figure 6.3 is that of a put backspread— selling one in-the-money put and buying two at-the-money puts, for example. You can see by the straight lines on the graph that the backspread is very similar to the long straddle, except that the profit potential is truncated on the upside.

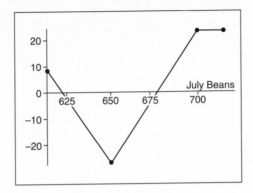

Delta neutral: 0.73/0.35 = 2.09
So buy two 650 puts and sell one 700 put
Credit = 45 − (2 × 11) = 23 credit

Figure 6.3   Neutral trading: Put backspread.

As you can see from the graph, the put backspread has large profit potential to the downside. The maximum loss of the backspread is *less* than that of a corresponding long straddle because of the profit potential that is forsaken on one side of the backspread.

A *call* backspread has somewhat similar characteristics. It is constructed by selling an in-the-money call and buying two at-the-money calls, for example. It has a limited profit potential on the *downside* (where *that* side of a straddle purchase is "lopped off") and has unlimited profit potential to the upside.

You might use a backspread instead of a long straddle if there is a volatility skew in place, or if you think the particular market is more likely to move in one direction or the other. But the neutral strategist is not normally interested in price projection initially. Rather, the strategist would use the backspread when the implied volatilities of the *individual* options in the spread differ. When there is a forward volatility skew, as we have been discussing in this section, then a *put* backspread is the one to use because it involves buy options with a lower strike and *selling* options with a higher spread. That construction takes advantage of the forward volatility skew. Later, we will see that in the *reverse* volatility skew situation, such as exists with index options, a call backspread is the strategy to use.

In Figure 6.3, an example of a put backspread is shown. In this particular case, utilizing July soybean futures and options, the futures themselves are trading at 665. The option prices are:

Option	Price	Delta	Implied Volatility
July 650 put	11	0.35	16.0%
July 700 put	45	0.73	19.8

Once again, we use the deltas to determine the initial neutral ratio. Here, the division of the deltas (0.73 / 0.35) is 2.09. Still, this is close enough to 2-to-1 that we will use that particular ratio. In this case, we would *buy* two of the July 650 puts and *sell* one of the July 700 puts. That transaction would bring in a credit of 23 points, less commission: the sale bringing in a credit of 45 points, the purchase of the two costing 22 points. A one-point move in soybeans is worth $50, so the 23-point credit is worth a credit of $1,150.

As for profitability, there are several important factors. First, notice that if July soybeans rally strongly, then all of the puts will expire worthless and the spreader will keep the initial credit—a profit of $1,150, less commissions.

The next thing to do is to compute the *worst case scenario*. That would occur if the underlying were exactly at the strike price of the long puts at expiration. The formula for computing the maximum risk is:

$$\text{Maximum risk} = \text{Net credit} - \left(\begin{array}{c} \text{Difference in strikes} \times \text{Number} \\ \text{of } \textit{short} \text{ options} \end{array} \right)$$

In this example,

$$\text{Maximum risk} = 23 - (50 \times 1) = -27$$

Hence, we could lose 27 points (or \$1,350, plus commissions) if July soybeans were exactly at 650, the striking price of the long options, at expiration. It is, of course, unlikely that the futures would be at exactly that price at expiration, but even if they're in the neighborhood, a loss will result.

Finally, we can compute our breakeven points. On the downside, the formula is:

$$\begin{array}{l}\text{Put backspread} \\ \text{downside} \\ \text{breakeven point}\end{array} = \begin{array}{l}\text{Strike} \\ \text{price of} \\ \text{long options}\end{array} - \left(\frac{\text{Maximum loss}}{\text{Number of } net \text{ long puts}}\right)$$

In this example,

$$\text{Downside breakeven point} = 650 - \left(\frac{27}{1}\right) = 623$$

So, if July futures fall below 623, large profits are possible, and they would accumulate in greater amount the farther that the futures are below the breakeven point.

There is also an upside breakeven point—somewhere between the two strikes involved in the spread. In general, the formula for that is:

$$\begin{array}{l}\text{Put backspread} \\ \text{upside} \\ \text{breakeven point}\end{array} = \begin{array}{l}\text{Strike} \\ \text{price of} \\ \text{long options}\end{array} + \left(\frac{\text{Maximum loss}}{\text{Number of short puts}}\right)$$

In this example,

$$\text{Upside breakeven point} = 650 + \left(\frac{27}{1}\right) = 677$$

Hence there will be losses if the July soybean futures are between the two breakeven points—between 623 and 677 at July
expiration. Outside of that range, profits will accrue although
they are limited on the upside to the amount of the initial credit
(23 points). Look at the profit graph in Figure 6.3 and you will
see that it corresponds exactly to the figures that we have computed on this page.

So, in summary, when you spot a forward volatility skew,
you can attempt to use a bullish vertical spread to take advantage of it. However, if you prefer a less directional and more
neutral approach, you can utilize either a call ratio spread (if
the options are on the expensive side) or a put backspread (if the
options are cheap).

TRADING THE REVERSE (NEGATIVE) SKEW

When implied volatilities are skewed in the negative direction,
two strategies that are the exact opposite of the previous ones
are appropriate: either the *put* ratio spread or the *call* backspread. In these two strategies, you are buying the option with
the lower strike, which has the higher implied volatility. Once
again, there is a statistical advantage, since you are selling an
option that is "expensive" on the same security on which you are
buying an option. If implied volatility is low, the call backspread is the preferred strategy, but if implied volatility is near
the high end of its range, then the put ratio spread would be the
better choice of a strategy to trade the reverse skew.

The reverse volatility skew is very prevalent in broad-based
index options. (But this wasn't always the case—prior to 1987,
there was a slightly forward skew—and it may therefore disappear once again someday.) It also appears with some frequency
in futures options markets that experience a sudden decline in
price. In recent years, it has appeared in cattle, T-bond, and
crude oil options. In these cases, the reverse skew disappears as

soon as the underlying commodity stabilizes in price. However, with the broad-based index options, the skew has persisted for years—mostly due to margin and supply/demand factors.

Backspreads are the preferred strategy in OEX options when implied volatility is low and the reverse volatility skew is present. Since 1987, the call backspread in OEX options has served very well as a strategy with which to take advantage of the reverse volatility skew. This is partly due to the fact that OEX options have, for the most part, traded near the lower end of their volatility range. If you wait for those opportunities to establish the backspread, the rewards are worthwhile.

However, if implied volatility is high—options are relatively expensive—then a *put* ratio spread is the best neutral strategy to use. The put ratio spread contains naked puts and therefore has substantial risk if the underlying should fall by a great deal. Hence, the put ratio spread strategy requires monitoring and often needs follow-up action.

If you prefer a directional approach—one in which an attempt is made to predict the direction of movement of the underlying instrument—then a bear spread is useful when a reverse, or negative, volatility skew exists. Such a bear spread can be established with puts or calls, it makes no difference profit-wise. In a bear spread, you buy the option with the higher strike and then sell an option in the same expiration month at a lower strike. The implied volatilities of the individual options *decrease* as the strikes move higher. Thus, when there is a reverse volatility skew, you would be buying an option with a lower implied volatility than the one you are selling—a theoretical advantage.

Finally, note that there is a bullish bias in a reverse volatility skew. What this means is that if the reverse skew persists when the underlying moves higher, your position will do better than if the skew were eliminated. For example, suppose that with OEX at 600, you bought a July 600 call, and at the time, it had an implied volatility of 15%. Later, assume that OEX moves up to 610 and that volatility skew remains the same up and down the line. Thus, a July 610 call (which is *now* at-the-money) would have an implied volatility of 15% with OEX at 610. However, the July 600 call that *you* own would have a higher implied volatility than 15% because of the reverse volatility skew. Hence, not only do you own a call that has risen in value because the underlying made a bullish move, but you have the added benefit of seeing it *gain* implied volatility because of the reverse volatility skew. That additional gain due to volatility is the bullish bias imparted by the volatility skew.

Call Backspreads

As noted earlier, a call backspread is often the best way to "buy volatility" in the index options because they usually display a reverse volatility skew. In Figure 6.4, we have an illustration of an OEX call. Its profitability is similar to that of the put backspread, a strategy that was discussed earlier, except now the limited profit is on the downside and the unlimited, large profit potential is on the upside. In the graph shown in the exhibit, OEX is at 670 and the option prices are:

Option	Price	Delta	Implied Volatility
October 640 call	35	0.88	16.0%
October 675 call	8	0.44	19.8

As before, the deltas are used to determine the initial neutral ratio. Here, the division of the deltas (0.88 / 0.44) is exactly 2.00. So, we would *buy* two of the Oct 675 calls and *sell* one of the Oct 640 calls. That transaction would bring in a credit of 19 points. This is a credit of $1,900, less commissions. One point that was not made earlier about backspreads—and it is an important one—is that the initial position should ideally be established for a fairly decent credit because that credit represents your profit

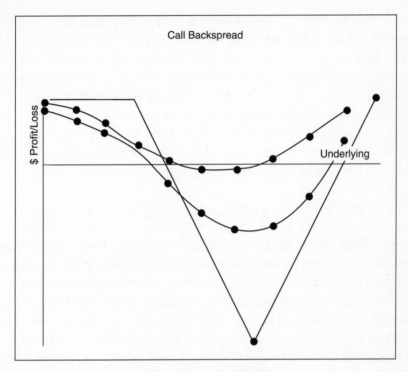

Delta neutral: $0.88 / 0.44 = 200$
So buy two 675 calls and sell one 640 call
Credit $= 35 - (2 \times 8) = 19$ credit

Figure 6.4 Neutral trading: Call backspread.

potential on one side of the backspread (upside for calls, down-side for put). If you don't have that nice initial credit to start with, you will really only have profit potential in one direction; that means that you would be employing more of a directional strategy than a hedged, neutral strategy.

In this case, if OEX declines below the lower strike—640—at expiration, then all of the calls will expire worthless and the spreader will keep the initial credit—a profit of $1,900, less commissions.

As was the case with the put ratio backspread discussed ear-lier, the worst result would occur if the underlying were exactly at the strike price of the long options at expiration. The formula for computing the maximum risk is exactly the same:

$$\text{Maximum risk} = \text{Net credit} - \left(\begin{array}{c} \text{Difference in strikes} \times \text{Number} \\ \text{of } \textit{short} \text{ options} \end{array} \right)$$

In this example,

$$\text{Maximum risk} = 19 - (35 \times 1) = -16$$

Hence, we could lose $1,600, plus commissions, if OEX were exactly at 675, the striking price of the long options, at expiration. While OEX might not be exactly at that price, there would still be fairly large losses if it were anywhere *near* that price at expiration.

Finally, we can compute our breakeven points. On the upside, the formula is:

$$\begin{array}{c} \text{Call backspread} \\ \text{upside} \\ \text{breakeven point} \end{array} = \begin{array}{c} \text{Strike} \\ \text{price of} \\ \text{long options} \end{array} + \left(\frac{\text{Maximum loss}}{\text{Number of } \textit{net} \text{ long calls}} \right)$$

In this example,

$$\text{Upside breakeven point} = 675 + \left(\frac{161}{1} \right) = 691$$

Hence, a move by OEX above 691 could produce very large profits. There is also a downside breakeven point somewhere between the two strikes involved in the spread. In general, the formula for that is:

$$\begin{array}{c} \text{Call backspread} \\ \text{downside} \\ \text{breakeven point} \end{array} = \begin{array}{c} \text{Strike} \\ \text{price of} \\ \text{long options} \end{array} - \left(\frac{\text{Maximum loss}}{\text{Number of short calls}} \right)$$

In this example,

$$\text{Downside breakeven point} = 675 - \left(\frac{16}{1}\right) = 659$$

Thus, with these calculations, we now have a complete picture of the profitability of the OEX call backspread. If you look at the profit graph in Figure 6.4, you will see that the calculations we have just made all agree with where the lines fall on the graph: there will be losses if OEX is between 659 and 691 at expiration; there is unlimited profit potential above 691, and there is *limited* profit potential of $1,900 less commissions below 640. Once again, the profit graph looks like that of a straddle with one side lopped off.

A Put Ratio Spread

Typically, you would construct a put ratio spread in much the same way that was shown in the prior example of a call ratio spread: buy some puts at one strike, sell a larger number of puts at a lower strike. However, there is a variation that can sometimes be used to create a wider profit range and thus reduce the probability of the naked put(s) ever running into the danger of becoming in-the-money puts. That variation involves using three strikes in the spread using the prices shown in Table 6.4.

With March S&P futures at 973.70, the specific put ratio spread is this:

Option Position	Price	Delta	Implied Volatility
Buy 1 March 940 put	18.10	−0.32	22.1%
Sell 1 March 910 put	11.90	−0.22	24.2
Sell 1 March 860 put	6.50	−0.11	28.0

Table 6.4 Reverse Volatility Skew: March S&P Futures Options

| | | | | | | | Ratio ▼ | | | |
Strike	Call	VTY	Delta	Gamma	Theta	Vega	Put	PUTDEL	CVOL	PVOL
725	249.00	32.8	0.99	0.02	0.02	0.08	1.30	−0.01	1	1
750	224.50	33.8	0.98	0.03	0.05	0.17	1.90	−0.02	1	71
775	200.10	32.9	0.97	0.05	0.08	0.25	2.50	−0.03	1	1
780	194.75E	30.6	0.98	0.05	0.06	0.22	2.70	−0.02	0	20
790	185.04E	30.3	0.97	0.06	0.07	0.26	2.90	−0.03	0	100
800	175.90	31.6	0.96	0.08	0.10	0.36	3.30	−0.04	1	40
810	166.40	31.3	0.95	0.09	0.12	0.41	3.70	−0.05	1	1
820	156.80	30.6	0.94	0.11	0.13	0.46	4.10	−0.06	1	6
830	147.20	29.7	0.93	0.12	0.14	0.51	4.50	−0.07	1	11
840	137.66E	28.8	0.92	0.14	0.15	0.56	5.10	−0.08	0	6
850	128.50	28.5	0.91	0.16	0.17	0.63	5.70	−0.09	1	225
860	119.40	28.0	0.89	0.18	0.19	0.71	(6.50)	−0.11	1	15
870	110.12E	27.1	0.88	0.21	0.20	0.77	7.30	−0.12	0	4
880	101.20	26.4	0.86	0.23	0.21	0.85	8.20	−0.14	1	310
890	92.40	25.8	0.83	0.26	0.23	0.93	9.30	−0.17	1	22
900	83.60	24.9	0.81	0.29	0.24	1.01	10.50	−0.19	1	47
910	75.10	24.2	0.78	0.33	0.25	1.09	(11.90)	−0.22	1	17
920	(66.90)	23.4	0.75	0.37	0.26	1.17	13.60	−0.25	1	6
930	59.00	22.8	0.72	0.40	0.27	1.25	15.70	−0.28	1	29
940	51.50	22.1	0.68	0.44	0.28	1.32	(18.10)	−0.32	5	13
950	44.40	21.5	0.63	0.48	0.29	1.38	20.90	−0.37	4	119
960	37.60	20.8	0.59	0.51	0.29	1.43	24.00	−0.41	7	14
970	(31.30)	20.1	0.54	0.54	0.28	1.46	27.60	−0.46	3	29
980	25.50	19.4	0.48	0.56	0.27	1.46	31.70	−0.52	101	5
990	20.40	18.8	0.42	0.57	0.26	1.44	36.60	−0.58	31	1
1,000	16.00	18.3	0.36	0.56	0.24	1.38	42.10	−0.64	171	1
1,010	12.20	17.7	0.30	0.54	0.22	1.30	48.19E	−0.70	25	0
1,020	9.10	17.3	0.25	0.50	0.19	1.18	55.01E	−0.75	60	0
1,030	6.50	16.8	0.20	0.45	0.16	1.04	62.40	−0.80	32	1
1,040	4.50	16.3	0.15	0.39	0.13	0.88	70.24E	−0.85	10	0
	▲ Back									

March Futures: 973.70

First, you can see that this is still a delta neutral position initially. The delta of the long put that we are buying is −0.32 (recall that put deltas are stated as negative numbers to show that they move in the opposite direction of the underlying), while the sum of the deltas of the puts that are being sold is 0.33. Thus, the two effectively offset each other for a position delta of nearly zero to begin with. Also, note that the reverse volatility skew is present in these options and makes the position theoretically attractive, in that the option being bought has a lower implied volatility than that of the options being sold.

The profitability of this position at expiration can easily be determined. First, notice that the spread can be established for a slight credit: the option that is being purchased cost 18.10. Meanwhile the sum of the prices of the two put options being sold is 18.40. Thus, the spread is established for a 30 cent credit ($75), which is probably just about enough to cover commissions. So, if the underlying futures rally and are above 940 at March expiration, then all of the puts will expire worthless—meaning that the profit of this spread is $75, less commissions. However, if the futures are below 940, larger profits and/or losses are possible.

If the futures are anywhere between 910 and 940 at expiration, the short options will expire worthless and the profit will be equal to the value of the long put at that time, up to a maximum of 30 points with the futures at 910. Between 910 and 860 at expiration, the short March 860 put will expire worthless, and the profits will be equal to the difference in the strikes of the remainder of the position, which is a bear spread—30 points. Below 860 at expiration, the naked March 860 put kicks in and begins to detract from the profits and eventually could cause large losses. The actual downside breakeven point is 830—the lower strike, 860, minus the 30 point profit that was achieved at that price. Below 830, large losses could occur.

Since the futures are currently at 973, the place where risk begins—830—is quite a long way below, and if the spread has only a reasonably short period of time remaining until expiration, the probability of realizing that risk is small. Meanwhile, if a decline of smaller magnitude should take place—one that drives the futures down to between 940 and 830 at expiration—profits would result.

SUMMARY

Identifying abnormalities in the implied volatility of option prices and analyzing them correctly allows traders to establish profitable trading strategies. In general, when implied volatility skew is positive, either the call ratio spread or the put backspread is the preferred strategy. However, when implied volatilities are skewed in the negative direction, either the put ratio spread or the call backspread is the appropriate strategy, depending on whether the volatility is high or low.

Please take time to answer the review questions before proceeding on to a more generic discussion of volatility trading.

REVIEW QUESTIONS: TRADING VOLATILITY

1. When valuing an option, which of the following are true (mark all that apply)?

   a. Dividends are irrelevant for index options.

   b. Implied volatility is an input to the option pricing model.

   c. Interest rates are virtually irrelevant for valuing futures options.

2. What can be said about volatility (mark all that apply)?

   a. Market makers determine implied volatility.

   b. Implied volatility is a fairly accurate measure of forthcoming volatility.

   c. Historical volatility is computed by observing past option prices.

   d. Historical and implied volatility can be at substantially different levels.

3. What happens when a volatility skew exists (mark all that apply)?

   a. Implied volatilities vary at different strikes, usually in a uniform manner.

   b. The skew predicts which way the underlying is going to move during the life of the option.

   c. Out-of-the-money options are more expensive than at-the-money options.

   d. The underlying does not behave according to the normal or lognormal distribution.

4. When a dual skew exists (i.e., there is a forward skew at higher strikes and a reverse skew at lower strikes), which are true (mark all that apply)?

   a. Out-of-the-money puts are more expensive than out-of-the-money calls.

   b. At-the-money calls are cheaper than out-of-the-money calls.

   c. Out-of-the-money puts are cheaper than at-the-money puts.

   d. Out-of-the-money options are more expensive than at-the-money options.

5. Given the following data, mark all of the following statements that are true.

Stock price: 56.

   Apr 50 call has implied volatility = 32%.

   Apr 55 call has implied volatility = 35%.

   Apr 60 call has implied volatility = 40%.

   a. This is a positive skew.

   b. This is a negative skew.

c. A call backspread would be a good strategy for these options.

d. A call ratio spread would be a good strategy for these options.

6. Which of the following strategies has unlimited profit potential to the *upside* (mark all that apply)?

   a. Put backspread.

   b. Call backspread.

   c. Straddle buy.

   d. Call ratio spread.

7. Which strategies listed have extremely large risk (mark all that apply)?

   a. Put ratio spread.

   b. Call ratio spread.

   c. Put backspread.

   d. Straddle sale.

8. Given the following call backspread, answer the following questions.

   You establish this backspread: Buy 2 July 70 calls @ 2.

   Sell 1 July 60 call @ 10.

   a. What is your *upside* breakeven point?

   b. What is your greatest risk (in dollars), and at what stock price does it occur?

   c. What happens if the stock drops precipitously by expiration and is below 40?

7

BUY LOW AND SELL HIGH—VOLATILITY, THAT IS

LEARNING OBJECTIVES

The material in this chapter helps you to:

- Determine when volatility is out of line.
- Use the percentile approach to determine if options are cheap or expensive.
- Analyze the reasons behind volatility changes.
- Apply the criteria for straddle buying.
- Calculate "ever" and "closing" probabilities.
- Know when to use strangle sales and call ratio spreads.
- Understand the criteria for selling naked options.

The best situations for trading volatility occur when implied volatility is considerably out of line with where it has been in the past. We are often tempted to think that it is sufficient to compare historical volatility with implied volatility in order to find volatility trades. However, it is not enough that there is a big discrepancy between these two types of volatility. We also need to know where both implied and historical volatilities have been over the past months, or maybe even a year; that is, we want to know what range they have been trading in. Even if implied is much higher than historical, we should not automatically sell the volatility unless the trading range of implied volatility confirms that it is high with respect to where it's been in the past. This chapter gives you some general principles to use in forming your volatility trading strategies.

DETERMINING WHEN VOLATILITY IS OUT OF LINE

Let's begin our discussion with an example of volatility analysis. The following are readings of OEX volatility, taken from February 1995 just before the market embarked on an upside explosion of historic proportions.

If the implied volatility of OEX was 11% and the historical volatility was 6%, a trader might want to sell options because of the differential between historical and implied. From this limited bit of information, that *does* seem like a logical conclusion. However, on further investigation, it will be obvious that it is an incorrect conclusion.

OEX options traditionally trade with a higher implied volatility than the actual (historical) volatility of the OEX Index. There is probably not a logical explanation for this fact, but it *is* a fact. Thus, it is not sufficient to base analysis on the fact that OEX implied volatility is currently 11% and historical is 6%. Rather, look at past levels of both implied and historical volatility.

In fact, over the past year or even several years, OEX implied volatility had ranged from a low of 10% to a high of 22%. So you can see that the current reading of 11% is actually quite low. In a similar fashion, historical volatility had ranged from a low of 6% to a high of about 15% over that same period. Hence, the current reading of 6% is at the absolute low end of the range.

Given this information, strategies oriented toward *buying* options clearly would be more prudent because volatility is currently low by both measures—historical and implied. This strategy was proven correct by the upward market movement that followed.

This example demonstrates that knowing the previous range of volatility is much more important than merely comparing current values of implied and historical volatility. Using only the latter can lead to incorrect conclusions and losing trades. Moreover, since strategies in which you are selling volatility often involve the use of naked options, you should be extremely careful in your analyses before establishing positions.

USING PERCENTILES IN ANALYSIS

An approach to this analysis that works well is to use *percentiles* in comparing the volatilities. You should be familiar with percentiles. They are often used to describe demographics. Essentially, the concept is this: if you have 200 past observations of something and one current observation, and the current observation is greater than 194 of the 200 past observations, then we can say the current observation is in the 97th percentile—it is greater than 97% of all past readings.

What can specifically be done with options is to use the daily implied volatility readings and this percentile approach to determine situations where options are cheap or expensive. While it is true that individual options on a particular stock or futures contract have different implied volatilities, we can combine these into one *composite* implied volatility reading. This is done by weighting the individual options by their trading volume and distance in- or out-of-the-money. This formula is discussed in some detail in the book *Options as a Strategic Investment*. Essentially, we have a composite implied volatility reading for every stock, index, or future every day. If we keep that data in a database, then it is a simple matter to compare those past readings with the current reading.

Suppose, for example, as in the earlier $OEX example, we know that the *current* implied volatility daily reading is 11%.

Now, in our database, we have daily readings of implied volatility for $OEX going back hundreds of trading days. When we line them all up, we find that the current 11% reading is higher than only 20 of the past 600 days' readings. That means that the current reading is in the third percentile. Not only that, it indicates that most of the time $OEX implied volatilities are much higher than the current reading. Hence, we should probably be thinking about *buying* these options since they are cheap.

In addition, you may want some confirmation from historical volatility. But not necessarily a percentile confirmation. What you would like to know is, if you assume a reasonable historical volatility for this underlying—based on where historical volatility has measured in the past—does it still make sense to make this trade? That is, if you are thinking about buying options, then does historical volatility support your contention that the stock can actually move far enough to make a straddle buy profitable? In order to make this assumption about historical volatility, you would look to see where it's been in the past and then use those figures to make a "conservative" estimate about where it might be in the future. Hence, if you are buying options, you might look at the 10-day historical, 20-day historical, 50-day historical, 100-day historical, and then perhaps the median historical volatility of similar measure over a much longer time period—say, 600 trading days.

Continuing with the previous OEX example, these are the historical volatility summaries:

Decile:	1	2	3	4	5	6	7	8	9	10
Implied =	10.3>	11.4	11.8	12.3	13.0	13.7	14.5	15.3	16.0	16.7	17.7
10-day =	4.3	5.2	6.2	6.6	7.0	7.7	8.6>	9.4	10.1	10.8	16.5
20-day =	5.4	5.8	6.2	6.6	6.8	7.9>	8.6	9.1	9.8	11.1	12.9
50-day =	6.3	6.6	7.2>	7.5	7.7	8.0	8.6	9.1	9.9	10.3	11.1
100-day =	7.4>	7.7	7.8	8.0	8.5	8.9	8.9	8.9	9.0	9.1	9.1

The implied volatility numbers are the 20-day moving average of implieds. These go back one year, and there are about 250 trading days in a year. So there would be 231 20-day observations in that time period. The ">" character indicates that the current reading is in the 1st decile.

The other four lines refer to historical volatility. There are four separate measures of historical. You can see that the 10-, 20-, and 50-day historical averages are all in higher deciles than the implied volatility is. The 100-day is in the same 1st decile as implied.

Overall, this is an attractive picture of volatility for option buying strategies: implied is at its lowest point, and historical is more normal with the 10- and 20-day actually being in deciles slightly above average (the 6th and 7th deciles, respectively). Thus, if implied were to return to the middle deciles as well, implied volatility would increase and option buying strategies would benefit.

A similar situation holds for determining when implied volatility is too high. You would compare its percentile with the historical volatility's percentile. There is one exception about high implied volatility that should always be taken into consideration: very expensive options on a moderately volatile stock may signal an impending corporate news event such as a takeover or earnings surprise. In fact, when options get expensive, it may often mean that someone knows something—someone with a lot more (inside) information than you have. Therefore, volatility selling should probably be confined to:

1. Index options—where there can't be takeover, and earning surprises have only a minimal affect on a whole index of stocks.

2. Stock options where news has already been released—bad earning, for example—that has caused a large increase in implied volatility.

A good rule of thumb is to only sell implied volatility if it is at the high end of a previously determined *range*. But should the volatility break out of that range and rise to new highs, you should probably be very cautious about selling it and should even consider removing existing positions. Thus, you should generally not engage in volatility selling strategies when the implied volatility exceeds the previous range, especially if the stock is on the rise. The one exception would be if a stock were dropping rapidly in price, and you felt that that was the reason for the increase in implied volatility. In this situation, as we saw in the section on using options as a contrary indicator, covered writes or naked put sales can often be very effective.

LOOK FOR REASONS BEHIND VOLATILITY CHANGES

If you are considering volatility selling, a good dose of skepticism will probably stand you in good stead. If there is no news to account for an increase in option prices, and if the stock is not in a steep downtrend, then you should seriously ask *why* these options are suddenly so expensive. As we know, there not only may be insider information circulating in the marketplace, but there may be other things that are not readily publicized—such as a hearing by a government regulatory body (FDA, FTC, etc.) or a lawsuit nearing completion. The chart of Cephalon (CEPH) in Figure 7.1 is another illustration of what can happen to a biotech company when the FDA rejects its application for approval: in this particular case, the stock fell from 20 to nearly 12 in early May 1997 after an FDA rejection. Along the bottom of the chart, implied volatility is shown. It had risen dramatically from late March until early May, as the option market makers and other traders factored in the possibility of an extremely large gap move by the underlying. As a volatility trader, you would have been wise to avoid this situation because, even

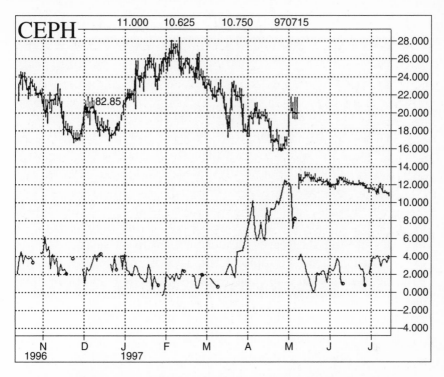

Figure 7.1 Cephalon volatility reaction to FDA action.

though implied volatility was rising to very high levels, there was a *reason* for that increase in volatility (the FDA hearings). In fact, as pointed out earlier in this book, that is the type of situation in which we sometimes *buy* straddles (the "event-driven" straddle buy). It is certainly *not* a situation where we'd want to *sell* volatility.

Can there be something similar as far as *buying* volatility? That is, can there be a situation where implied volatility is low and it looks like the stock has a good chance to be volatile, yet you should avoid the purchase? That is a very rare situation. Usually when volatility is too low, it can be bought without much worry. There is no guarantee that it will increase, of course, but statistics would normally be on that side in such a case.

However, there *are* occasionally times when volatility is low and perhaps deserves to be, and most of these have to do with fundamental changes in the company. A very obvious situation would be if the underlying company had received an all cash bid, or tender offer. The stock would still be trading—supposedly quite near the price at which the offer was made—but the options would have lost nearly all of their implied volatility because the stock would not be expected to either rise or fall in price, assuming that the cash bid was expected to go through to completion without much problem. So, from a purely statistical basis, the options would look cheap, but there is a fundamental reason why they are cheap. Consequently, straddle buys or other volatility buying strategies cannot be used in this case.

Iomega is a good example of this (see Figure 7.2). When the company was a start-up, the implied volatility on its options went through the roof. As Iomega matured, the implied volatility sank into the 10th percentile. However, this is probably where it belongs, and consequently, straddle buying is not appropriate.

Another situation in which implied volatility might justifiably decrease below historical standards would be where the underlying stock is undergoing a change of behavior: it *used* to be a volatile stock but now, for one reason or another, something has changed fundamentally at the company and the stock can no longer be expected to move as rapidly as it used to. This might occur after one company takes over another—especially if a smaller, more volatile company takes over a larger, less volatile company. The resulting entity would be less volatile than the original company was.

Finally, if the stock is trading at a substantially higher price than it used to, it can be expected to be less volatile. It is a general rule of thumb that higher-priced stocks are less volatile than lower-priced stocks. For example, a 5-dollar stock often trades up or down a half point on any given day. However, a $100 stock rarely moves 10 points in a given day. Hence, lower-priced stocks are more volatile than higher-priced ones. So, if our history of volatility encompasses mostly times when a

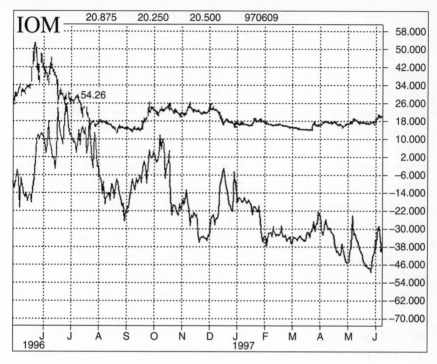

Figure 7.2   IOM.

stock was trading at low prices, and then the stock climbs to a much higher price, we would probably expect to see a decrease in the options' implied volatility. In that case, it might look like the options were a good buy—that implied volatility is too low—but in reality they would not be. For a summary of appropriate trading actions when volatility is out of line, see Table 7.1.

Table 7.1   Capitalizing When Volatility Is Out of Line

1. If it's cheap, buy straddles.
2. If it's expensive, sell out-of-the-money options.

A few variations
1. Cheap: Backspreads.
2. Expensive: Credit spreads.
    Ratio spreads.

MY FAVORITE STRATEGY

My favorite strategy for both novice and experienced option traders is straddle buying. As you know, a straddle buy is the simultaneous purchase of both a put and a call with the same terms, generally established with the underlying stock, futures, or index at about the strike price of the options. The basic features of a straddle purchase are (1) limited risk and (2) large profit potential, as long as the underlying moves far enough in one direction or the other. First, let's discuss the risk. The limited risk feature comes from the fact that you cannot lose more than you pay for the straddle initially. In fact, either the put or the call is normally worth *something* at expiration, for the underlying would have to be *exactly* at the strike price at expiration in order for both of them to expire worthless. Still, even with limited risk, the loss can be large, percentage-wise—you can lose 100% of your investment in a relatively short period of time. Thus, you should be judicious about what straddles you buy. More about that later.

As for the large profit potential, it is fairly easy to see that if the underlying rises dramatically in price while the straddle is owned, then the call will appreciate substantially (the put will be virtually worthless). So, the call's profit could theoretically be many times the initial investment. Similarly, if the stock should *fall* precipitously while the straddle is held, then the *put* will make a great deal of money (while the call expires worthless). In either case, a large percentage return is possible. Consider the following example:

$$
\begin{array}{ll}
\text{XYZ:} & 50 \\
\text{XYZ July 50 call:} & 5 \\
\text{XYZ July 50 put:} & 4
\end{array}
$$

This straddle costs 9 points, or $900. This means that if XYZ is more than 9 points higher than the strike price at expiration (i.e., above 59), the call will *have* to be worth more than 9 and hence the straddle buyer will have a profit. In addition, if XYZ falls more than 9 points *below* the strike price (below 41), the *put* will have to be selling for more than 9 points. Once again, that would mean the straddle buyer has a profit. These points, outside of which profits can be made, are called the *breakeven points:* 41 and 59 in this case. So, if XYZ falls below 41 or rises above 59 before July expiration, then this straddle buyer would have a profit. The risk is the entire $900 that was paid for the straddle, although XYZ would have to be *exactly* at 50 on expiration for that to occur. More likely, XYZ will be somewhere above or below 50—even if only fractionally—so that either the put or the call will have some value on expiration day. As we shall see later, it is probably not wise to hold the straddle all the way until expiration day anyway.

Now that we see how the straddle purchase works, we want to lay out some criteria for exactly which straddles are good buys and which are not. Perhaps a word about what is *not* sufficient would be a good starting point. *Do not* just look at some straddle prices and say to yourself, "Oh, I think XYZ can move that far in the required time. I think I'll buy that straddle." You need to be more rigorous than that.

Criteria for Buying Straddles

Criterion 1

The first criterion for straddle buying is to find cheap options to start with (See Figure 7.3 for an illustration of a straddle purchase when implied volatility is below the 10th percentile). Since we are buying options in this strategy, we want the options to be underpriced so that we have some advantage. In addition, we want the options to have at least three months' life remaining when we buy them, which will prevent time decay from becoming a problem right away. By insisting on this criterion, we are practicing volatility trading in the form of buying volatility.

One way to find out what options are cheap is to visit our Web site, www.optionstrategist.com, and look on the "Free

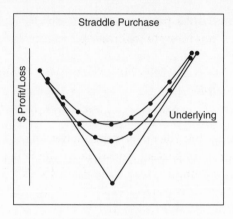

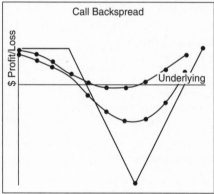

Also advantageous if implied lower than historical.
Implied: 25%
Historicals: 10-day 32%; 20-day 35%;
50-day 39%; 100-day 37%

Figure 7.3 Trading volatility implied below 10th percentile: (Options are cheap).

Stuff—Options Data" page. There, you will find a figure called the *implied volatility* for each underlying (IBM, for example). In addition, there is a *percentile* number given as well. If the implied volatility reading is in the 10th percentile or lower, then the options are cheap. In real time, if you have an option pricing service, you may want to check the current prices in order to compare the current implied volatility levels with what you found on our free data page in order to verify that the options are still cheap. Consider the following example:

Suppose, for IBM, you look up the free data on our Web site and find the following:

IBM: Curiv 29   9%ile

This means that the current implied volatility for IBM was 29 when the data was posted, and it is in the 9th percentile of all past readings of implied volatility for IBM. Thus, these options are cheap (or underpriced) because the percentile is below the 10th percentile. At this point, if you have option evaluation software of some sort, you would want to look at the current prices of the IBM options to verify that they are still trading with implied volatility somewhere near 43.

Suppose that you do so and find that the implied volatility of the at-the-money Apr 125 call is 30. The Apr 125 put should have the same implied volatility. Since this is less than or equal to the 29 we find on the Web site—and we know that the 29 figure is cheap—we can conclude that the options are still cheap. If the real-time prices revealed an implied volatility that was much *higher* than the Web site reading, then we might figure the options have gotten more expensive and the straddle wouldn't be worth buying if that happened. However, in this example, the straddle *is* cheap, so we would consider buying it.

Criterion 2

Once options that are trading in the 10th percentile or lower of past implied volatility readings have been identified, then we want to perform a couple of checks to ensure that the stock actually has the ability to move the required distance in the required time. This first of these two checks is Criterion 2, and it involves the use of a probability calculator. There are a couple of different types of probability calculators available to stock traders. Most are of a simple nature that give the probability of the stock trading at or beyond a target price *at the end* of a certain time period.

Typically, these could be used to answer the question: "If I buy the IBM April 140 call, with IBM at 125, what is the probability that IBM will be above 140 at April expiration?"

In reality, though, that isn't sufficient for most option traders. What you'd *really* like to know is "what is the probability that IBM will *ever* trade at 140 (or some other price) *at any time during the remaining life of the April 125 call?*" That is an entirely different question, and its answer is considerably larger than the question asked in the previous paragraph.

Let's call this second probability the *ever probability,* for it answers the question regarding the probability of the stock *ever* trading at the target price at any time during the option's life. The previous probability—that of the stock being above the target at the *end* of the time period—will henceforth be referred to as the *closing probability.*

The ever probability is particularly important for option *sellers,* for they would not stick around to expiration if the stock moved through the strike price of an option that had been written naked. Typically, that option would be covered as soon as the stock went through the strike price, and the option seller wouldn't even be around to see what happened at expiration. Hence the need for the closing probability—it doesn't accurately reflect what would really happen in the actual trading strategy.

The ever probability is much harder to calculate than the closing probability is. In fact, the closing probability is really the option's delta. That is, if the delta of an IBM April 140 call were 0.30, then that is saying that the probability of IBM being above 140 at April expiration is 30%. Hence, you don't need to buy a closing probability calculator (some of which sell for very expensive prices) if you have any sort of option evaluation software. The option evaluation software will give you the value of the option's delta, and hence a closing probability.

To calculate the ever probability, a simulation is necessary for there is not a specific formula that can do it. A simulated process created by a computer program that attempts to duplicate events that might happen in the real world is called a

Monte Carlo simulation. With such a simulator, you can get a handle on the ever probability. The following examples are taken from a product that we sell—the Probability Calculator 2000 and that is available to subscribers of The Strategy Zone portion of our Web site, www.optionstrategist.com.

Perhaps a couple of simple examples might be useful, whether you're interested in buying straddles or not. Again, we'll use the IBM example that was begun previously.

IBM: 125   IBM Apr 125 call: 12

IBM Apr 125 put: 10

Furthermore, let's assume that these options have six months of life remaining, or, to be specific, 130 trading days. There are five inputs required (or four if you only want to evaluate the probability of the stock hitting one target price, not two): stock price, upside target (which for straddles is the strike price plus the straddle price), downside target price, number of *trading days* until expiration (the Probability Calculator 2000 has a built-in function to calculate the number of trading days remaining until any expiration), and the volatility to use during the study.

Inputs   Stock price: 125.

Upside target price: 147.

Downside target price: 103.

Trading days until expiration: 130.

Volatility: ???

The volatility to use during the study is something that requires a little discussion. As stated earlier, if you are interested in option *buying* strategies, you should use a conservatively *low* estimate for this input. In that way, you will not overstate the probabilities. If they look good under the conservative assumption, then you probably have found an excellent position. On the other hand, if you are interested in option *selling* strategies, you should use a *high* estimate for that will also be a conservative estimate for an option seller.

This volatility should be based on *historical volatility*. So, this is where historical, or statistical, volatility enters the equation. As mentioned previously in the $OEX example, you would first look at the 10-day, 20-day, 50-day, and 100-day historical volatilities (of IBM, in this case). An option buyer would choose the *minimum* of those four numbers as the volatility estimate for the Monte Carlo simulation (whereas an option *seller* would choose the maximum of the four). If you suspect that even the minimum of those four numbers is overstating things—as might be the case if the stock has been especially volatile of late—then you should go farther back and look at a histogram of past historical volatilities (as was done in the earlier OEX example) to choose an appropriately conservative estimate of volatility for use in the Monte Carlo simulator. In this example, suppose we find the following historical volatilities for IBM:

10-day historical:	31%
20-day historical:	39%
50-day historical:	54%
100-day historical:	45%

The minimum of these is 31%, so we would use that in the probability calculator if we were an option buyer.

Using the five inputs, then, the Probability Calculator 2000 returns the following information:

Probability of *ever* hitting *either* target:	85%
Probability of *closing* outside of *either* target:	48%

These two outputs starkly contrast the two probabilities: ever versus closing. The ever shows that you have an 85% chance of making money—that is at *some* time between now and expiration, the stock will hit one or the other of the breakeven points. That is a pretty good probability and one would normally take a trade of this type. However, if you only looked at the closing probability, then you would see that there is only a 48% chance that the stock actually closes *outside* of the breakeven points. That isn't as favorable and you might pass on what is actually a very favorable trade.

What causes the discrepancy between the ever and the closing? Mathematically, it is due to the random probability of the normal curve that says it is difficult for a stock to move too far, too fast. The closing probability is based on the normal distribution and it has problems, as was stated earlier. In fact, most markets do *not* conform to the normal or (lognormal) distribution, so the probabilities of a stock hitting a target are usually larger than that distribution would have you believe. We don't have space here to get into a lengthy discussion on the merits and demerits of the lognormal distribution, but suffice it to say that stocks often make moves of much greater size than the confines of the lognormal distribution would allow for.

Another thing that contributes to the closing probability being much lower than the ever is that the lognormal distribution assumes a randomness to stock prices, whereas in reality there is a memory. If you are an experienced trader, you know that if a stock or futures contract breaks out to new highs—especially if there was multiple resistance before the breakout—then there is a good chance that the stock will continue in the upward direction for awhile: shorts cover (buy), momentum traders buy, and technicians buy the breakout. This is not random, and such things increase the probability of a stock's moving farther than the lognormal distribution assumes it can.

The Monte Carlo simulation can be used to evaluate an outright option purchase, too. Let's use the IBM example again, but this time we'll just look at the call. With IBM at 125, and the IBM Apr 125 call selling for 12, we can figure any number of probabilities, but the one that would guarantee a profit would be

"What is the probability of IBM *ever* trading at 137 (the strike price plus the call price) at *any time* between now and expiration?" The same Monte Carlo probability calculator says that there is a 68% chance of that happening—not great, but not terrible. At the same time, the closing probability for the same event is only 35%. So, if you only knew the 35% probability, you might be tempted to sell the option. In reality, there is about a two-thirds chance that the stock will hit the strike *at some time between now and expiration*—certainly not a good probability for an option seller. Once again, the closing probability gives misleading results.

One final point on this subject, not that it is now sufficient to use the delta of the IBM April 125 call as the closing probability in the preceding example. That delta is 0.59. But what that means is that, with IBM at 125, there is a 59% probability of IBM closing above 125—the strike—not 137, the target.

So this is the second criterion for straddle buying: *the Monte Carlo probability calculator must determine that there is at least an 80% chance that the underlying will hit one or the other of the breakeven points at any time prior to expiration.*

Now let's move on to the third criterion.

Criterion 3

Look at the chart of IBM's past movements and verify that the stock has been able to move the required distance in the allotted amount of time. Does it appear that a 22-point move by IBM over the course of six months is a reasonable proposition? If so, then you have found a good straddle to buy.

If you have charting software with historical pricing data, you could write a program to actually determine statistically just how often IBM has been able to move 22 points in one direction or the other over a 130-day trading period, in the past.

If you don't have access to such software, then you can attempt to do the same thing with a chart. If you see that there have been frequent periods when the stock stagnates and can't move 22 points in six months, then you would probably reject this as a straddle buy—even if the first two criteria were satisfied. However, if it appears that the stock has bounced back and forth—or even better, made straight-line moves—in moves that are at least 22 points in magnitude within a six-month time frame, then this criterion would be satisfied.

Criterion 4

Finally, if all three of the previous criteria are satisfied, the fundamentals should be checked in order to make sure that there isn't a cash takeover bid, or a takeover bid by a less volatile stock—things that would create what appear to be cheap options, but which are in reality fairly priced because of the takeover. This change in fundamentals was mentioned a few pages ago, and it is certainly one that is valid.

Once all four of these criteria are satisfied, an attractive straddle purchase candidate has been found:

1. Option implied volatility is currently in the 10th percentile or lower.

2. The Monte Carlo probability calculator gives an 80% chance or greater of the stock *ever* hitting one or the other of the breakeven points at any time during the options' life.

3. Using past prices, verify that the stock has frequently been able to make a move of the required distance in the allotted length of time.

4. Check the fundamentals to ensure that there is no fundamental reason why the options should be so cheap.

See Figure 7.4 for two examples of ideal conditions for buying straddles. Figure 7.5 shows tremendously cheap straddles purchased on 10-year note futures.

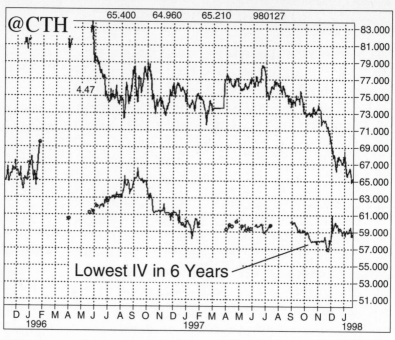

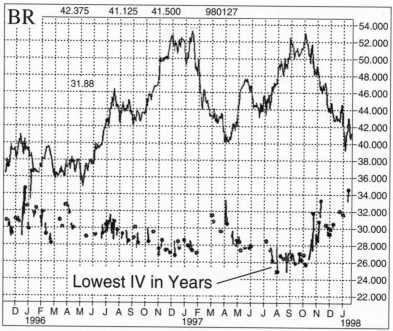

Figure 7.4 Buying straddles for March Cotton and Burlington resources.

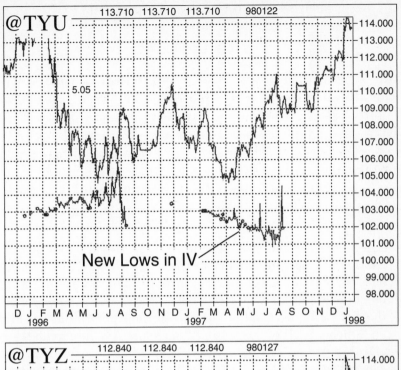

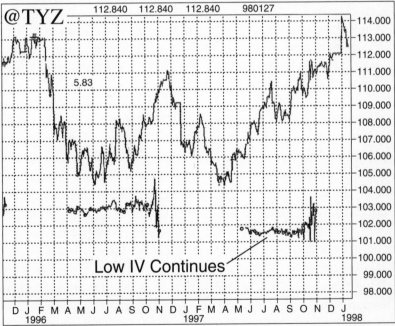

Figure 7.5 Straddles on 10-year note futures.

Follow-Up Action

Once the straddle is in place, we prefer to leave it alone to see if it can hit one or the other of the breakevens. We will risk 60% of the initial price, which is usually enough room to allow you to hold the straddle until about one month of life remains. If you are fortunate enough to have profits develop, take some partial profits on the winning side, sell out the losing side, and ride the remainder of the winning side, using the 20-day moving average of the stock as a trailing stop. Look at the following example:

> Again, suppose you buy the IBM Apr 125 straddle for 22 points. Later, IBM moves up and trades through resistance at 149. It is now beyond the upside breakeven point, which was 147, and it has broken bullishly out over resistance. At that time, suppose the Apr 125 call is selling for 27 and the Apr 125 put is selling for 2. Sell out all of the puts (taking a loss, but recouping the remaining value), sell out a portion—perhaps one-third—of your long calls (taking a profit). Then, hold the remaining calls, using the 20-day moving average of IBM as your stop price. If, on any day, IBM closes below its 20-day moving average, then sell the rest of your calls.

There are, of course, other ways that you could take follow-up action with a straddle. Some traders prefer to "trade against" the straddle. That is, when the underlying stock rises in price and nears a resistance point, say, then the trader would sell some of the long calls (or would sell stock short against the long calls), figuring that the stock will decline toward the strike price. I don't like this approach because it limits gains on a real strong breakout. Furthermore, it forces you to stay on top of the position almost constantly.

This "trading against the straddle" strategy is really a way of keeping the straddle more or less neutral. But, once again, it takes a lot of work and any neutrality adjustments limit the profits on big, breakout moves. It is my philosophy that trying to ride the trend is a better strategy, especially for a commission-paying public customer, because it keeps costs down and allows for the occasional very large gain.

One of the nice things about straddle buying, with the follow-up approach outlined in the above example, is that it is a strategy that can be operated by the layman. You do not have to have access to a trading screen all day long. You merely need to check the stock's closing price each day and make any adjustments that are necessary the next morning (alternatively, you could call your broker just before the close of trading each day and make any necessary adjustments at that time).

Any surprises are good news. A takeover? Great! Bad earnings? Just as good! Surprise government crop report in a futures position? Super! Anything that makes the stock or futures make a gap move is welcome to a straddle buyer.

As for risk, most of the time nothing happens when you own a straddle. A little time passes each day, and that's about as bad as things get. If too much time passes, and the straddle loses 60% of its value, then we would terminate the position and go on to look for another position. On any given day, there are usually plenty of straddle buys to choose from—just be sure you stick rigidly to the four criteria set forth above. A deviation from that strategy will usually lead to an inferior position, thereby increasing the probability for losses.

"WATCHING PAINT DRY"

Buying volatility can sometimes be an arduous occupation. First, you do a lot of "fancy" analysis to determine that options are cheap. Then—convinced that you are about to take advantage of the other option traders' inaccurate projections of volatility—a straddle (or other long position) is taken. However, often nothing happens for a while. Expectation turns to boredom. It's like watching paint dry before, hopefully, the stock finally makes a move. I'm exaggerating a little, of course—sometimes the stocks move right away—but the point is that buying volatility is often a strategy where not much happens for fairly long stretches of time. This can sometimes cause (novice) practitioners to abandon a strategy when perhaps they shouldn't.

One trader recently commented, "I now can acknowledge that it takes a certain type of person to endure these strategies." *Endure* is an interesting choice of words, but it *does* describe the "watching paint dry" effect. Of course, no strategy is apropos for every investor. You *must* feel comfortable with any strategy you are using—no matter what I, or any other supposed expert, tells you about how profitable it is.

Assuming that you have decided that buying volatility *is* an appropriate strategy, you might still have doubts, much as expressed by the following comments: "Somewhere, I remember reading that the most (statistically) probable thing for any issue is to do nothing (and also that there is about a 99% chance [editor: actually, it's 97%] of its being within two standard deviations). It's bothersome to note the high probabilities that your [Monte Carlo] probability calculator gives vis à vis the aforementioned statistical fact. Does your calculator somehow take this into account?"

The 97% probability mentioned is a totally fictional thing as far as the stock market is concerned. It is based on normal (lognormal) distribution, and stock prices don't conform to that model at all. It is just used as a convenience by certain mathematicians because the "real" distribution—whatever it is—can't be determined.

Chaos theory may come closer than anything else to describing this theoretical distribution, but the fact is that each stock or sector or market may have its *own* distribution so that no broad approach will actually work across the board.

As for the normal distribution, how many stocks move more than two standard deviations in any time period? Some daily price moves are eight standard deviations or more—so unlikely by the normal distribution that we shouldn't see more than one or two per century. Yet we see several every day. So the lognormal distribution is clearly wrong. For example:

> On Monday, April 5, 1999, there were five stocks that had moves of eight standard deviations or more, including one of over 30 standard deviations. The article also cited that, on the day of the *lowest* $VIX reading in history (July 25, 1993), there were 12 stocks that moved four standard deviations or more that day. This is just more evidence that the normal distribution is not correct. It should also make you very scared if you're a seller of stock options (futures, options sales, while better, might be problematic as well).

Nevertheless, some sort of distribution has to be assumed for general studies, and the lognormal distribution is used as the best fit by many analysts and mathematicians. In fact, we use it in our volatility buying analyses as well. Because, if an option looks like a good buy under the lognormal distribution, then it must surely be a terrific buy under the "real" stock market distribution. Hence, if our calculator is giving a high probability of success, it is actually *understating* things because it hasn't factored in the possibility of any eight standard daily moves!

It is for this reason that I think our straddle buying analyses are done in a manner that they should make money even if the underlying conforms to a normal distribution. If the stock in fact should behave chaotically, then the straddle should be nicely profitable.

So, if owning these straddles is like watching paint dry, I guess that's just the price you'll have to pay while waiting for a sizeable move by the underlying. On the other hand, you're not glued to your trading screen with such positions, so you can have a life—play golf!

SELLING VOLATILITY

Selling volatility is a riskier endeavor because, if the options are sold naked, then large losses could occur. Furthermore, even if a spread is established to reduce risk, some unwanted things can make it difficult to profit. In general, selling stock options naked is asking for trouble because of their penchant for making the large moves discussed above. Even if you establish a spread in stock options, or a covered write, you may be limiting your profits too severely because of the possibility that the long side of the spread (or the long stock) could actually make far more money if it weren't inhibited by the presence of a short option. Nevertheless, there are sometimes situations where it makes some sense to sell options—particularly index options, which aren't subject to large gap moves. See Table 7.2 for a summary of trading volatility when options are expensive.

When the implied volatility is too high, the strategist wants to sell volatility, intending to capitalize when it returns to more normal levels. When I want to *sell* volatility, I favor one of two strategies—the sale of a naked combination (a strangle) or a

Table 7.2 Trading Volatility Implied about 90th Percentile (Options Are Expensive)

---

1. Selling out-of-the-money options.
   "Sell combo" or "Sell strangle."

   Example: XYZ: 50
                  Sell May 55 call: 2 and
                  Sell May 45 put: $1\frac{1}{2}$
                  Take in $3\frac{1}{2}$ credit

                  Breakeven points at expiration:
                  Upside: higher strike + Credit = $55 + 3\frac{1}{2} = 58\frac{1}{2}$
                  Downside: lower strike − Credit = $45 - 3\frac{1}{2} = 41\frac{1}{2}$

                  Quick losses can occur on fast movements.

2. Maximum profit anywhere between strikes at expiration. (Between 45 and 55 in this case.)

3. Margin: allow 20% of higher strike + credit.
   $(20 \times 55 + 350 = 1,100 + 350 = 1,450)$
   Some firms require substantially more.

---

ratio spread. Since both strategies involve the sale of naked options, some traders prefer to purchase deeply out-of-the-money
options as disaster protection. That may or may not be a good
idea. On the one hand, it allows you to be worry-free about large
gap openings, but on the other hand it costs money, and if you
have done your analysis correctly, you should be selling inflated
volatility, not buying it. I also tend to keep the options relatively
short term in nature when selling volatility.

In a naked combination **(strangle)** sale, an out-of-the-money
call is sold, as well as an out-of-the-money put. I favor this over a
straddle sale because of the wider price range of profitability
that is attained. A straddle sale can make more money if the underlying is near the striking price at expiration, but a strangle
sale makes money over a wider range of prices of the underlying
instrument. Since you are often forced to make adjustments to
naked positions when the underlying makes adverse price movements, the use of the combination sale lessens the odds of having
to adjust so often.

When selling high volatility, you expect that volatility will
return to more normal levels. In most cases, when this happens,
you will make money and can then exit the position. This return
to normal volatility may occur quickly, or it may take awhile (or
may never happen at all). The trader's statistical "edge" is that
you are selling inflated volatility, and your profit potential—as
represented by that "edge"—is the amount of money that you
could make if volatility returned to normal levels.

The top graph in Figure 7.6 shows the general shape of a combination (strangle) sale, with two curved lines inside of it. The
straight lines are where the profits or losses would lie if the position were carried all the way to expiration. The curved lines are
profit projections if the position were held only halfway to expiration. The reason that there are *two* curved lines is that one represents the results with volatility remaining at high levels (the
lower curved line), while the other depicts the results if volatility
were to return to normal levels (the higher curved line).

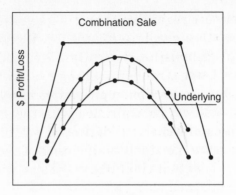

Also advantageous if implied higher than historical
Implied: 32%
Historicals: 10-day 19%; 20-day 21%;
50-day 22%; 100-day 21%

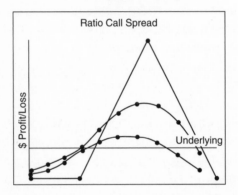

Figure 7.6 Strangle sale and call ratio spread: Options are expensive.

You can see that there are profits under both curved lines if the underlying is near the center of the graph. Likewise, there can be losses as well, as both curved lines penetrate below the zero profit line if the underlying rises or falls too far. What is most important, however, is that there is a definite space between the two curved lines. This space is the statistical advantage that the seller of high implied volatility has, for if volatility returns to its normal level, he or she will profit by the amount of the shaded area.

A similar picture regarding the ratio spread strategy can be observed in the other graph in Figure 7.6. It is the graph of a *call* ratio spread. Simplistically, a call ratio spread involves buying one call at a lower strike and selling more calls at a higher strike. Notice that the maximum profit area of all three scenarios—expiration, halfway to expiration with the same volatility, and halfway to expiration with decreased volatility—is at the higher striking price (i.e., the striking price of the short options in the spread). It is at that point where the statistical edge is the largest; the area between the two curved lines is widest at that point.

As for the criteria for selling naked *index* options, I would essentially use ones similar to those for straddle buying:

1. The options must be expensive—in the 90th percentile or higher of implied volatility.

2. The Monte Carlo probability calculator should be used to determine that there is a 25% chance or less of the underlying *ever* trading at the strike price of the naked option *at any time* prior to expiration. In fact, 25% might be too high; something like 10% or 15% might be more reasonable since it is safer. Moreover, when the calculator is run, the user should input a *high* estimate of volatility so that a conservative output is obtained. You don't want to delude yourself into thinking that there is only a small chance of the index's hitting the breakeven points, if that result is obtained by inputting an overly low volatility estimate into the calculator.

If you are selling naked *stock* options, which I don't normally recommend, then I would also check the fundamentals to make sure that there isn't some obvious reason why implied volatility is high (even if that reason is a takeover rumor).

In the graph in Figure 7.7, a series of $OEX options were written naked when they were expensive. Except for one foray in

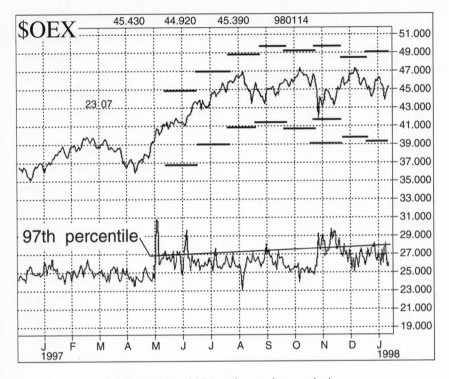

Figure 7.7 $OEX options written naked.

October 1997, OEX never hit either of the breakevens during the time that the naked strangles were in place. In each of these cases, the two criteria were rigidly adhered to before the options were sold. First they were expensive. You can see from the line at the bottom of the graph in Figure 7.7 that they were often near or above the 97th percentile of implied volatility. (The reason that the 97th percentile line on the graph is not exactly horizontal is that, as more and more expensive daily readings were added to the OEX data, it took a higher level to reach the 97th percentile—hence the line is rising as time passes.)

Second, the probability of the index's reaching the break-even points was calculated. In general, a 15% chance of *not* ever hitting the breakeven points was used, and a conservatively high estimate of volatility was used (usually something on the order of 25% to 30% volatility, when in reality OEX was trading with a statistical volatility closer to 15% in those days).

As a result, you can see that there were eight months on the chart (eight sets of parallel horizontal lines, which represent the holding periods of eight separate strangle sales). Only once did the index hit any of the lines. So that is an actual rate of 6.25% of the index *ever* hitting the breakeven points, as compared to the ever estimate of 15% which we were striving for with the calculator. Thus, in this limited sample, our results were better than the statistics indicated we should expect.

Note: We will also *not* sell a fractionally priced option naked. You will never cover such an option until it expires totally worthless. Rather, if we sell naked options, we prefer to sell ones that are priced at least as high as 1½ or more. In that way, if the option declines to a quarter point, we can cover if we are nervous and still make a good profit.

Follow-Up Action for Sellers of Naked Options

Sellers of naked options should be careful to take defensive action as soon as the underlying hits the strike price of the option being sold. To facilitate this, enough margin should be allowed initially for a move to that adjustment point. When you sell an out-of-the-money option, your margin requirement is not as large as it will be if the stock moves to the strike or if the option becomes an in-the-money option. Still, if you sell naked options, you should allow enough margin for the stock to bounce around and do whatever it wants to do, as long as it doesn't hit the adjustment point. For you want to be able to dictate adjustments based on factors such as where the stock price is and how much the option is worth, as opposed to being forced to make adjustments because of margin considerations. For example:

$OEX is trading at 600, and you want to sell the Jan 550 put naked. The margin requirement for selling a naked index option is 15% of the index price, plus the option premium, minus any out-of-the-money amount. There is usually a *minimum* requirement, too, and it currently is 10% of the value of the index.

$OEX: 600   OEX January 550 put: 3

Margin requirement for selling the January 550 put (which represents a put on 100 shares of OEX):

15% of the index:	$9,000
Plus option premium	+300
Less out-of-the-money amount (50 points)	−5,000
Total	$4,300

However, 10% of OEX's value (for 100 shares) is $6,000, so the actual margin requirement is $6,000 since this is the minimum margin required.

Nevertheless, I would want to allow enough margin for the stock to fall to 550. If it did, there would be a requirement of 15% of 550 (times 100), plus the put premium. We could use an option model to estimate the put premium, and let's say that estimate is 10 points. That is, if OEX makes a sudden fall to 550, we would probably expect implied volatility to increase, and the put would thus be selling for about 10. If that happened, our possible margin requirement would be:

Margin to allow, if OEX falls to 550:	
15% of OEX price (550):	$8,250
Plus option premium	1,000
Total to allow	$9,250

So, rather than allow the minimum requirement of $6,000 for each naked option sold, you should *really* allow $9,250 apiece. In that way, you won't have to make any unwanted adjustments until and unless the index falls to 550.

As for what adjustment to make, it is often quite easy with index options. Recall that in earlier sections we saw that (1) index options have a negative volatility skew, and (2) options tend to increase in implied volatility when the underlying experience a sudden drop in price. Thus, if OEX were to fall to 550 within a month from its current price of 600, it is likely that the puts would get quite a bit more expensive (in terms of implied volatility) and the reverse volatility skew would also steepen. These things, if they come to pass, actually aid in follow-up action. For you should be able to buy back your Jan 550 put and roll down and out to a much lower strike for a credit or even money. In this way, you defer making your 3-point credit that you had hoped to capture by January expiration, but keep alive "hope" that the credit will eventually be realized.

Here is another example:

OEX falls to 550 in just a couple of weeks and the following prices then exist:

Jan 550 put: 16

Feb 520 put: 17

You could buy back the January put for 16 (incurring a realized loss of 13 points) and sell the Feb 520 put for 17 points. Thus, you have lowered your "danger point" by 30 OEX points (550 to 520) and have received a slight credit for doing so. Now, if OEX stays above 520 until Feb expiration, you will make four points total (the original three-point credit, plus the one-point credit from this follow-up action).

In fact, you could roll down out farther if you wanted. For example, a *March* 500 put would probably be selling for about 17 at the same time. This would decrease your probability of having to adjust again, but would lengthen the amount of time you would have to wait for the option to expire.

Finally, it should be noted that profits equal to those available from selling OEX options are available from selling S&P 500 futures options, but the margin requirements are more favorable in the futures market. Hence the seller of naked index options can operate more efficiently in futures (Table 7.3).

A description of some more complex strategies that professionals use to wrestle with the concept of selling volatility, but hedging it as well is found in more detail in the book *McMillan on Options*.

Table 7.3   Complex Neutral Strategies

Characteristics:

Neutral to market movement

Have volatility risk

(Delta and gamma neutral; with vega exposure)

Examples:

Position you might establish in the month of April:

> *Call ratio spread (negative vega)*
> Buy 10 June 50 calls
> Sell 17 June 60 calls
> Buy 3 June 50 puts
> *Note:* Ratio is less than 2-to-1 sold.

> *Call calendar spread (positive vega)*
> Buy 16 September 50 calls
> Sell 12 June 50 calls
> Buy 3 June 50 puts
> *Note:* Extra amount of long calls gives position upside potential.

> *Short straddle with long "wings" (negative vega)*
> Sell 10 September 890 calls
> Sell 10 September 810 puts
> Buy 12 August 900 calls
> Buy 12 August 800 puts
> *Note:* Longer-term sale is hedged with shorter-term "wings" (naked in OEX options, but *not* in futures options).

The above positions are examples, and the exact quantities needed in any given situation may differ from the above quantities.

SUMMARY

Much material has been presented in this book. I encourage you to supplement this information with more reading if you are unfamiliar with these concepts. Furthermore, remember the number one principle of trading: use only trade systems and strategies with which you are comfortable—those that agree with your philosophy of life and/or trading. Do not undertake trades that keep you awake at night or require you to feel uncomfortable while they are in place. For no matter *who* tells you how to make money, only you can decide which is the suitable approach for you.

REVIEW QUESTIONS: BUY LOW AND SELL HIGH—VOLATILITY, THAT IS

1. Suppose that we know that XYZ options are trading with an implied volatility of 22%, and that the 20-day historical volatility of XYZ is 30%. What can we surmise (mark all that apply)?

   a. The options are cheap.

   b. Implied volatility will move higher until it reaches 30%.

   c. The stock will become less volatile over the next few months, since statistical volatility is too high in comparison to implied volatility.

   d. Longer-term measurements, such as the 100-day historical volatility, are probably lower and more on the order of 22%—near the implied volatility.

2. Why can historical and implied volatility differ so substantially?

   a. They are measured over different time periods.

   b. One is a leading indicator, the other is lagging.

    c. One is based on hard statistics, the other is a matter of opinion.

    d. It is caused by the lognormal distribution.

3. By observing past daily implied volatility readings, you can assign the current reading to a percentile. Generally the 90th percentile or higher identifies expensive options, and the 10th percentile or lower identifies cheap options. However, if you notice that there are a *significantly* large number of stocks with expensive options at the current time, which of the following might you do (mark all that apply)?

    a. Make no change to the definition of cheap (10th percentile) or expensive (90th percentile).

    b. Adjust upward: define *cheap* as the 15th percentile and *expensive* as the 95th.

    c. Adjust downward: define *cheap* as the 5th percentile and *expensive* as the 85th.

    d. Adjust only the definition of *expensive,* leaving the definition of *cheap* as is.

4. Which of the following could be a valid reason for expensive options on a particular stock—indicating that you probably shouldn't initiate volatility selling strategies at the current time (mark all that apply)?

    a. A corporate board meeting is set for tomorrow.

    b. The company has announced that the FDA will review its product application soon.

    c. Internet chat rooms are touting the stock as a takeover candidate.

    d. The jury in a patent infringement case against the company has retired to deliberate the evidence.

5. Which of the following might be a valid reason for *cheap* options on a stock (mark all that apply)?

    a. Earnings are to be announced tomorrow.

    b. The company has rejected an unfriendly takeover bid.

c. The company has accepted an unfriendly takeover bid.

d. The company has acquired a larger company, whose stock is less volatile.

6. When options are cheap, you generally have the choice between buying a straddle or establishing a backspread. What might entice you to use the backspread instead of buying a straddle?

a. A reverse volatility skew is in place.

b. A positive volatility skew is in place.

c. The margin requirements are more favorable for a backspread as opposed to a straddle.

d. The breakeven points are closer together for a backspread, so there is a higher probability of making money.

7. With a stock right at the strike price, you buy a four-month straddle. Is your position biased with respect to market movement? Explain your answer fully.

8. You are given the following information:

Stock	Options	Price	Delta
XYZ: 51.25	July 50 call:	6.00	0.60
	July 50 put:	4.50	−0.40

You are going to buy the July 50 straddle, but you want to remain delta neutral. What ratio of puts to calls should you buy to remain neutral? How many total calls and puts should you buy if you have a *maximum* of $11,000 to spend and still want to remain neutral? What are your breakeven points for this position?

9. What is the probability of losing your entire investment when you buy a straddle?

a. Greater than 80%.

b. About 50%.

c. About 5%.

d. Less than 2%.

10. You buy a straddle, when the options are in the 10th percentile of implied volatility and hold it. After about a month, the stock is pretty much unchanged—trading near the striking price of the options in the straddle. However, implied volatility has moved up to the 50th percentile after the month has passed. Which of the following are true (mark all that apply)?

    a. The straddle is probably about unchanged in price from where you bought it.

    b. You most likely have a loss of about 10% on your long straddle.

    c. You have a profit, and you should take it since the stock is unchanged.

    d. There is no way to tell from the information given if there would be a profit or not.

11. If you are selling naked options, you should (mark all that apply):

    a. Never sell call options naked.

    b. Allow enough margin to allow for the stock to get to your adjustment point (usually, the strike price).

    c. Only sell overpriced options.

    d. Never sell futures options naked.

12. IRA rules state that only a fixed amount can be contributed in a given year. With this rule in mind, what option strategies would be allowed in an IRA account (choose all that apply)?

    a. Call buying.

    b. Put buying.

    c. Selling naked puts, using minimum margin requirements.

    d. Selling naked calls if you put up the full value of the stock value at the strike price as margin (i.e., if you sell a Jan 50 naked call, you put up $5,000).

13. Assume you establish a call spread—one in which you buy calls at one strike price and sell an equal number or *fewer* calls at *another* strike price. What can be said (mark all that apply)?

    a. The naked calls in such a spread mean there is large, theoretically unlimited, risk.

    b. The worst result at expiration will occur if the stock is exactly at the strike price of the long calls.

    c. You can't fully assess answer *b* unless you know the expiration dates of the calls in the spread.

    d. If these are cash-based index options, you can't accurately assess your risk.

14. What can be said about neutral positions (mark all that apply)?

    a. It is virtually impossible to keep a position neutral.

    b. Public customers would lose a great deal in commissions in keeping a position neutral.

    c. "Neutral" positions eliminate the necessity to predict the direction of the underlying stock.

    d. Only a change in the price of the underlying will change an option's delta.

ANSWERS TO REVIEW QUESTIONS

———

Not every one of these questions has a *definitive* correct answer. Some are intended to provoke thoughts regarding the choices one must make in the real world when dealing with options. The explanations given with the questions are important for you to read, so please take the time to study them as you would any other portion of this course.

CHAPTER 1   INTRODUCTION

1. *(c)* The Options Clearing Corp. is *not* a brokerage/trading firm. The others are.

2. *(b)* Secondary market is the only completely correct answer. Many over-the-counter options are traded by institutions and thus have very low commission rates and *huge* open interest. Choice *d* is probably not correct in today's environment either, since the majority of over-the-counter business is actually being done by the *most* reputable brokers (Salomon, Morgan, etc.). In the days *before* listed options, *(d)* would have been a correct answer as well, but no longer.

3. *(a), (b),* and *(c)* are all true; *(d)* is not.

4. *(a)* and *(b)* have unlimited profit potential, and thus are the correct answers. *(c)* and *(d)* are equivalent, and both have only limited profit potential but large loss potential.

5. *(b)* In-the-money options have less time value premium than at-the-money options do, and—unless there is an especially large dividend—in-the-money puts have less time value premium than do in-the-money calls.

6. *(d)* is the answer. *(a)* and *(c)* are the same thing and they use the fixed mathematical formula for standard deviation. There is also agreement for *(b),* as to the correct way to *measure* implied volatility (it is the volatility that must be plugged into the option model in order to make the model's answer be equal to the current option price). But *(d)* is open to question, for different traders may have different *estimates* of the forthcoming volatility of the underlying and hence the option's implied volatility.

7. Both *(b)* and *(d)* are correct. *(b):* Statistically speaking, a 30% annual standard deviation means that there is a two-thirds chance that the underlying will rise or fall 30% (lognormal) in the next year (*not* the next 20 days—choice *a*). *(d)* is also correct, for obvious reasons. Choice *c* is wrong because there is no guarantee or requirement that implied and statistical volatility be equal.

8. *(a)* is correct. The in-the-money options (choices *c* and *d*) are trading very near parity and thus have a low implied volatility. Choice *b* has three more months of life than choice *a,* but has only 1/4 more point of time value premium. Thus, choice *a* has the higher implied volatility.

9. *(a)* is the only correct answer, and even it expires on the third Friday in certain months (by coincidence).

10. *(b)* and *(d)* are correct.

11. *(d)* is a bear spread. The others are all equivalent versions of bull spreads.

12. You would show a profit graph, because it shows exactly what your supervisor wants to see—potential gains and losses from the position at various points in time. A *pricing curve* just shows how the price of a particular *option* varies over time. As a further measure of risk, you could show the delta of the position, and even some of the other "greeks" (gamma, theta, vega).

13. This position is the same as a long put, and this position is called a *synthetic put.*

14. This position is equivalent to short stock.

15. The option position allows you to be equivalently short stock (1) without having to borrow the stock as a short seller would, (2) without requiring an uptick to get short. The fact that the option position has more leverage (a smaller margin requirement) is not necessarily an advantage.

16. *(a)* The implied futures price = strike + call – put. That is 81.80, using any of the three pairs of put and call prices given. *(b)* Buy 5 May calls and sell 5 May puts with the same strike price. The fact that cotton futures and options are worth $500 per point is an irrelevant piece of information.

17. *(c)* is correct. Satellite has the largest band width of the choices given, at least in the year 2002. Standard phone lines may one day exceed satellite—who knows?

18. *(a), (d), (b), (c).* Delayed quotes are free and can be obtained by just a local phone call in many cases. However, since most people access delayed quotes over the Internet, *(a)* and *(d)* could be considered to be equal. So if you said D = A, B, C, for your answer, it is acceptable.

19. *(c)* is correct. *(a)* can be determined by iteration with the model. *(b)* is a first derivative by-product of the model. *(d)* can be determined by assuming that the current market option prices are in their true arbitrage state. *(e)* is what the model is used for most frequently.

20. The points you might raise would be (1) a need for real-time pricing to gauge risk during a volatile trading day; (2) a need for real-time pricing to figure your profits and losses intra-day; (3) a need for a model that can assess the theoretical values, implied volatilities, and "greeks" on a whole array of options at one time, rather than doing them one at a time on the CBOE site. Actually, this point is useful for analyzing new positions to be established, as well as analyzing the ones currently in the portfolio; (4) the more sophisticated software pulls the prices right into the model, therefore saving a vast amount of time and eliminating the mistakes that would occur if you had to look up the prices yourself and then type them in the free CBOE model, one at a time (including strike prices, expiration dates, etc.); and (5) the advanced software allows a lot of what-if analyses to be done easily, such as

"What happens to our positions if implied volatility skyrockets over the next month?"

CHAPTER 2   OPTIONS AS DIRECT INDICATORS

1. *(b)* is the correct answer; *(d)* has no relevance to the matter.

2. I would favor the one with the *in-the-money puts* as the one that the insiders are working. This is because a favored strategy of theirs is to buy the in-the-money puts and buy stock at the same time. This can be done in size because an arbitrageur will take the other side of the trade. Then the stock can be sold on downticks, because they own *long* stock. They not only force the stock down by doing this (thereby raising rumors along the street), but they wind up with a bunch of long puts that they can hold or exercise to turn into short stock. Even in *this* case, though, I would want to see the stock *fall* in price before I bought puts for my own account. As for the other choice, out-of-the-money puts are usually bought by common public speculators and are not reliable as predictors of some pending negative corporate news release.

3. *(d)* is the correct answer. It looks like approximately 900 puts and calls traded with the same terms (an equivalent arbitrage—reversal or conversion). Subtracting that volume out leaves about average volume.

4. The answer is no for both.

5. *(d)* is correct.

6. *(a)* is my best choice. *(b)* makes you a risk arbitrageur, which you are *not*—you would be out of your league with those guys; *(c)* makes little sense; *(d)* is reasonable but still makes you a risk arb; *(e)* is totally irrelevant.

7. *(b)*. Since the option volume is still high on some days, and since option implied volatility is still high on most days, I would roll my position out to the next month, despite the cost, because it seems there is still a decent possibility that this stock will be taken over.

8. *(c)* is the most likely answer. *(a)* is a by-product of *(b)*, but they wouldn't be heavily buying puts for an event

that they expect to take place a month from now. *(b)* and *(d)* are possible, but quite unlikely for listed companies.

9. *(d)* is correct.

10. *(d)* is correct. The sale of puts in these situations has two main disadvantages, even if you're right about the takeover: (1) you only have limited profit potential and the takeover comes at a much higher price, you will be unhappy, and (2) many deals are done with "back ends" or "stock for stock"; in those cases, the puts may have some actual value and therefore won't trade down as much as you might expect. Not only that, if the rumor proves to be completely false, the stock might fall a great deal, and the puts have large risk if that happens.

11. *(a)* is correct. If you do the research, you will know if it's a takeover rumor or if it's the subject of an event, such as an FDA hearing or a legal trial. *Then* you make your decision about whether to buy more stock or sell covered calls.

CHAPTER 3   OPTIONS AS CONTRARY INDICATORS

1. *(d)*. Stock volume is the only correct answer, since it is not a contrary indicator. Option volume *(a)* is used to calculate put-call ratios, while *(b)* and *(c)* are essentially the same thing—option prices, which *can* be contrary indicators.

2. *(b)* because election surveys reflect what one is going to *do*—not an opinion about something over which he has no control. The others are all opinions, and when a majority reaches that opinion, it can be treated as a contrary indicator.

3. *(a)* $VIX uses only the options at the nearest two expiration months, and the nearest two strikes to $OEX's current price.

4. *(c)*

5. *(a)*, *(b)*, and *(c)* are all conditions. In any market where prices are falling rapidly *and* implied volatility is sharply increasing, a buy signal occurs when implied volatility reaches a peak.

6. *(b)*, *(c)*, *(d)*, and *(e)* are all bullish strategies, so they are correct. *(a)* is a bearish strategy.

7. *(c)* is the best answer. Sometimes *(a)* can be correct, but it is really a subset of *(c)*. *(b)* and *(d)* are completely incorrect.

8. *(b)* is the correct answer. Even though all grain futures have *something* in common, they are really different markets that can trade in substantially different directions. Thus, each one's put-call ratio should be calculated separately.

9. *(d)*.

10. *(d)*.

11. A *static* interpretation of an indicator requires that one buy and sell when the indicator reaches predetermined fixed levels. A *dynamic* interpretation, however, allows one to alter the levels at which one interprets the indicator as a buy or sell signal, depending on market factors. Specifically, for the put-call ratio, we look for peaks in the ratio as buy signals—at whatever absolute level they may occur—and we look for troughs as sell signals.

12. In a certain sense, all of these answers are true. The most obvious are *(b)* and *(c)*, which have increased in the 1990s and those activities—not being reflective of the public's opinion of the market—distort the usefulness of the $OEX put-call ratio as a contrary indicator. But *(d)* is a contributor, too, because the public's decreased trading of $OEX options has only made the effects of *(b)* and *(c)* more distorting. Finally, *(a)*—the bull market—is partially to blame, too, because the public has seen that it is often easier to make money in stocks since they have risen so fast in the long bull market—and thus have lessened their trading of $OEX options, thereby exacerbating *(d)*, which as shown above contributes to *(b)* and *(c)*.

13. *(a)* is the best answer. *(d)* would be nice, but it is rarely true that the public is buying puts heavily on a stock making new highs. *(b)* is irrelevant—it's the ratio between puts and calls that's important. *(c)* is not recommended, because one wants to see *some* signs of stability by the underlying before stepping in to take a bullish position.

14. *(b)*, *(a)*, *(c)*. *(b)* is an immediate signal which should see the stock move right away; *(a)* is more vague than *(b)*, but should see some results in a fairly short period of time; *(c)* has no timing value at all.

15. *(d)* is the best answer, but *(c)* is true as well. *(a)* and *(b)*—while they might seem logical—are not true. There is little, if any, correlation between the level at which the put-call signal occurs and its result in terms of stock price.

16. Infinity is an unacceptable value to include in a moving average, so one must find a way around using it. The standard way that this is handled for illiquid indices is to compute the 21-day average in a slightly different way:

$$\frac{\left(\text{Sum of all put volume over the last 21 days}\right)}{\left(\text{Sum of all call volume over the last 21 days}\right)}$$

However, the formula shown in Question 17 would suffice as well.

17. One thing that should be pointed out is that this ratio ranges between +1 (100% of the volume is puts) to −1 (100% of the volume is calls) on a daily basis. In this way, the put-call ratios for *all* stocks, indices, and futures would range between +1 and −1 and could theoretically be compared with one another. That is, if AXP has a reading of +0.5 and AOL has a reading of +0.4, we could say AXP is more "oversold" than AOL. Some back-testing would have to be done, though, to determine if that were a useful thing to be able to know. One problem might be that very liquid ratios—such as the equity-only put-call ratio—where heavy put and call volume is seen daily would not deviate from 0 very much at all. Therefore, one might be deluded into thinking that a "small" number, such as +0.3 is not significant, whereas it might actually be *very* significant in practice. The ratio calculated in this manner would still be interpreted in the usual way: peaks are buy signals, troughs are sell signals.

18. *(b)* and *(c)* are true. *(a)* is called a "nearby futures" chart and is different from a continuous futures chart because the gaps are left in. *(d)* is just plain false—again because of the gaps. Consider a commodity where there is *never* any price movement, except that each successive futures contract is more expensive than the previous one by 1.00 point. A continuous chart would be exactly flat because that's the result a trader would have if he bought the futures, held them while they

remained flat until they neared expiration, and then rolled to the next series which in turn remained flat while he held it, and so forth. However, a long-term chart of either one series of a "nearby futures" *(a)* would show a series of stair-steps rising 1.00 point in price each time expiration neared.

19. *(b)*. There is no single formula for the desired calculation, so *(a)* is wrong. Moving averages need not be computed with a computer; they are quite simple, so *(c)* is wrong, too.

20. This is the exact opposite of contrary theory, and it is wrong. In fact, when the editors of *Investors Intelligence* first began to survey investment advisors in the 1950s, they thought that they would be following along with these "wizards of Wall Street." They were somewhat surprised to find that the investors were *wrong* at the major turning points, and so they became adherents of contrary investing. The reason that contrary trading works is that everyone is uniformly bullish, they have probably already finished their buying before they "tell" the public. So there isn't any more money to fuel a further bullish move, and the market begins to reverse and go down as soon as everyone is bullish (i.e., as soon as everyone is "in the market"). There is also the more cynical viewpoint that the brokerage firms, hedge funds, and big traders want to sell near the top, so they put out a lot of bullish opinions to entice the public to buy, so they can sell to the public (at the top).

CHAPTER 4   SYSTEM TRADING

1. *None* of these statements are true. There are many, many profitable trading systems that pertain to all types of markets, and they can range from day trading to long-term trading.

2. *(c)*.

3. *All* of these would be criteria that you should consider before using a trading system.

4. The best answer is *(a)*. *(c)* is a poor choice, but there is some truth to it; *(b)* is completely false; *(d)* is also false because Dow Jones *futures* options can't be trading in a stock account—Dow Jones *stock* options, as listed on the CBOE, can.

5. *(d)*, because the others are all composed of relatively similar large-cap stocks, while the Russell is not.

6. *(a)* and *(b)* are true; *(c)* is false, since one only needs a *single* piece of historical information—yesterday's exponential moving average value—in order to calculate today's value, while a 20-day simple moving average, say, would require knowing the prices for each of the last 20 days.*(d)* is just plain false.

7. *(a)* = (2); *(b)* = (3); *(c)* = (4); *(d)* = (1). Essentially the longer-term the system, the less delta we want to own.

8. *(d)*. The others are patently false.

9. Only *(b)*. The others are irrelevant for this determination.

10. *(d)* is the best answer, although we really can't expect arbitrage buy programs unless the net call open interest is large enough—usually over 40,000 contracts. *(a)* is false, but there is a modicum of truth in both *(b)* and *(c)*. However, as a practical matter, *(b)* and *(c)* can never be determined, so in the normal course of attempting to estimate arbs' intentions, only *(d)* really pertains.

11. *(b)*. $SPX and most other index and sector options are *European* style, which means that they can *only* be exercised on their expiration date, and not before. $OEX options, however, are *American* style, which means that they can be exercised at any time during their life.

12. *(d)*. The net open interest of in-the-money calls minus in-the-money puts is +70,219. Since it is greater than +40,000, we can expect arb buy programs if $OEX is *above* the given striking price.

13. *(a)* and *(c)* could both be contributing factors. The other two choices are false.

14. *(a)* is the only true answer of the four given.

15. Since the premium of 14.00 is only one point (1.00) above fair value, which is 13.00, there would *not* be any arbitrage programs instigated at this time. Generally the premium must differ from fair value by at least 2.00 points before the arbs can make money.

16. *(d)*. *(b)* can be simply done with a hand-held calculator. *(a)* and *(c)* are not relevant to the fair value calculation.

17. *(c)* is the only option advantage. The others are all advantages of the underlying, *not* the options.

18. All except *(b)* are true. Each of the others moves higher as the stock you own moves higher, thus fulfilling the definition of a trailing stop. *(b)* would never move higher as the stock does and thus would not "trail."

19. *(a)* is correct. *(b)* is totally false. *(c)* is also false; while it may be true that experienced traders can make an accurate estimate of the model's output, they still use the model anyway. *(d)* should also be considered false; even though the model may use the lognormal distribution (which is not really the way prices behave) it does not change the fact that a model is needed for evaluation.

20. *(c)* is the most important. While *(a)* and *(d)* might generate profits, if they are not compatible with your personal investing philosophy, they will not work for you. *(b)* is unnecessary—it is perfectly acceptable to rely on other's research; you don't need to reinvent the wheel.

CHAPTER 5   PROTECTING A STOCK PORTFOLIO

1. She would most likely use *(c)*, S&P Index options. *(a)* is an unlikely choice, because it removes all possibility of making money if the market rises. She wouldn't use sector options *(b)* for a diverse portfolio of large-cap stocks. She *might* use individual stocks *(d)*, but that is a lot of work, so she would most *likely* use *(c)*.

2. The beta must be used in order to ensure that the quantity of insurance purchased—puts or futures—adequately insures a portfolio that might be more or less volatile than the broad stock market.

3. *(a)* since everything else is the same (portfolio actual value, strike price, and shares per option). A more volatile index requires less options to hedge a portfolio. The ratio of the volatilities is 3/4 (0.15 divided by 0.20), so the value line will require 3/4 times 60, over 56 options as a hedge.

4. All four are possible, and all four occurred at one time or another during Monday or Tuesday of the Crash of 1987 (October 9 and October 20).

5. *(b)* $500,000. The formula is: actual worth×beta = adjusted worth.

6. *(c)* 120. The number of puts to buy is determined by the formula: adjusted worth divided by (strike price × shares/option). Since shares per option is 100, using the data given results in an answer of 120.

7. *(d)* 6%. If he buys 120 options and pays $2,500 each for them, that's an insurance expense of $300,000. That represents 6% of the value of his *actual* net worth of $5,000,000.

8. There are two possible reasons. One is that the adjusted for beta requires a greater quantity of index options to be bought and that raises the overall cost of insurance beyond that required by purchasing individual stock options. The second is that there is generally a reverse volatility skew in index options; that is, out-of-the-money index puts are quite overpriced and thus cost more on a statistical basis than stock options, which do *not* display that same characteristic.

9. *(c)* is the best answer, because it is the most generic. Technically, *(b)* could be considered correct in some sense as well because it describes what happens in the case where the market falls and you have insurance in place.

10. All of these options could be used to construct a collar, depending on what you want to insure.

11. *(d)* is the only correct answer. *(a)* is the opposite of *(d)* and is thus incorrect. *(b)* is also incorrect—there is risk when the collar is in place, but the risk is limited. Finally, *(c)* is not correct either since a collar placed on stock results in a position that is similar to a bull spread.

12. If you are not willing to sell the stock, you must always take action to counter the price of a rising short call if the underlying stock rallies, just as a naked call writer would do. A true covered writer would just let it be called away. Furthermore, there are the psychological similarities between a naked call writer and one who is unwilling to sell the stock that the calls

are written against. The most prevalent is the fact that when the stock rises above the strike price of the call, the call writer begins to worry, has sleepless nights, and generally acts as if he is losing money—when in fact, he is "flat" since the stock gains (in theory) are offsetting any losses in the short call.

CHAPTER 6 TRADING VOLATILITY

1. *(c)* is the only one that is true. The interest rate component of a futures option is not used for its theoretical value (recall that you can set the interest rate in the model to 0% for futures options) but *does* have some meaning as to the present value discount of owning an expensive futures option. *(a)* is false; dividends are very important for index options, and for many stock options as well. *(b)* is false; implied volatility is a *byproduct* of the model, not an input.

2. *(d)* is the most true, since historical and implied volatilities can be—and often are—at very different levels. *(a)* is partly true, but implied volatility is determined by *all* traders in the marketplace, not just the market makers. *(b)* is pretty much false; implied volatility often *fails* to accurately predict just how volatile the underlying will be during the life of the option. *(c)* is completely false; historical volatility is computed using past *stock* prices.

3. *(a)* is certainly true. *(c)* is somewhat true, although it's not specific enough: in a forward (positive) skew, out-of-the-money calls are more expensive than at-the-money calls, and in a reverse (negative) skew, out-of-the-money puts are more expensive than at-the-money puts. *(b)* and *(d)* are false in that the underlying can do anything it wants—the skew is not an accurate forecaster of the underlying's movements.

4. *(b)* is certainly true, and so is *(d)*. *(c)* is false, since it describes a forward skew at the lower strikes, which is opposite to the assumptions. *(a)* is indeterminate, since there really isn't any necessary relationship between the out-of-the-money puts and out-of-the-money calls in a dual skew situation.

5. *(a)* is true, so *(d)* is true as well, for in a call ratio spread, we would be buying options with lower strikes (and hence lower

implied volatilities in this example) and selling options with higher implied volatilities. *(b)* is false, and *(c)* is the preferred strategy for a negative skew, not a positive one such as in this example.

6. *(b)* and *(c)* have net long calls and thus have unlimited profit potential to the upside.

7. *(a)*, *(b)*, and *(d)* all involve naked options and thus have extremely large risk.

8. *(a):* 76; *(b):* loss of $600 (plus commissions) at 70; *(c):* profit of $400 (less commissions).

CHAPTER 7   BUY LOW AND SELL HIGH—VOLATILITY, THAT IS

1. None of the answers are true, in general. *(a)* comes closest to being true, but the real measure of whether an option is underpriced would be to compare the current implied volatility with past measures of *implied* volatility. *(b)*, *(c)*, and *(d)* are just plain false. If they were true, it would just be coincidence.

2. *(b)* and *(c)* are both true. Implied volatility is a leading indicator but is based on the opinions of the traders in the marketplace. *(a)* and *(d)* are false.

3. I would think that, if there are too many expensive options showing up, we would want to temporarily tighten our definitions—raising the thresholds for what constitutes expensive and also possibly raising the definition for what constitutes a cheap option (especially if we aren't finding many cheap options at this time). Therefore, *(b)* would be the correct answer, and *(d)* would be correct if you didn't want to adjust the definition of *cheap*. I usually find that, when it is necessary to temporarily make such adjustments to the definitions, I change *both* of them.

4. All of the above answers are true. *(b)*, *(c)*, and *(d)* were discussed in the text. But *(a)* could be valid as well, for a board meeting might mean there is rumor of a stock split, or perhaps an announcement related to earnings—both of which could cause the options to become more expensive temporarily.

5. *(c)* and *(d)* could both be true, if the company that is being merged with is a less volatile company. *(a)* and *(b)* are false—they would normally make the options expensive, not cheap.

6. In certain situations, all the answers are true. *(a)* is true if you are talking about call backspreads as opposed to a straddle. *(b)* is true if you are talking about put backspreads vis-a-vis the straddle. *(c)* is probably not true, in general, but it could be if the options were high-priced. Finally, *(d)* is true but the backspread has a limited profitability on one side, so it may not have as high of an *expected return* as a straddle buy would.

7. Yes, your position would have a bullish bias in almost all cases. Since stocks can rise farther than they can fall, the at-the-money call has a higher delta than does an at-the-money put. Hence your position is delta long—biased to the upside. Stated alternatively, say you paid 10 points for the straddle. There is a higher probability that a stock can rise 10 points than there is that it can *fall* 10 points.

8. Since the ratio of the deltas is 3-to-2 (0.60 to 0.40, forgetting the minus sign), we would want to buy three puts for every two calls that are purchased. If we bought three puts at 4½, that's $1,350. And two calls at 6 cost $1,200. So the "base" 3-by-2 positions cost $1,350 + $1,200 = $2,550. Hence if we have $11,000 to spend, we can buy four "base" units at a cost of $2,550 each, for a total of $10,100. The breakeven points are 61¼ on the upside and 42½ on the downside. These are determined by using the "base" unit cost of 22½. That would be our theoretical maximum loss if the stock were exactly at 50 at expiration.

$$\text{Upside breakeven} = \text{Strike} + \left(\frac{\text{Maximum loss}}{\text{Number of long calls}} \right)$$

$$= 50 + \frac{22.5}{2} = 50 + 11.25 = 61.25$$

$$\text{Downside breakeven} = \text{Strike} - \left(\frac{\text{Maximum loss}}{\text{Number of long puts}} \right)$$

$$= 50 - \frac{22.5}{3} = 50 - 7.5 = 42.50$$

9. The correct answer is *(d)*, because the only way you can lose the *entire* investment is for the stock to end up *exactly* at the strike price at expiration. The probability of that happening is a very small number.

10. Most likely, *(a)* is true—the increase in implied volatility from the 10th percentile to the 50th percentile will generally wipe out about a month's time decay. However, *(d)* has some credence as well because we don't know the absolute volatility numbers that represent the 10th and 50th percentiles (if they are very close together, then perhaps *(a)* is not true). *(c)* could be true if there were a big increase in volatility from the 10th to the 50th percentile, although that once again lends credence to *(d)* as being the best answer. Normally, *(b)* would be false.

11. *(b)* is the best answer, for it is invariably true. *(c)* is also a good practice to adhere to, and it would certainly be considered a correct answer. Both *(a)* and *(d)* are false. Futures are actually less volatile than stocks, so there shouldn't be any prejudice against selling futures options. Also, if one is willing to sell naked puts, why not calls? The underlying could fall as well as rise.

12. While some brokerage firms bend the rules, these are the strict interpretations. *(a)* and *(b)* are true for once the call or put is paid for in full, there can be no other demand for money. Admittedly, you cannot exercise the call or the put, for that would require a lot more margin and hence some firms won't let you trade long options—figuring that if you're unreachable at expiration, an automatic option exercise could violate the IRA rules. *(c)* is most certainly false. Putting up the *minimum* margin for a naked put sale would be a disaster if the underlying stock dropped dramatically in price. Finally, *(d)* is false, too, for if the stock were to *rise* dramatically, and you were then assigned, you might be required to put a lot of margin into the account, or—if you decided to cover your short stock or calls instead—to pay a large debit.

13. *(c)* and *(d)* are always true. *(c)* is true because an early assignment on a cash-based option may cause the spread to incur more risk than the distance between the strikes in the spread, since you can't get out of the other side until the next trading—by which time the market may have moved dramatically.

(b) is true if the spread is a vertical spread—that is, if the options expire in the same month. Meanwhile, *(a)* is false—there are no naked options under the assumptions in this question.

14. *(a)* and *(b)* are true. *(c)* is false because a neutral position is only neutral until things begin to change—including the price of the underlying. *(d)* is false; both time remaining and implied volatility affect the delta of an option, as well as the price of the underlying.

GLOSSARY

---

calendar spread   different expiration months, same strike

call option   the right to buy the underlying at the striking price until the expiration date

collar   the protection strategy of simultaneously buying puts and selling calls on stock; results in limited risk below the striking price of the put and limited profit potential at the striking price of the call

composite implied volatility   weighted average of the implied volatility of each of the options on a particular underlying instrument; weighted according to trading volume and distance from the strike

contrary indicator   an indicator that measures market sentiment, which is usually wrong, and tells the trader to take the opposite position

delta   the amount by which the option will move if the underlying instrument moves one point

derivative security   a security—option—whose price movements are determined by the movements of another security (e.g., underlying stock)

direct indicator   an indicator that shows the way the market is actually going to move

drawdown   the worst losing period that a system has faced

equity-only put-call ratio   put-call ratio calculated by using the volume of all stock options; the most useful major put-call ratio

event-driven straddle buying   strategy of buying a straddle on the stock on the exact day before the decision on a corporate event, such as a lawsuit or hearing before a federal agency, is made public

exercise the option   convert the option into the underlying instrument

expiration date   date on which the option holder's rights cease to exist

first notice day   the first day that the holder of a long futures contract can be made to take delivery of the physical commodity; speculators are usually out of the market by that date

gamma   the amount of change in the delta of the option when the stock changes in price by a point; the delta of the delta

historical volatility   a strict statistical measure of how fast prices have been changing

implied volatility   an estimate of how volatile the underlying will be during the life of the option

index and sector options   options on an index or a sector such as the S&P 500 or the Semiconductor Index

insider trading   trading with advance knowledge of a corporate event

in-the-money   trading price of the underlying is higher than the strike price of a call option, or is lower than the strike of a put option

in-the-money amount   the amount by which the underlying exceeds the strike price of a call option, or by which the strike of a put exceeds the underlying price

intrinsic value/time value   the two elements of an option's complete price

LEAPS   acronym for an option that has more than nine months of life remaining

lognormal distribution   distribution in which stock prices could rise infinitely, although with great rarity, but cannot fall below zero; generally accepted as a reasonable approximation of the way that prices move

long stock   is equivalent to a long call and a short put with the same terms

noise   trading volume that has nothing to do with insider trading activity and that can be misleading

OEX ($OEX)   the S&P 100 Index; uses 100 major stocks whose options trade on the CBOE; the primary speculative vehicle for option traders who want to trade the broad market

open interest   the number of contracts that exist—opened by traders and not yet closed

option model   a mathematical formula used to give some accurate estimates of an option's price based on its components

out-of-the-money   trading price of the underlying is below the strike price of a call option, or above the strike of a put option

over-the-counter option   direct link between buyer and seller; no secondary market; an option traded over-the-counter rather than listed; usually traded by large firms such as Morgan Stanley or institution such as mutual find; biggest type is interest-rate trade (swap)

premium of futures   difference between the futures contract and the cash index ($SPX) itself

pricing curve   the picture of a single option's value depicted over a range of stock prices

profit graphs   graphs depicting the potential profits and losses from a position

put-call ratio   all the puts traded on a particular day divided by the total of all the calls traded on that same day

put option   the right to sell the underlying at the striking price until the expiration date

relative beta   measure of how each stock in the portfolio relates to the index being used as a hedge

rho   amount of change in the option price when the risk-free interest rate increases

sector index   index whose stocks belong to a certain sector such as the gold and silver index or the oil and gas sector

serial option   an option on a futures contract that has an expiration month different from that of any of the futures contracts

settlement price   the price that the market makers post as the middle of the closing range at the end of the day

short stock is equivalent to a short call and a long put with the same terms

slippage the amount of extra money you lose when you enter or exit the market

spot underlying cash index

straddle the simultaneous purchase of both a put and a call with the same terms

strangle a put and a call with the same expiration date, where the call has a higher strike price than the put

strangle sale an out-of-the-money call is sold, as well as an out-of-the-money put; a naked combination sale

strike price the price at which the option holder has the right to buy the underlying (for calls) or to sell it (puts)

theta the amount of change in the option price when one day passes; time decay

tracking error the performance differential between a stock portfolio and the index underlying the futures contract (usually the S&P 500)

trading system a methodology that has well-defined rules for entry and exit, plus perhaps some rules for taking partial profits

trailing stop a stop that moves with the position when it is making money but remains static if it begins to lose money

underlying instrument (underlying) stock, index, or futures contract on which options are traded

vega the amount of change in the option price when volatility moves up or down by 1 percent

vertical spread same expiration month, different strikes

VIX ($VIX) CBOE's Volatility Index; measure of implied volatility; can be used as a measure of contrary sentiment

volatility skew a pattern of varying implied volatilities among the options of a particular underlying instrument

warrants exchange-traded derivatives similar to options but less liquid and generally without standardized terms

zero cost collar the proceeds from the call completely cover the cost of the put

INDEX